MYTHS AND LEGENDS

OF THE

NEW YORK STATE IROQUOIS

MYTHS AND LEGENDS OF THE NEW YORK STATE IROQUOIS

by

Harriet Maxwell Converse
(Ya-ie-wa-noh)

edited by

Arthur Caswell Parker
(Ga-wa-so-wa-neh)

YESTERDAY'S CLASSICS

ITHACA, NEW YORK

ISBN: 978-1-63334-241-5

Yesterday's Classics, LLC
PO Box 339
Ithaca, NY 14851

CONTENTS

PART I
IROQUOIS MYTHS
AND LEGENDS

TABLE OF CONTENTS

TABLE OF CONTENTS

PART II
MYTHS AND LEGENDS
BY HARRIET MAXWELL CONVERSE

PART III
MISCELLANEOUS PAPERS

BY HARRIET MAXWELL CONVERSE

TABLE OF CONTENTS

BY A. C. PARKER

Harriet Maxwell Converse

PREFATORY NOTE

One may not hope to read a primitive culture from the record of its workmanship alone, although this is often the only avenue remaining by which a lost culture may be approached. The mentality of a primitive people living close to nature mirrors the supreme law of the universe in its simplest and most elemental expressions; it clothes with individuality the manifestation of this law, gives words to its unconscious forces and thoughts to its living agents; it reads, suffused in a wealth of imagery, the spiritual law in the natural world or embellishes some historical event. Such simple and unembarrassed expressions, transmitted not by records of hand but from mouth to mouth through the generations, are priceless to the student who finds in a progressed and complicated civilization the obscuration of natural law by the artificial conditions erected on the rebellious logic of human society.

The labors of Mrs. Harriet Maxwell Converse in recording the legends and nature myths of the New York Iroquois are, for these and other reasons, most worthy of conservation. She was devoted in her love for her adopted people; she shared their spirit and could record their folk tales with perfect sympathy.

Mr. Parker, who has edited the manuscripts of Mrs. Converse and prepared the introductory portion of this work, has been prompted not only by fidelity to the memory of a friend but by the piety and inspiration of inheritance.

JOHN M. CLARKE
(Ho-san-na-ga-da)

INTRODUCTION

No people can long exist as an ethnic group without consciously, or otherwise, creating a philosophy of things which becomes the common belief of that body of people—becomes their science and religion. The more permanent the people, the more enduring and greater the influence of their system of belief. Viewed in the light of exact science, as we know it, these primitive philosophies become mythologies. A myth may appear to us puerile and without any basis in logic, it may appear as a worthless fancy or a child's tale and yet a deeper study of the myth reveals within it the beginning of physics, philosophy and theology. Unfamiliar with the real cause of the phenomenon of mind or matter, the primitive mind, being a reasoning mind seeking to satisfy its curiosity and allay its fears, hypothecates the causes of visible effects in the form of myths. The primitive mind, believing all things the result of some intelligence, personifies and deifies the causes of effects, and thus has arisen the multiplicity of gods and guardian spirits.

Once crystallized and diffused, myths become working factors of human action. They become the science and religion of the ethnic group which entertains them. They become the basis of reasoning.

A treatise on a cause, they become a cause. They become so ingrained in the minds of their believers that, when in other generations they are rivaled by more rational systems, they are not easily supplanted, for they bear the approval of the religious leaders and the wise men of the generations past. To the great body of people the old myth was a part of common religion; the new myth which attempted to explain the thunder or the wind's fury was the science of the day and few would have aught to do with it, and here we have a glimpse of the conflict of religion and science. Religion was the conservative element and clung to the sacred beliefs of its fathers; science (so called), which brought the innovation, denied all precedents and struck out afresh to establish new ideas. Years passed by and the religions of the day accepted the new beliefs until the throes of their birth became forgotten in the haze of many years. Then again the critical minds of the time, comparing the experiences of the past and analyzing as best they could, sought to find new explanations that appealed more to their ideas of logic. Then old myths were scoffed at, a new system established, and again the conflict. Nor is it strange that men should be loath to deny that to which they have become accustomed; there is always a feeling of uncertainty about new systems and they are cautiously experimented with at first.

In reviewing myths of the ancients or of modern primitive men we may sometimes wonder how any large body of rational men could hold as sacred truths such fictions as we may regard unworthy of serious consideration. If such is the case it is because we have forgotten that the human mind has not always been of the same texture as it is today in the modern man of civilization. The minds of men, we should recall, through the varying grades of culture, from lower savagery to civilization, are characterized by wide differences. They are not uniformly susceptible to the same stimuli, for each culture grade gives to the mind of the man which it characterizes a different viewpoint, different capacities and different associations. It is always well to keep in mind the fact that our present enlightened beliefs, our sciences and our civilization are the product of a long period of evolution under favorable circumstances, and that they are not things that men were always able to grasp. It is well, also, to remember that our ancestors were once barbarians and rude savages, scarcely more intelligent than the other animals of the forest. All this might be hard to believe were it not that primitive savages still are to be found, and that all the various culture stages can be illustrated by groups of living peoples. There is little doubt that the man of five centuries hence will find plenty to laugh at, if he feels so disposed, when he reads the annals of our times and gets an insight of our customs and beliefs, some of which he may term myths. While he may appreciate our achievements he will certainly deny our claim to enlightenment and choose to bestow it upon himself. There can be no true enlightenment, and the age of fable will not cease to be, until the laws which govern all phenomena are known to men. Until then men must theorize. Myths were originally theories adduced from the best information at hand. Surviving in more enlightened ages they were still held even though inconsistent with the known objective experience of the time. Even so they were regarded as sacred truths. A myth must be regarded, therefore, as a primitive theory, as a rude attempt to reach truth, as a tentative hypothesis upon which to fasten one's belief, for one must believe something.

Legends and traditions. No people of any intellectual life can exist in social bodies without building up out of their experiences and especially out of their imaginations a vast body of oral fiction. Among peoples, widely separated in point of time and space, the same general myths and legends are found. This by no means necessarily implies contact. Rather does it illustrate the fact that illimitable as imagination seems to be in its power to combine and create, in reality it is limited by certain suggesting factors which may be common to all people of a given cultural stage and to all times. We have dwelt upon this feature at some length in a note on the Celestial Bear myth. It is not to be supposed, however, that some myths have not been derived by contact directly or indirectly in times more or less historic. On the other hand it seems quite feasible to believe that certain myths have been transmitted from one stock to another, the elements to be preserved and the details to be recast, in local molds. Some myths are plainly derived from external sources and are easily traced to their originating sources. Others are more difficult to trace.

Certain individuals among tribes in the lower culture stages become the story-tellers of their people and are the tribal libraries of this oral fiction. Legends differ from myths in that they are wonder stories told for the amusement of those who hear them and are recognized as ingenious creations of imagination. There is, however, a class of legends that relate to localities and which explain some local phenomenon, but these are traditions rather than legends. Traditions differ from legends in that they pretend to be and often are the relations of actual occurrences. They are the histories of the peasantry and the tribes that have no system of writing.

Iroquois folklore

The North American Indians possessed a vast oral literature of mythology, legendary lore and tradition. The field of American folklore has scarcely been touched by anthropologists, and even tribes that have been known the longest have received comparatively little attention. True, much has been recorded, but this much is but a small portion of the total. That this should be the case is not due to the lack of energy on the part of students but to the inaccessibility of the greater part of the material.

Much is known of the material culture of the Iroquois and much also of their governmental system and their social laws. That not all is known is conceded, but enough to place them conspicuously before historians and ethnographers as the Indians of

Indians, as the most splendid of barbaric men. It will be found of interest, therefore, to bring before students for correlation the small portion of their literature contained in this volume.

The mythology of the Iroquois differs in form from that of many other of the American races. Iroquois tales were of strength, of great deeds, of nature and the forces of nature, "standing out in striking contrast to the flimsy conceptions of the Algonquins," as someone has remarked. They are the classics of all the unwritten literature of the American aborigines.

The Iroquois were a people who loved to weave language in fine metaphor and delicate allusion and possessed a language singularly adapted for this purpose. They were unconscious poets, and some of their tales seem to have been chanted in blank verse, the rhythm and swing of the meter in their estimation giving an added delight to the story. When the legends are told to white men the delicate word-weave is seldom revealed, and never if the legend is told in English. The translation robs it of much of its intended charm and grace, for the Indian seems to think that the pale invader may laugh at his metaphors or deride him for revealing that such fine emotions exist within a stoic's breast. Thus it is that so many legends appear puerile and without pertinency which in the vernacular are strong and full of meaning.

Story-telling customs of the Iroquois. Each settlement had its official story-teller whose predecessor had carefully taught him all the legends and traditions of the mysterious past and his listeners who gathered about him never tired of the narrative though repeated again and again.

According to ancient traditions no fable, myth tale, or story of ancient adventures might be told during the months of summer. Such practice was forbidden by "the little people" (jo-gä-oh), the wood fairies. Should their law be violated some jo-gä-oh flying about in the form of a beetle or bird might discover the offender and report him to the jo-gä-oh chief. Upon this a sign would warn the forgetful Indian. Failing to observe the omen, some evil would befall the culprit. Bees might sting his lips or his tongue would swell and fill his mouth. Snakes might crawl in his bed and choke him while he slept, and so on, until he was punished and forced to desist from forbidden talk.

The wood sprites enacted and enforced this law for two purposes: first, that no animal should become offended by man's boasting of his triumph over beasts, or at the same time learn too much of human cunning and fly forever the haunts of mankind; and second, that no animal, who listening to tales of wonder, adventure or humor, should become so interested as to forget its place in nature, and pondering over the mysteries of man's words, wander dazed and aimless through the forest. To listen to stories in the summer time made trees and plants as well as animals and men lazy, and therefore scanty crops, lean game and shiftless people resulted. To listen to stories made the birds forget to fly to the south lands when winter came, it made the animals neglect to store up winter provisions and grow their warm winter coats of fur. All the world stops work when a good story is told and afterwards in marveling forgets its wonted duty. Thus Oñ-gweh′-o-weh-ka′, the Iroquois, loyal to old-time custom, reserves his tales of adventures, myth and mystery for winter when the year's work is over and all nature slumbers.

When the story-teller finds an audience about him or wishes to call one, he announces his intention to recite a folk tale (ga-gä′, or in the plural, ga-gä′-sho-ŏ) by exclaiming "Ha-nio′!" and the eager reply is "Hĕh," which is an ardent request that his "Hanio" take immediate effect, and the relation of a ga-gä′ ensues.

At intervals during the relation of a story the auditors must exclaim "Häh!" This was the sign that they were listening. If there was no frequent response of "Häh," the story-teller would stop and inquire what fault was found with him or his story.

It was not only considered a breach of courtesy for a listener to fall asleep, but also a positive omen of evil to the guilty party. If any one for any reason wished to sleep or to leave the room, he must request the narrator to tie the story, "Si-gä′-hah." Failing to say this, and afterwards desiring to hear the remainder of the tale, the narrator would refuse him, for if he related it at all it must be from the beginning through, unless *tied*. Thus *si-gä′-hah* was the magic word by which a legend might be told as a serial.

Methods of recording folklore

There are several ways in which folk tales may be recorded, as indeed there are several purposes for which they are written. To satisfy strictly scientific requirements, the method employed by the Smithsonian Institution and other progressive ethnological institutions, is undoubtedly the best. The native text is recorded with an exact translation interlined, word beneath word. This method is most satisfactory to the student of languages but from the standpoint of literature it falls short. The resulting English is extremely awkward as it must necessarily be in an attempt to parallel two radically different systems of grammar and word compounding. No idea of the native beauty is preserved in such translations, which are often inelegant and difficult to read and understand. To remedy these defects the whole translation must be rewritten in accord with current methods of expression.

Another method of preserving a myth is to record it exactly as told, in the broken English of its narrator. The most poetic conception is thus sometimes reduced to grotesque caricature, and the value of the record lies not so much in its subject-matter as it does in the estimation which is formed of the narrator's ability of expressing in our tongue the thoughts of his own. The charming Uncle Remus stories are of this character but the result is only a study in brogue or dialect, and fails to convey to our minds the ideas which exist in the mind of the native myth teller. From the standpoint of literature and psychology it is the impression, its form, its spirit that we wish to apprehend. The same medium may produce different results if employed on different substances. The mind of the modern progressive man of today is of a different texture from that of the savage or the peasant, and the same idea produces different emotions and associations in these classes of intellect.

Many have employed the method of entirely recasting primitive ideas in their own thought molds, eliminating all the original idioms and picturesque eccentricities of expression and presenting the folk tale in all the verbiage of contemporary literature. The plot and motive of the original relation is warped and modified to fit modern requirements, the original elements are lost and the story becomes simply a modern one built upon the shattered skeleton of the old. The use of this method has produced a mass of florid, ocherous, recast and garbled folklore, which nevertheless, is presented as genuine.

There is yet another method which embraces some of the worthy features previously suggested. It may have its drawbacks to be criticized but it is full of merit notwithstanding. By this method the transcriber attempts to assimilate the ideas of the myth tale as he hears it, seeks to become imbued with the spirit of its characters, and, shutting out from his mind all thought of his own culture, and momentarily transforming himself into the culture of the myth teller, records his impressions as he recalls the story. His object is to produce the same emotions in the mind of civilized man which is produced in the primitive mind, which entertains the myth without destroying the native style or warping the facts of the narrative. If in the vernacular the ideas convey tragic, mysterious, or horrifying impressions, and the style is vigorous, metaphorical or poetic, the transcriber employs every consistent art to reproduce the same elements in his own language. There is virtue in this method if honestly followed but it can only be used by one familiar with all the incidents of the culture which produced the tale, by one who is familiar with the language, life and psychology of the myth maker. A myth tale recorded in this way is neither mechanical, dialect or affected in style, but on the other hand, the same living, sentient story, though dressed in the garments of another speech.

It is substantially this method which has been employed by Harriet Maxwell Converse in recording the myths and legends contained in this volume, and for this reason her work is eminently worthy of the consideration of students. Her great love for the Indians, her sympathetic nature, her scientific training and her psychic temperament enabled her to get at the heart of the stories her Indian friends told her. With her poetic mind schooled in all the arts of literature she has interpreted the ideas and impressions in a matchless style which enables the reader to feel all that the red man felt when he listened to the ancient stories of his forefathers.

The editor has endeavored to arrange the various myths and legends systematically and add such notes as will illuminate some of the obscure passages and to suggest by other notes the wealth of material which is opened up by the study of Iroquois folklore and American folklore in general.

As a loving friend and grateful student of Mrs. Converse, the editor has aimed in putting forth this work to rear from her own material a worthy monument, both to the memory of the gifted writer and to the people whom she loved.

ARTHUR C. PARKER

BIOGRAPHY OF HARRIET MAXWELL CONVERSE

To the late Mrs. Harriet Maxwell Converse, the State of New York owes a debt of lasting gratitude. The reason is apparent to even the superficial visitor to the Indian collections in the State Museum where in striking prominence are to be seen hundreds of rare and priceless relics of the aborigines of New York, her gift to the State in memory of her father, Hon. Thomas Maxwell of Elmira. Her unselfish work in preserving the record and relics of the first claimants of New York State has resulted in preserving much of immense value for students of culture, history and ethnography. Her great interest in the Indians and her wonderful influence with them made it possible for her to mingle with them as a trusted and beloved friend. Indeed so greatly did the Indians esteem her that they bestowed upon her every possible honor within the gift of the clan and the council, hailed her as a sister and a mother, called her Ya-ie-wa-noh, She Who Watches Over Us, adopted her as a member of the nation and gave her a seat in their councils. There is a very great difference between merely receiving a complimentary name and an actual national adoption.

The life story of so remarkable a woman can not fail of pertinent interest from any viewpoint. Mrs. Converse was not a woman who was given to saying much concerning herself and although the writer was associated with her more or less from his childhood, the notes which he has relating to her earlier history are few and fragmentary, but from them and from the records which he has at hand, a brief account of her life's history has been prepared.

To get at the ancestral elements which contributed to the construction of her mind and personality, we must go to the Highlands of Scotland where in the romantic days of history, "the Maxwells maintained the splendor of their name in the baronial towers of Caerlaverock." A splendid name was that of Maxwell, and proudly borne by brave Highlanders from days of old.

Alexander Maxwell. Back in the early years of the 18th century, in the Scottish valley of the Nithe was, born Alexander Maxwell. He married Jane McBratney, she too a Highlander, and of the clan McPherson. The charm of America had reached the ears of Alexander Maxwell and in June 1770 he and his good wife set sail, from the port of Partick, for the new world where adventure and fortune, good or ill, awaited every daring pioneer. But summer seas are not always smooth and June breezes sometimes become gales that lash the waves to fury and bring disaster to unwary barks. This the emigrating couple discovered almost at the outset of their voyage. A violent storm came up as they coursed down the North channel which wrecked the ship and tossed it upon the shores of County Down in Ireland. The unfortunate couple found refuge in a fisherman's cottage on the shore where, about a month later, June 15, 1770, a son was born, whom they named Guy. The Maxwells and their baby son continued in Ireland for months when, in 1772, they embarked again for America. Upon their arrival they settled in Carlisle, Pa., but soon removed to Virginia, where they made their home in Martinsburg, Berkley Co., and where today are many descendants of the Scots, and prominent among them, descendants of the Maxwells.

When young Guy Maxwell was 18 years of age he took up his residence at Tioga Point where he entered into the firm of Colonel Hollenback. His extraordinary acumen is attested by the fact that Governor Mifflin in 1788 appointed him justice of the peace, then an office of greater importance than at the present day. He was less than 19 years of age when he took the appointment which he held for many years. Guy Maxwell occupied many positions of trust during his early years and contemporary history tells us that he was a shrewd business man. He removed from Milton, Pa., in 1794 to the present site of Elmira where he purchased a town lot. He dealt extensively with the Indians especially the Senecas, by whom he was greatly esteemed because of his uniform courtesy and strict honesty. In those days it was a common thing to treat Indians with respect but the quality of honesty was oftentimes a rare one when dealing with them. The Senecas appreciated his integrity and sought to express their regard by bestowing upon him the name, Ta-se-wa-ya-ee, meaning Honest Trader.

His love for the red men of the forest was shared by his son, Thomas, who was born in Athens, Pa.

Thomas Maxwell. Thomas Maxwell during his early boyhood became a great friend and favorite of the Indians who made Elmira a trading post and often spent days in the forest with them. His skill with the bow and his speed on the trail excited their admiration. Finally after some deed of heroism and endurance, they acclaimed that he was a red man at heart, though his skin was white, adopted him in the Wolf Clan, told him to call Red Jacket his father and that his name was henceforth, He-je-no and meant Brave Boy. For years Thomas Maxwell was county clerk of Tioga and Chemung counties and he also served in Albany as assemblyman for his district and afterward as congressman in Washington. He was a man of exceptional literary ability and contributed widely to the periodical publications of his day. When in 1812 his country was threatened he enlisted with the American army and fought with all the traditional ardor of a Scottish American. During all his public life he never lost interest in the Indians who had been his boyhood friends but frequently mingled with them until the day of his death in 1864.

Harriet Maxwell Converse. The second wife of Hon. Thomas Maxwell was Marie Purdy, a lady of culture, education and refinement. She was the mother of the seven children of Thomas Maxwell. The youngest was Harriet Maxwell, born in 1836 in Elmira. One of the old family scrapbooks contains a clipping which

18

relates that Harriet left Elmira, at the age of 9, after the death of her mother, went to Milan, O., "where she was duly put to school." It was at this time she first began to write verse for publication. A gentleman who was her playmate in the days before her departure says he has

RED JACKET

Taken from a steel engraving of the painting by R. W. Wier

a distinct and vivid recollection of her in a white dress and a broad red sash tied in an immense bow. "I can shut my eyes and see her as she appeared then, one of the most graceful little girls I ever saw."

In 1861 Harriet Maxwell Clarke, then the young widow of G. B. Clarke, one of the owners of Congress Spring, Saratoga, married Frank Buchanan Converse, of Westfield, Mass., a friend and playmate of her early childhood. For five years after her marriage she traveled in Europe, Asia and Africa and toured the United States. Her husband, Mr. Converse, was an inventor and musician. He had spent his early days in the west where he experienced all the adventures of the early pioneer. He lived with the Indians and became a great favorite with them. His skill as an athlete, and his dexterity with the rifle and bow won their admiration.

After the return of Mr. and Mrs. Converse to the East they took up their home in Mott Haven, afterward removing to West 46th street. New York City.

Mrs. Converse's interest in Indians may be described as hereditary. It is quite possible, however, that although she might ever have been a loyal friend to them, she might never have known them intimately had it not been for her acquaintance with Gen. Ely S. Parker, himself a Seneca Indian of the Wolf Clan, to which Red Jacket belonged. Oftentimes when environments are foreign we fail to appreciate the circumstances of others, nor are we able to do so, for it is experience which makes one able to appreciate the white man's metropolis and the Indian's reservation are the opposing extremes of civilization and there is little in the bustling complex city to remind one of the quiet simple reservation. Thus, although Mrs. Converse had within her all the elements which were capable of knowing sympathetically, understanding appreciatively and loving steadfastly the Indians whom her father and grandfather had loved,

Ely. S. Parker
Donehogawa
The Wolf

it required an awakening stimulus to arouse her interest in this direction. And once awakened there could be no turning. The moment Mrs. Converse met the Iroquois sachem her life and thought took a new direction. The great mind of the Indian had furnished the impulse.[1]

For years Mrs. Converse had written for the best periodicals in America and Great Britain, and her essays and poems were widely copied. Her poems written in the old Scottish for the Edinburgh journals awakened the fires of Highland patriotism and received an abundance of warm praise. Subsequently she was a regular contributor to the *Ladies Journal* (Edinburgh), the *Scottish American* and the *British Advertiser*. She became a regular contributor to several American magazines and her literary career became assured. Her book of poems. *Sheaves,* passed through several editions and was enthusiastically received by the most rigid critics. Her friend John G. Whittier, read and reread the volume and then wrote her, "It is a sheaf in which there are no tares." The gifted authoress received also a complimentary letter from Tennyson and the volume even inspired Dom Pedro, the Emperor of Brazil, to write a letter of appreciation. The press was universally warm in its praise and even the *New York Independent,* usually so severe in its criticism of poetical aspirants, copied several of her poems and said that at least one of the number was worthy of Keats.

It was this promising literary career which Mrs. Converse relinquished to devote the remainder of her life to the study and defense of the Indians of New York. General Parker took her to his reservation and to the Tuscarora Reservation where she met his sister, Mrs. Caroline Mountpleasant, wife of Chief John Mountpleasant of the Tuscaroras. In 1881 she visited the Cattaraugus Reservation where she became acquainted with the descendants of Red Jacket.

For many years her knowledge of the Iroquois had been gleaned solely from the manuscripts left by her father and from the *League of the Iroquois*, the joint work of Lewis H. Morgan and General E. S. Parker. With the insight of Indian character which these works had given her, her actual experiences among the Indians themselves fanned her interest into a passion. She admired their laws and customs, she marveled at their wondrous national vitality, their endurance, and she loved them. And they, finding her a friend, loved her.

Mrs. Converse's untiring activity in behalf of her red friends won their esteem and confidence. Her labors both at Washington and Albany, before the federal and state legislative bodies, at once placed her conspicuously before the public as a friend of the Indians and those who planned adverse legislation feared the forces she was able to muster in opposition. The best men in private and in public life were her friends and anxious to fight as she directed.

The Indians were grateful and thus expressed themselves, but were unable for a time to find a suitable way for expressing it by other means than words. Then they began to shower their ancient heirlooms upon her, articles of embroidered buckskin, chieftains' belts, ceremonial regalia, strange musical instruments, beadwork and wondrously wrought silver brooches.

This was not enough, however. Bearing in mind the record of two generations past, of Honest Trader, her grandfather, and Brave Boy, her father, and with the evidence of her loyalty fresh in their minds, they planned to make her a sister and a clanswoman. This could be done only by a family adoption and naming. The matter impressed Tho-na-so-wah, one of the national Seneca sachems, whose English name was William Jones, who with his wife, Jo-on-do-oh, planned to adopt Mrs. Converse as a sister. The adoption ceremony took place on the Cattaraugus Reservation on June 15, 1885; Mrs. Converse was received into the Snipe Clan and given the name Ga-ya-nes-ha-oh. Bearer of the Law. This was one of the ancient hereditary names of the Snipe Clan honondiont, *faith keepers,* and was once borne by Ruth Stevens, Red Jacket's stepdaughter.

Mrs. Converse at the time of her adoption

The naming ceremony was elaborate and impressive. All the modern innovations which the Senecas had acquired were added to the ancient usages to increase the interest of the occasion. In accordance

24

with the ancient custom the council was held out of doors in a council square, made by bounding a grassy spot with huge logs and benches, which served as seats for the throng. The council fire crackled within the square and the chiefs and matrons moved about within the space. This square was arranged in the Jones orchard and may be seen even today. Only once again was it used for council purposes. At this ceremony two others were "named" and one "confirmed." Hon. George S. Conover of Geneva, a student of Indian lore, received the name, Hy-we-saus, Seeker of History; Maj. Fred H. Furniss of Waterloo was named To-an-do-ah, Inventor; and Hon. Charles H. Hutchinson, ex-mayor of Utica, who had received an honorary name from an individual Indian, received the confirmation of his honorary title.

It is well to note here that the conferring of a name or even a family adoption carries no national rights with it. National adoption and honorary naming are honors widely different. Yet those who have received names often believe themselves adopted tribesmen. Naming, does not necessarily imply adoption, nor does family or clan adoption imply national adoption. Considered in the true light, few have ever been adopted into an Indian tribe, although many have claimed to be. There are even grades of names, so that to have an Indian name does not necessarily mean that one bears an ancient Indian title. Persistent name seekers often have been danced around by a grinning Indian with a rattle, who demanded $5 in return for a name which no Indian would translate, but which the donor assures

25

the recipient means Great Big Eagle Chief, or some like fiction. The white man or woman who has persisted in his quest for an Indian name is satisfied and ever after boasts himself an adopted Indian. The Indians, however, only laugh and think of the greenback which somebody received and of the ludicrous name that no one will translate. A true Indian name is not easily obtained by a white man or woman nor is it often given to those who ask for it. It is, however, given those who have shown themselves worthy of the honor and who know how to bear it. Such were the names given by the sachems, chiefs, and warriors, the faith keepers and women of the Senecas at the Tho-na-so-wah ceremony.

Mrs. Converse's reception in the Snipe Clan and into the family of William Jones, placed her in a position to secure extensive information regarding the customs and institutions of the Iroquois. The more she studied, the greater her enthusiasm became. She contributed generously to all their festivals and attended the various ceremonies on all the reservations in New York and Canada, each time the guest of the chiefs. Her home in New York became the stopping place of Indians visiting that city and the writer has met at her home Indians not only of the Iroquois nations of New York, but Indians from all over North America, from Hudson bay to Yucatan, from Dakota to Arizona and from Maine to British Columbia.

Naturally, simple minded Indians in a great city were wont to get into complications. Sometimes they would not hesitate to strike down an inquisitive inhabitant of the Bowery who ventured a disparaging remark. The Bowery inhabitant went to Bellevue and the Indian to the police station. Fortunately for the Indian the next morning found Mrs. Converse in court to plead for his release, and while Mrs. Converse lived the cases against Indians almost without exception were dismissed. Most of the cases are extremely humorous and an examination of the court documents will reveal that when an Indian in New York spoiled a white man's face the white man was usually fined and the Indian discharged, though sometimes with a mild reprimand.

Mrs. Converse not only was the Indians' defender in the courts, but was constantly busy relieving unfortunate Indians who had been robbed, swindled or injured. She always managed to find a ticket home for Indians who were destitute and disgusted with the big town. Sometimes they returned with a new pocketbook well lined and clean new outfits.

Those who were stricken with diseases or injured in accidents found her quick to discover their plight and to furnish relief. Mrs. Converse kept track with all the solicitude of a mother of the 50 or 100 Indians who lived in New York and those who came temporarily. The writer has four or five large scrapbooks full of clippings telling of the humorous, tragic and pathetic experiences of Indians in New York City, most of them from the pen of Mrs. Converse herself.

Her activities, however, were not confined to the Indians who dwelt in the city. She constantly watched bills before legislative bodies and was always on hand with a good fight when an adverse bill came up. The forces which she marshaled were formidable and the framers of the bills were obliged to capitulate every time.

Soon after her naming Mrs. Converse was initiated into the Pleasant Valley Lodge of the "Guards of the Little Waters," popularly known as the Secret Medicine Society. She also became a member of the Ye-ih-dos, the Society of Mystic Animals, one of the Little Water fraternities. The writer is a member of the first named order and of the lodge which she subsequently joined, Ga-nun'-da-sē.

CHIEF JOHN SANDY

*One of the Canadian chiefs who welcomed
Mrs. Converse to the Six Nations Reservation in Ontario*

With the Indians the term "medicine" means a mystic potence, or to use Hewitt's word, it means *orenda*. There is no English equivalent of the word which the Indians term "orenda," though it is erroneously and ambiguously interpreted *medicine*. The "Medicine" Society, therefore, does not necessarily imply an organization devoted to the compounding of drugs or the mixing of nostrums. Mrs. Converse was probably the first white woman ever to have become a member of this fraternity and to have actually held the great Ni-ga-ni-ga'-ah in her possession.

The love which all the Iroquois nations of New York had for her amounted to a passion. She was their one strong arm in every trial. They could do nothing to express their appreciation, but to plan more to honor her. Her first naming had only been a complimentary honor and at the time considered the highest ever given a white woman by the Iroquois. Now they planned to give her a national adoption and to ratify and seal it with the consent of the council and the seal of the nation.

In April 1890, the Name Holders of the Snipe Clan held a council and decided to change Mrs. Converse's name. Thus on the following June there was another ceremony. Mr. Converse was present with Mrs. Converse and was given a clan adoption. He was named Ha-ie-no-nis, Music Maker, in allusion to his ability to wring melody from any musical instrument which he chose to touch. Mr. James Kelly of New York City, an American sculptor of note, at this ceremony was named Ga-nius-kwa, Stone Giant, a name consistent with the sculptor's profession. Mrs. Converse was received with great ceremony and named Ya-ie-wa-noh. The next spring the Indians planned to advance her still further in the honors of the nation.

She had just succeeded in bringing about defeat to a particularly objectionable bill. The *New York World*, April 8, 1891, in an article entitled "Named Ya-ie-wah-noh," describes the action which was taken as follows: "After the bill was killed, when the Seneca Council, now in session at Carrollton, Cattaraugus Co., New York,

*An Ostowa-gowa officer who presides over
adoption and naming ceremonies*

in the Allegany Reservation was called, an application was laid before that body to the effect that 'by love and affection' it was the desire of the Indians that Mrs. Converse should be received into their nation as a legal member of it. Upon this appeal a vote was taken and it was unanimously resolved that she should at once be invited to appear before the council and receive her Indian name. To this summons Mrs. Converse immediately responded and on her arrival at Carrollton was met by a delegation of the Indians and escorted to the Council House where she was received by the Marshal of the nation and presented by him to the President and Board of Councilors.

The council was in session but immediately adjourned to welcome her and after a prayer had been offered to the Great Spirit, thanking him for her safe journeying through the dangerous trail of the white man (a railroad accident detained her), she was offered a seat by the side of the President and the hour of the adoption ceremony was appointed.

A runner was immediately sent out to notify the people and 300 of them had gathered at the Council House when Mrs. Converse was nominated by the Indian matrons to sit with them. Taking her place between two of the 'mothers' at the head of the Council House, the ceremony proceeded, conducted by the head chief of the Snipe Clan of which Mrs. Converse had been made a family member in 1884. The resolution of the council was then read in the Seneca language and interpreted to her as follows:

Chauncey Abrams, Sachem of the Tonawanda Snipe Clan

Whereas, Harriet Maxwell Converse has through her kindness and tender feeling to our Nation exerted herself to the uttermost in behalf of the protection and welfare of our Nation, and is always ready to stand at the helm of the canoe to avoid the crash of extinction of the Indians; it is

Resolved, On account of our appreciation and love thereof, she shall be honorable admitted as a member of the Seneca Nation of New York Indians.

The new name and title which was given was Ya-ie-wa-noh meaning She Watches Over Us. This name had once been borne by the wife of the celebrated Chief Cornplanter."

The next year, 1892, the Onondaga chiefs, the

legislative body of the Six Nations, determined to share in the honors which were due Mrs. Converse.

The plan was inaugurated at the Condolence Council held at the Tonawanda Reservation in September 1891. There Mrs. Converse had joined in the national condolence for the lost chief of the nation. After the ceremony of official mourning, the Onondaga chiefs nominated and elected Mrs. Converse for the office formerly held by the dead chief of the Tonawanda Senecas, but as the ceremonies were conducted entirely in Indian languages, Mrs. Converse did not learn of the action until the following spring when she was

Daniel La Forte, President of the Six Nations in 1892

summoned to the Six Nations Council at Onondaga Castle.

A personal invitation was sent by Chief Daniel La Forte. At the council she was unanimously confirmed a chief of the Six Nations, an honor never before conferred upon a white woman. The certificate which was afterward handed the newly elected chief read as follows:

Onondaga Castle, Mar. 25, 1892

This is to certify that Harriet Maxwell Converse has been duely elected & Installed to the Chieftain Ship of the Six Nations of the New York Indians on the 18th day of September, in the year 1891, at the Condolence held on the Tonawanda Indian Reservation. And she is therefore recognized as one of their Chiefs — to look after the interest of the Six Nations & also is recognized as Ya-ie-wa-noh.

Witness	*Principal Chiefs*
Rev. ALBERT CUSICK	*his*
Vice President *Six Nations*	MR. ABRAM (x) HILL
	mark
	THOMAS WILLIAMS
	THOMAS WEBSTER
	his
	BAPTIST (x) THOMAS
	mark

President of Six Nations, DANIEL LA FORTE

The chiefs of the Six Nations of Canada then invited her to honor them with a visit and once again she was received with an ovation.

After this culmination of honors her Seneca friend, Do-ne-ha-ga-wah (Gen. Ely S. Parker) wrote:

> I am extremely delighted to receive your brief note telling how bountifully honors have been showered upon you by the remnants of the Iroquois, both in New York and Canada. You deserve these honors empty and shadowy though they be and a great deal more, for the service you have rendered them. Accept, please, my hearty congratulations on your triumphal tour among these simple but honest hearted children of our ancient forests.

Mrs. H. M. Converse's national adoption and chieftainship certificate

The people you have been visiting have never been understood nor fully comprehended. I say that to study them satisfactorily needs a life time and at the end of life one has hardly begun the study. The study of the race is extremely kaleidoscopic. Your opportunities have been grand and rare. You have improved them well, and today are the best informed woman on Indian lore in America.

Mrs. Converse continued her studies and wrote many interesting articles about the Indians and Indian lore for the newspapers of the country.

The death of General Parker in 1895 was the first great sorrow which Mrs. Converse had experienced since the commencement of her active interest in Indians and for a long period she mourned the loss of the friend whose counsel and suggestions had been an inspiration.

Starting out to carry on the labors and researches of her father Hon. Thomas Maxwell, she now had as a legacy the work and plans which General Parker left. He had been a stanch friend of his people, an able sachem and a true Seneca. His counsel had been sought in all national matters by his people and his advice by the legislators of the white men when Indian law was involved. Mrs. Converse therefore must redouble her vigilance and perfect her knowledge of the Indians. The necessity of collecting material to illustrate their culture impressed her and she began to complete her collection. About this time the State Museum was given an appropriation with which to establish an Indian museum. Mrs. Converse's interest was awakened and she saw her opportunity to place the State in possession of a magnificent collection of articles illustrating the culture of the Iroquois. The collection was given in memory of her father Thomas Maxwell and is known as the Converse-Maxwell memorial. Subsequently her services were sought by the State as a collector for the museum and to her the State Museum is indebted for an interesting portion of the ethnological exhibit. It was largely through Mrs. Converse's influence that the National Council of the Onondagas passed the wampum belts of the Five Nations into the keeping of the State Museum. To her we owe a matchless collection of ceremonial paraphernalia and more than a hundred specimens of Iroquois silver work which include brooches, buckles, disks, arm bands, bracelets, earrings, beads and crowns or head bands. It was planned that Mrs. Converse should write several museum bulletins relating to her collections, but because of a change in arrangement she was able only to publish one paper, "Iroquois Silver Brooches" [N. Y. State Mus. 54th An. Rep't, v. i].

Secretary Dewey of the Board of Regents, when Mrs. Converse's work for the museum had been finished, wrote:

> DEAR MRS. CONVERSE: I want to thank you on behalf of the State for the great services you have so unselfishly rendered it in building up our new Indian museum. Much that has been accomplished could hardly have been brought about by any other agency. Desirable as it was, no one had the confidence of the Indians and could guide them to wise decisions so well, and you have done them a great service

in getting into fireproof quarters the relics of their wonderful career. I hope our Indian day and the good feeling shown on both sides was but the beginning of more satisfactory relations between the white and red men of the Empire State.

I am sure that as long as you have strength you will be deeply interested in anything that advances the best interests of the Iroquois and we shall rely on you in all these matters as our adviser. Perhaps we shall baptize you with the name, say "The Woman Who Works for the Indians," thus making you an honorary member of the University staff as the Indians so wisely have made you a chief among them.

Pray accept my own thanks personally as well as officially for all you have done, with the hope that even more will be accomplished in the future. We all appreciate the value and unselfishness of your labors and shall not soon forget you in this department of the University activities.

Yours very truly

MELVIL DEWEY

After Mrs. Converse had finished her work for the State Museum she placed a number of interesting and valuable series of relics in the American Museum of Natural History of New York City, and in the Peabody Museum of American Archeology and Ethnology of Cambridge, Mass.

Mrs. Converse's philanthropic work consumed almost her entire time, although she found moments which she utilized for the preparation of newspaper and magazine articles.

Most of the immense volume of data which she had collected rested in rough fragmentary notes illegible to any one but herself. The time which might have been devoted to getting them in form was consumed by her practical work for the Indians.

To the writer was left Mrs. Converse's library of Indian subjects and most of her manuscripts. He has been able to rescue from her notes more than a dozen myth tales, intended for incorporation in her "Myths and Mystics," and also several other manuscripts relating to Indian matters. These are included in this volume among the miscellaneous papers, but the greater part of her data can never be used.

In October 1903 Mrs. Converse was prostrated by the death of her husband. As a man of fine literary

Prominent Cattaragus Senecas who were Mrs. Converse's friends and advisers

tastes, a deep student of human nature, he had been her invaluable aid for many years. His sudden death was a shock from which Mrs. Converse never recovered. It seemed impossible for her to banish the sorrow from her mind. Her Indian friends in New York City used every means within their power to comfort her. They brought presents of strange relics to revive once again her interest in her collections, they gathered at her home and sought to entertain her with stories of old, they brought their native delicacies to her home and prepared them for her table, but all in vain. Interest was but momentary and the memory of her bereavement would settle again like a clutching shroud that could not be shaken off. The Indians never ceased, however, to minister to her. Her grief had also robbed her of her genius and she could no longer use her pen with her customary fluency. Her journalistic work became neglected and she was unable to finish her work on myths and mystics of the Iroquois, which now forms the basis of this volume.

On the evening of November 18th she was invited to take dinner with Chief Tahamont of the Abenakis, his family and friends at the chief's residence on West 26th street. The Indians waited anxiously for her appearance and finally fearing that something serious had detained her dispatched one of their number, a young Mohawk, to her home. Upon his arrival at the house he entered, there being no response to his rapping, and found her unconscious where she had fallen. She was yet breathing but expired before a physician arrived. Upon her desk was an almost illegible note which she had left for the writer of this sketch just before she fell. She wrote that she felt death upon her and left directions as to certain matters. The day of her death was the first on which the writer had been absent from her home for several weeks.

The Indians of New York were immediately notified and 50 came from all parts of the State to attend the funeral. Some were engaged in their farm work when the telegram was handed them and in order to reach New York in time some came just as they were, rather than miss the only train which would bring them to the funeral. Her faithful friends to the last were the "pagans" who allowed neither ceremony nor convention to prevent them from carrying out the honors due the noble dead. After their ancient way they addressed her as she lay in state and poured out their grief to the spirit which they believed hovered over the body. The Indian matrons who were present placed about her neck the sacred beads and the men placed a pair of moccasins at her feet. Charms and death journey requisites were also placed at her side. The chieftain emblem, a string of purple wampum which had lain above her was lifted and outspread again in the form of "the horns" of a chief's office. The wampum was then handed to Joseph Keppler, a New York publisher who for several years had studied with Mrs. Converse and to whom the Senecas had given a national adoption. His clan name is Gy-ant-wa-ka, the name once held by the celebrated Cornplanter. Mr. Keppler accepted the wampum and his election as the successor of Mrs. Converse afterward was confirmed by the Indians on the reservations.

*Part of the Harriet Maxwell Converse collection
of silver brooches now in the State Museum*

After the funeral ceremony (November 22) which was held in the Merritt Chapel on 8th Avenue, Rev. Dr Sill of St. Chrysostom's Chapel, of which Mrs. Converse was a member, officiating, her body was shipped to Elmira for interment.

The writer was placed in charge of her estate by the heirs and an examination of her accounts showed that her fortunes had dwindled almost to nothing. Her life had been spent in giving and in doing for others. Her charity extended not only to the unfortunate red race, but to the distressed of every race and class. She never neglected an opportunity to do good and oftentimes placed herself in embarrassing positions in her zeal to better the condition of the unfortunate.

Mrs. Converse was a woman of remarkable personality and her nature was entirely unselfish. Her friends have not ceased to mourn her loss for the influence of her fine personality has imbued them far too deeply to be soon forgotten.

Part I

IROQUOIS MYTHS AND LEGENDS

BY

HARRIET MAXWELL CONVERSE

PREFACE

In these legends, which I have gathered from time to time during the 22 years of my adoption among the Seneca Indians, I have endeavored to adhere to the poetical metaphor of these people. Of the 40[2] which will be included in the volume, save four or five, none of them have been published; and it has been my privilege to listen to these stories during the winter season, which is the only time when an Indian will relate his mystery tales. They have descended to me first through my grandfather, then my father, finally to be corroborated and recited to me by the Indians themselves.

HARRIET MAXWELL CONVERSE

In Mrs. Converse's text the English method of spelling Indian names has been used. In his footnotes, however, the editor has used the phonetic system generally adopted by students of American languages.

CREATION[3]

Hah-gweh-di-yu, Spirit of Good. Hah-gweh-da-ĕt-găh, Spirit of Evil. Ata-en-sic,[4] the Sky Woman. Hah-nu-nah,"[5] the Turtle.

The floating island

By Iroquois mythology, the earth was the thought of the Indian Ruler of a great island which floats in space. In all the Iroquois myths, the natural and the supernatural are so closely blended that they seem of one realm. Yet in the story of the creation, the Ruler bestowed universal authority upon the two Spirits, Good and Evil, who remain on the earth always.

The Ruler, the Great Creative Being, is known by various names, Sho-gwa-yah-dih-sat-oh (He Who Created Us), Ha-wen-ni-yu (He Who Governs), Hah-ni-go-e-yoo (Good Mind), Great Spirit and Tha-nio-do-oh or To-no-do-oo, the latter being generally adopted by the Iroquois.[6]

This mythical island of the Iroquois is a place of eternal peace. In its abundance there are no burdens to weary; in its fruitfulness all needs are endlessly provided. To its perpetual calm death never comes, and to its tranquillity, no desire, no sorrow nor pain.

The council tree

In the far away days of this floating island there grew one stately tree[7] that branched beyond the range of vision. Perpetually laden with fruit and blossoms, the air was fragrant with its perfume, and the people gathered to its shade where councils were held.

One day the Great Ruler said to his people: "We will make a new place where another people may grow. Under our council tree is a great cloud sea which calls for our help. It is lonesome. It knows no rest and calls for light. We will talk to it. The roots of our council tree point to it and will show the way."

Having commanded that the tree be uprooted, the Great Ruler peered into the depths where the roots had guided, and summoning Ata-en-sic, who was with child, bade her look down. Ata-en-sic saw nothing, but the Great Ruler knew that the sea voice was calling, and bidding her carry its life, wrapped around her a great ray of light[8] and sent her down to the cloud sea.

Hah-nu-nah, the Turtle

Dazzled by the descending light enveloping Ata-en-sic, there was great consternation among the animals and birds inhabiting the cloud sea, and they counseled in alarm.

"If it falls it may destroy us," they cried.

"Where can it rest?" asked the Duck.

"Only the oeh-da (earth) can hold it," said the Beaver, "the oeh-da which lies at the bottom of our waters, and I will bring it." The Beaver went down but never returned. Then the Duck ventured, but soon its dead body floated to the surface.

Many of the divers had tried and failed when the Muskrat, knowing the way, volunteered to obtain it and soon returned bearing a small portion in his paw. "But it is heavy," said he, "and will grow fast. Who will bear it?"

The Turtle was willing, and the oeh-da was placed on his hard shell.

Having received a resting place for the light, the water birds, guided by its glow, flew upward, and receiving the woman on their widespread wings, bore her down to the Turtle's back.

And Hah-nu-nah, the Turtle,[9] became the Earth Bearer. When he stirs, the seas rise in great waves, and when restless and violent, earthquakes yawn and devour.

Ata-en-sic, the Sky Woman

The oeh-da grew rapidly and had become an island when Ata-en-sic, hearing voices under her heart, one soft and soothing, the other loud and contentious, knew that her mission to people the island was nearing.

To her solitude two lives were coming,[10] one peaceful and patient, the other restless and vicious. The latter, discovering light under his mother's arm, thrust himself through, to contentions and strife, the right born entered life for freedom and peace.

These were the Do-ya-da-no, the twin brothers. Spirits of Good, and Evil.[11] Foreknowing their powers, each claimed dominion, and a struggle between them began, Hah-gweh-di-yu claiming the right to beautify the island, while Hah-gweh-da-ĕt-găh determined to destroy. Each went his way, and where peace had reigned discord and strife prevailed.

The Sun, Moon and Stars

At the birth of Hah-gweh-di-yu his Sky Mother, Ata-en-sic, had died, and the island was still dim in the dawn of its new life when, grieving at his mother's death, he shaped the sky with the palm of his hand, and creating the Sun from her face,[12] lifted it there, saying, "You shall rule here where your face will shine forever." But Hah-gweh-da-ĕt-găh set Darkness[13] in the west sky, to drive the Sun down behind it.

Hah-gweh-di-yu then drew forth from the breast of his Mother, the Moon and the Stars, and led them to the Sun as his sisters who would guard his night sky. He gave to the Earth her body, its Great Mother, from whom was to spring all life.

All over the land Hah-gweh-di-yu planted towering mountains, and in the valleys set high hills to protect the straight rivers as they ran to the sea. But Hah-gweh-da-ĕt-găh wrathfully sundered the mountains, hurting them far apart, and drove the high hills into the wavering valleys, bending the rivers as he hunted them down.

Hah-gweh-di-yu set forests on the high hills, and on the low plains fruit-bearing trees and vines to wing their seeds to the scattering winds. But Hah-gweh-da-ĕt-găh gnarled the forests besetting the earth, and led monsters to dwell in. the sea, and herded hurricanes in the sky which frowned with mad tempests that chased the Sun and the Stars.

The Animals and Birds

Hah-gweh-di-yu went across a great sea where he met a Being who told him he was his father.[14] Said the Being, "How high can you reach?" Hah-gweh-di-yu touched the sky. Again he asked, "How much can you lift?" and Hah-gweh-di-yu grasping a stone mountain tossed it far into space. Then said the Being, "You are worthy to be my son;" and lashing upon his back two burdens, bade him return to the earth.

Hah-gweh-di-yu swam for many days, and the Sun did not leave the sky until he had neared the earth. The burdens had grown heavy but Hah-gweh-di-yu was strong, and when he reached the shore they fell apart and opened.

From one of the burdens flew an eagle guiding the birds which followed filling the skies with their song to the Sun as they winged to the forest. From the other there came animals led by the deer, and they sped quickly to the mountains. But Hah-gweh-da-ĕt-gäh followed with wild beasts that devour, and grim flying creatures that steal life without sign, and creeping reptiles to poison the way.

Duel of Hah-gweh-di-yu and Hah-gweh-da-ĕt-găh

When the earth was completed and Hah-gweh-di-yu had bestowed a protecting Spirit upon each of his creation, he besought Hah-gweh-da-ĕt-găh to reconcile his vicious existences to the peacefulness of his own, but Hah-gweh-da-ĕt-găh refused, and challenged Hah-gweh-di-yu to combat, the victor to become the ruler of the earth.

Hah-gweh-da-ĕt-găh proposed weapons which he could control, poisonous roots strong as flint, monster's teeth, and fangs of serpents. But these Hah-gweh-di-yu refused, selecting the thorns of the giant crab-apple tree, which were arrow pointed and strong.

With the thorns they fought. The battle continued many days, ending in the overthrow of Hah-gweh-da-ĕt-găh.

Hah-gweh-di-yu, having now become the ruler, banished his brother to a pit[15] under the earth, whence he can not return. But he still retains Servers, half human and half beast, whom he sends to continue his destructive work. These Servers can assume any form Hah-gweh-da-ĕt-găh may command, and they wander all over the earth.

Hah-gweh-di-yu, faithful to the prophesy of the Great Ruler of the floating island, that the earth should be peopled,[16] is continually creating and protecting.

Ga-oh, Spirit of the Winds

Though of giant proportions, Ga-oh,[17] who governs the winds, is confined in the broad north sky.[18] Were Ga-oh free, he would tear the heavens into fragments.

In the ages of his solitary confinement, he does not forget his strength, and punishes the winds to subjection when they suddenly rear for flight.

At the entrance of his abode and reined to his hands, are four watchers[19]: the Bear (north wind). Panther (west wind). Moose (east wind), and Fawn (south wind).

When Ga-oh unbinds Bear, it leads its hurricane winter winds to Earth; when he loosens Panther, its stealthy west winds creep down and follow Earth with their snarling blasts; when Moose is released, its east wind meets the Sun and its misty breath floats over the Sun's path blinding it with rains, and when Ga-oh unlocks his reins from Fawn, its soothing south winds whisper to Earth and she summons her Spring, who comes planting the seeds for the summer sunglow.

Though in his subjugation of the winds it is Ga-oh's duty to pacify them, frequently they are influenced by his varying moods. When Ga-oh is contented and happy, gentle and invigorating breezes fan Earth; when irritated by his confinement and Ga-oh is restless, strong winds agitate the waters and bend the forest trees; and when frenzied to mighty throes, Ga-oh becomes vehement, ugly blasts go forth, uprooting trees, dashing the streams into leaping furies, lifting the sea waters to

51

mountainous waves, and devastating the earth.

Notwithstanding these outbursts, Ga-oh is faithful in disciplining the winds to their proper seasons, and guarding Earth from the rage of the elements.

When the north wind blows strong, the Iroquois say, "The Bear is prowling in the sky"; if the west wind is violent, "The Panther is whining." When the east wind chills with its rain, "The Moose is spreading his breath"; and when the south wind wafts soft breezes, "The Fawn is returning to its Doe."

Naming the Winds

Ga-oh, Spirit of the Winds. Ya-o-gah, the Bear. Da-jo-ji, the Panther. O-yan-do-ne, the Moose. Ne-o-ga, the Fawn

When, in the creation of the earth, Hah-gweh-di-yu limited the duties of the powerful Ga-oh to the sky, assigning to him the governing of the tempests, he blew a strong blast that shook the whole earth to trembling, and summoned his assistants to a council.

Ga-oh chose his aids from the terrestrial because of their knowledge of the earth; and when his reverberating call had ceased its thunderous echoes, he opened his north gate wide across the sky and called Ya-o-gah, the Bear.

Lumbering over the mountains as he pushed them from his path, Ya-o-gah, the bulky bear, who had battled the boisterous winds as he came, took his place at Ga-oh's gate and waited the mission of his call. Said Ga-oh, "Ya-o-gah, you are strong, you can freeze the waters with your cold breath; in your broad arms you can carry the wild tempests, and clasp the whole earth when I bid you destroy. I will place you in my far north, there to watch the herd of my winter winds when I loose them in the sky. You shall be North Wind. Enter your home." And the bear lowered his head for the leash with which Ga-oh bound him, and submissively took his place in the north sky.

In a gentler voice Ga-oh called Ne-o-ga, the Fawn, and a soft breeze as of the summer, crept over the sky; the air grew fragrant with the odor of flowers, and there were voices as of babbling brooks telling the secrets of the summer to the tune of birds, as Ne-o-ga came proudly lifting her head.

Said Ga-oh, "You walk with the summer sun, and know all its paths; you are gentle, and kind as the sunbeam, and will rule my flock of the summer winds in peace. You shall be the South Wind. Bend your head while I leash you to the sky, for you are swift, and might return from me to the earth." And the gentle fawn followed Ga-oh to his great gate which opens the south sky.

Again Ga-oh trumpeted a shrill blast, and all the sky seemed threatening; an ugly darkness crept into the clouds that sent them whirling in circles of confusion; a quarrelsome, shrieking voice snarled through the air, and with a sound as of great claws tearing the heavens into rifts, Da-jo-ji, the Panther, sprang to the gate.

Said Ga-oh, "You are ugly, and fierce, and can fight the strong storms; you can climb the high mountains, and tear down the forests; you can carry the whirlwind on your strong back, and toss the great sea waves high in the air, and snarl at the tempests if they stray from my gate. You shall be the West Wind. Go to the west sky, where even the Sun will hurry to hide when you howl your warning to the night." And Da-jo-ji, dragging his leash as he stealthily crept along, followed Ga-oh to the furthermost west sky.

Yet Ga-oh rested not. The earth was flat, and in each of its four corners he must have an assistant. One corner yet remained, and again Ga-oh's strong blast shook the earth. And there arose a moan like the calling of a lost mate, the sky shivered in a cold rain, the whole earth clouded in mist, a crackling sound as of great horns crashing through the forest trees dinned the air, and O-yan-do-ne, the Moose, stood stamping his hoofs at the gate.

Said Ga-oh, as he strung a strong leash around his neck, "Your breath blows the mist, and can lead the cold rains; your horns spread wide, and can push back the forests to widen the path for my storms as with your swift hoofs you race with my winds. You shall be the East Wind, and blow your breath to chill the young clouds as they float through the sky." And, said Ga-oh, as he led him to the east sky, "Here you shall dwell forevermore."

Thus, with his assistants, does Ga-oh control his storms. And although he must ever remain in his sky lodge, his will is supreme, and his faithful assistants will obey!

He-no, the Thunderer[20]

As guardian of the heavens, He-no[21] is intrusted with the thunder, the voice of admonition, which can be heard above the turmoil of the tempests. It is also his duty to direct the rain for refreshing the earth. In the planting season, He-no has supervision of the seeds, and in the growing time renders beneficent aid in ripening the fruits and maturing the harvest.

He-no can assume the form of a human being and, as such, dressed as a warrior, he wears in his hair a magic feather, which renders him invulnerable to the attacks of Evil. On these occasions he is invested with authority to inflict dire punishment upon evil doers, and is dreaded as the avenger of vice.

He-no has two assistants,[22] one of whom is half human, the other, celestial. To aid them in their terrestrial travels, they have received no names, and so, unidentified by sign, they can faithfully serve his secrecy.

In his celestial travels. He-no carries on his back a great basket containing boulders of the chert rock, which he hurls at evil spirits whenever he discovers them in the sky. Sometimes the evil spirits evade these boulders and they fall to the earth enveloped in fire.[23]

Before He-no was transferred to the skies, he dwelt behind the great falls at Niagara, where he controlled the roaring of its waters. One of his assistants took there a beautiful Indian girl as his wife who, being

Hi' no, the Thunder Spirit

From a drawing by Jesse Cornplanter, a Seneca boy artist

transformed into a water spirit, lived in the spray of the lunar rainbow, which is often seen at Niagara. But when the storm spirits were warring in the heavens, and He-no was sent to quell them, the water spirit, following her companion and He-no, became a dweller of the clouds.

During the terrestrial life of He-no[24] the Iroquois people were terrified by the annual visits of a hideous serpent that lived in a cave near the Niagara cataract.

Toward the spring, when the rivers were loosing themselves and pouring their torrents into Lake Erie, this creature would emerge from its cave, and entering the burial places of the Iroquois, feed on the dead; and in the sinuous paths of its return, would poison the land with a pestilence to which large numbers of the people fell victims. He-no pursued it, and overtaking it as it wound through the De-gi-ya-goh (Buffalo creek) threw a terrific thunderbolt upon it, and in its writhings to escape, the monster pushed the shores of the creek into the bends which yet remain.

Slowly dying, it floated down the Niagara river to the verge of the great cataract where, in a final death throe, its bulky body arched backward in a semicircle extending from shore to shore.

The dead body restrained the rushing waters for a time, but finding an opening through the rocks, they dashed on, sundering the ledge which shelved over the river as they tumbled down the abyss in a riotous roar. And thus was formed the Horse Shoe fall of the great cataract.

Gun-no-do-yah, the Thunder Boy, and the Human Snake

He-no, the Thunderer, had hurled down a terrific rain storm which had flooded the land and overflowed the lakes and rivers, and, in pity for Earth, sent down Ha-de-ne-no-da-on, one of his aids, to pacify the waters.

As Ha-de-ne-no-da-on was passing over a canton of the Senecas, he heard a voice wailing in great distress, and descending, found a small child floating in the flood that had carried its parents away. Recognizing the child as Gun-no-do-yah, the son of a chief whom on his earth visits he had frequently seen, and who was a great warrior, he determined to save it, and carrying it to his home in the sky, laid it to rest on a strong black cloud and returned to earth on his peace mission. He-no, who had been out drilling his Thunderers, upon returning overheard the boy grieving the loss of his parents and, deciding to adopt[25] him, transformed him into a Thunder Hunter. Said He-no, "He has been sent to me; he is a human and knows all the paths of the earth, and can render me great service. There dwells in a lake a human monster that no mortal has been able to kill; my Thunderers, not being of earth, have sought him in vain; and he defies me and my thunderbolts while he ravages the lake of its fish, and frightening the fishers away deprives the people of their food. Gun-no-do-yah, having been human, can follow the trails of the earth. I will make him powerful, and give him a strong bow and arrow, and he shall follow my storms

58

when my black clouds[26] shadow the lakes, and hunt the monster to its death."

Now, Gun-no-do-yah, feeling that he owed his life to He-no, whose faithful Thunderer had rescued him from the water, was glad to do whatever he could to evidence his gratitude, and when He-no's black clouds descended to earth, he faithfully followed to the lakes.

But for many months his search was in vain. Only one lake (Ontario) remained to be searched, and, thought Gun-no-do-yah, "Its waters are deep and broad, it is there I will find this terrible serpent."[27] So, when He-no's black clouds hung heavy over the lake, obscuring the light of the sun, he stealthily approached the shore, when to his delight, he beheld the monster lashing the water with its great tail.

With steady aim Gun-no-do-yah drew his bow and sent swift his arrow, but before it could reach its mark, the monster had vanished, leaving a trail of foam in which the arrow harmlessly sank.

Many days Gun-no-do-yah had visited the lake and frequently had aimed at the monster floating on the water, but only to waste his arrows in the foam of its trail as it vanished. But one night when the Thunderers were savagely hurling their bolts over the lake which the clouds obscured in their blackness, and the fish swam deep in fear of the reverberating echoes, Gun-no-do-yah went boldly into the lake, and encountering the snake again drew his bow, when the snake beckoned to him to come closer and listen; and then it began to speak. "Come closer," it said, "and fear me not. I know you well, and I know your strong arrows; they can not reach me. He-no, your master, I fear not; I scorn his thunder, the lightning passes by me. Your task is useless and you need not serve him. I am your friend and will teach you how to shoot the fish in the night. I will reveal to you all the secrets of the waters. Come with me, I will guide you to my home in the rocks deep below which the sun never sees. Come and comb my long mane, it is tangled with fish and is heavy."

Gun-no-do-yah would not listen, he came to kill; but as he drew his bow with all his strength, the string snapped, the dead arrow fell to the water, and he was powerless. Raising its head high in the air, the monster opened its hissing mouth, and seizing Gun-no-do-yah, carried him down to the bottom of the lake.

He-no was sleeping, when Gun-no-do-yah appeared to him in a dream and related his misfortune, that he had found the snake monster in the lake Ontario and that it had devoured him.

The Horned Serpent

The dream caused He-no great anguish, and he determined to rescue Gun-no-do-yah; so hastily summoning his bravest warriors and relating to them the fate that had overtaken him, he sent them to earth to plough through the lake. Diligently they

ploughed through the deep caves under the water, where they found the monster sleeping; and drawing it from its hiding place carried it to He-no, who slew it and drew from its body the still living Gun-no-do-yah. And great was the rejoicing of the Thunderers and warriors.

Now, that Gun-no-do-yah had been saved, He-no would never permit him to revisit the earth, but that he might have him ever near him, made him one of his aids to accompany him during his storms and hurry the lightning.

Lake Ontario is noted for its violent winds, and when they drive the canoe high on the waves, the Indians know that the spirit of the snake is there "twisting the water" in its revenge and when the lightning darts quick across the sky, they whispered in awe, "Gun-no-do-yah is chasing it!"

O-se-ha-da-gaar[28], the Dew Eagle

He-no, the Thunderer. Ga-oh, Spirit of the Winds. The Fire Spirit, the Listeners, and Flame Bearers

In the myth lore of the Iroquois, where everything animate or inanimate is endowed with supernatural powers either evil or good, the myths relating to the sun, so fecund with life-giving power, have special significance.

Although never wandering from his path across the sky, the Sun[29] controls his broad dominion through

61

his assistants, Serving Spirits, whom he endows with various powers and sends down to Earth to fulfil his missions.

To some is given the care of the fruits, others guard the grains, nothing is overlooked; and these guarding spirits, ever watchful of their duties, faithfully serve the Sun.

But there are others. Spirits of Evil, who roam the Earth, and defying the Sun, seek to overthrow its beneficent power. Among these is the Fire Spirit who, malevolently jealous of the Spirits of Good, may summon his Flame Bearers and, descending to Earth, burn and destroy the harvests.

At the coming of the Fire Spirit, mountains shrink down, the thirsting valleys suck dry the streams and springs, Night pales her stars, and all Earth faints.

In vain Ga-oh searches the heavens for his hiding winds. In vain He-no hunts his thunderbolts to hurl at the Flame Bearers, and all seems hopeless and lost.

But to this desolation comes O-se-ha-da-gaar, a great bird, whose lodge is far beyond the west sky, and who carries a lake of dew in the hollow of its back.

O-se-ha-da-gaar is wise, and does not listen to every call. He knows his power and waits. He is faithfully guarded by a band of Listeners, great birds who fly far above the Sun and can see all that passes below. They hear every sound and know every voice in the heavens, and watch the soft winds which waft the summer clouds to gather the showers; and when the

Fire Spirit suffocates the Earth, they speed to her voice, and bear it to O-se-ha-da-gaar who waits in his lodge.[30]

Then O-se-ha-da-gaar hears; and pluming for flight, pushes the skies far apart, obscuring the Sun with his vast spreading wings as they dip to the east and the

The Dew Eagle
From a drawing by Jesse Cornplanter, a Seneca boy artist

west fanning gentle breezes, and mist veils the skies as through his fluttering wings he sifts down from his lake the dews to refresh the famishing Earth.

Then all nature revives, the Fire Spirit flees; the parching Earth bares her broad breast to the falling dews; her glad rivers and lakes rejoice, and her harvests rise to new life.

At the Harvest Feast of the Iroquois, the Creator is thanked for having bestowed upon the people the guarding vigilance of He-no, and is implored not to withdraw from them his power, which controls the gentle rains in the seedtime and the dews in the ripening.

O-ga-nyo-da and Sais-tah-go-wa, the Rainbow and the Serpent

Twins: Hah-gweh-di-yu, the Good Minded; Hah-gweh-da-ĕt-găh, the Bad Minded. Ga-oh, Spirit of the Winds. He-no, the Thunderer

In the creation of the earth, which the Turtle bears, upon its back, the Sky Woman gave birth to the twins, Hah-gweh-di-yu, and Hah-gweh-da-ĕt-găh; and with their birth, Good and Evil came upon the Earth; for Hah-gweh-da-ĕt-găh was bad minded, and between the brothers there was continual strife. Hah-gweh-di-yu, the Good Minded, was ever striving to create all things beautiful, which angered Hah-gweh-da-ĕt-găh, who sought only to disfigure and destroy.

Hah-gweh-di-yu created beautiful rivers, and planted high hills to guard their peaceful flow through the valleys, which enraged Hah-gweh-da-ĕt-găh, who brought forth Sais-tah-go-wa, a sea monster, directing him to enter and destroy them. Sais-tah-go-wa, accustomed to the freedom of the broad seas, was furious when restricted by the banks of the streams, and viciously strove to rend them apart, writhing his way through the waters and hurling great rocks upon them as they fled to the sea.

Bewailing the loss of his rivers should they be engulfed in the deep seas and his high lands and valleys perish from thirst, Hah-gweh-di-yu hastened to their rescue, whereupon, Sais-tah-go-wa, discovering his approach and dreading his power, sought to make his escape, and being unable to return through the rivers he had destroyed, fled to the sky.

The Sun was peacefully tracking its trail across the heavens when Sais-tah-go-wa appeared, and upon learning what the monster had done, determined that it should never return to the earth to injure the creations of Hah-gweh-di-yu, and throwing him across the sky, clasped him down to the east and the west.

It chanced at this time that He-no, the Thunderer, was passing on his way through a storm, and admiring the beautiful colors of Sais-tah-go-wa as he stretched across the sky, picked him up, saying, "My Lightning Hunter needs this for his bow," and straightway carried him up to his lodge.

Sais-tah-go-wa is restless in his captivity, and when He-no is busy directing his storms, endeavors to escape; but the ever watchful Sun detects him, and again bending him across the sky, paints him with his brightest colors that he may be discovered by He-no, who quickly comes and carries him back to his lodge.

In summer showers the red man sees Sais-tah-go-wa in the resplendent hues that arch the sky, and as they fade away and the sun comes forth, he exclaims, "The rain is past!—Sais-tah-go-wa tried to escape, but He-no has taken him back to his lodge!"

Ska-hai-we, Indian Summer

Ga-oh, Spirit of the Winds. Go-ho-ne, Winter. An-da, Day. Se-oh, Night. O-ga-nyo-da, the Rainbow. He-no, the Thunderer. Ga-o-no-uh, Canoe (new moon).

When in the late autumn the Sun "walks crooked," he is on his way to the south sky where during the winter solstice he rests, leaving his "sleep spirit" on guard during his absence.

Previous to his departure he smokes the ah-so-qua-ta (peace pipe) to veil the earth as he councils with the Great Mother.

Sun talks to Earth

"Earth, Great Mother, holding your children close to your breast, hear my power! Listen.

The days of my glowing are passed. I glare and I burn and I scorch no more. I am lighting my fire from you to kindle my ah-so-qua-ta, the pipe of my sleep. In the haze of my Indian summer I wrap you to silence while Ga-oh holds fast on your pillowing hills the flock of his jealous clouds. The smoke of my ah-so-qua-ta must not be driven back.

Soon I will travel my crooked sky trail. I hurry. I have heard the swift blast of Go-ho-ne's voice, and am flocking the fearing clouds of the Ska-hai-we closer together as they feather the stem of my ah-so-qua-ta.

See! Ga-oh floats gentle winds to the smoke of my ah-so-qua-ta. The north, east, south and west must smoke my peace pipe. I rule the sky! I summon An-da, and she watches my fields. I call Se-oh and she sends forth her stars to guard my dark paths. When He-no, the Thunderer, pours down his rain, I warn as I paint my O-ga-nyo-da to hang on the falling clouds, and He-no hushes his voice. When He-no is fierce and hurls his fire arrows across my path, I chase, and his arrows pale in my blaze.

When Ga-oh walks on his freezing way, my watchers hide from his howling blasts which lurk in the north. When I dream in my south land, Go-ho-ne grows strong, but the feet of my sky herd are speedy and free as they race with the winds; nor can the winds twist the horns of my stars with their fighting breath as they race, nor darken the track of my Moon with their mists; my Moon knows my power, and floats her ga-o-no-uh on my sky sea as her sign when she sets on her journey anew.

Earth, Great Mother, listen and hear my power!

Now your broad waters grow ugly and strong, roaming and fighting Ga-oh. Fear not. I look down into the dark where their monsters rage. I know the secrets of their deep places where Darkness is chained and will send it my light, as I go for a time to my sleep where gentler waters obey when my glow cradles on their waves.

Ga-oh will strike down your battling seas. When they rise and fight, he will hurl back their quarreling mountains. Ga-oh is mighty and will unlock his tempests when He-no lets loose his Thunderers to lash down the seas.

Great Mother, listen, I speak! Your stately mountains are watching my ah-so-qua-ta. Look at its smoke as Ga-oh craftily wafts it through shades where soft breezes creep in their hurried flight, for Ga-oh is whispering frosts in his wavering breath!

When I summon An-da, your mountains grow glad and red with my light as I crown them anew with plumes of my glow. Your mountains are proud, and push through the clouds to welcome me as I blaze the east and the west and the north and the south!

Great Mother, behold your valleys, the paths of your guarding hills! The smoke of my ah-so-qua-ta is searching them far where swift rivers run and lakes hide down. As the winds warn, the trees bend low and loosen their leaves to soften the bed for the winter snow; and the leaves fall fast. Mother Earth, red with your blood in their dying breath, and gold with my parting touch!

The trails of your valleys reach vast and long where your great rivers meet, and your willing breast flows and nurses its young. Great Mother, hug close your valleys while yet the smoke of my ah-so-qua-ta shields! Your deep-dwelling lakes are pale shadowed and dim in the hiding haze of my ah-so-qua-ta as it loses its way in their chasing waves; and over your face the mist falls low as Go-ho-ne is capturing my glow for his icy veil that will cover you down from my peering sky.

Great Mother, listen! The smoke of my ah-so-qua-ta drifts, my sleep spirit waits for its winter dream, and I speed as I go to the land of my rest. I hear the voice of Go-ho-ne, it is hindering and slow as it weaves your blanket of feathery snows. Shrink you strong from the stealing cold that chills your breast where your streams have fed.

Your veins will grow little and race no more, and your heart will hush slow when you turn from my gaze to the dark where your echoes hide. Their voices are stilled, they search no more for my Summer Day. Her feet are fastened with Ga-oh's thongs that bind her from the torturing winds. Ga-oh is kind.

Your mountains will wake when I come again, your mountains will wake, your rivers run fast, and lakes cradle low. Go-ho-ne will flee, I will burn his thongs. Your heart will hear my calling voice. Your seeds will climb to my waiting glow, and your breast flow swift to nourish your young.

Great Mother, listen! I am A-deka-ga-gwaa, the Sun! I rule the skies! I govern An-da. I chase Go-ho-ne. I frighten the shriek of the Thunderer's voice when he furrows my paths with his storms; but when I touch the wings of his flying clouds, they fold the rains fast and sift dews to your thirsting vales. I scorch and I burn, and I kill! I turn my face, and the tempests come. When I sleep in my South, Go-ho-ne is bold, when I open my eyes, Go-ho-ne flies, and He-no grows frightened and still!

I am A-deka-ga-gwaa! I reign, and I rule all your lives! My field is broad where swift clouds race, and chase, and climb, and curl, and fall in rains to your rivers and streams. My shield is vast, and covers your land with its yellow shine, or burns it brown with my hurrying flame. My eyes are wide, and search everywhere. My arrows are quick when I dip them in dews that nourish and breathe. My army is strong, when I sleep it watches my fields. When I come again my warriors will battle throughout the skies; Ga-oh will lock his fierce winds; He-no will soften his voice; Go-ho-ne will fly, and tempests will war no more!

As I sleep down to my dreams, the paths of my sky land slant crooked and small; the breath of my ah-so-qua-ta grows slow, its panting fire dies black, its ashes are pale, the trails grow dark, and my sleep spirit watches near!

Deh-oh-niot[31], the Evil Soul Gatherer

Sky color is the Deh-oh-niot, who haunts the tall tree tops and the high mountain crests.

With the face of a wolf, the wings of a vulture, the body of a panther and claws like a hawk, the Deh-oh-niot wanders in the "pathway of spirits,"[32] and is one of the emissaries Death[33] sends to the earth to gather souls.

The sick fear him, the dying hear him clawing at the door, where he whines like a cat if the spirit is departing, or barks like a wolf if it is not ready to travel.

Although Deh-oh-niot watches for his victims, and knows the death path which leads from every lodge door, there are other Invisibles, guardians of the departing soul, who guide it to its further condition where it may assume whatever form it is to inhabit before reaching its final rest place in the Happy Hunting Ground.

When watching the lodge of the dying, there is a continual struggle between Deh-oh-niot and these Invisibles.

By the law of Death, before whom all departing spirits must pass on their journey, Deh-oh-niot can seize only the evil of a spirit which enters his domain, and even then it may escape him if, in its earth existence, good has predominated. Yet, should Deh-oh-niot be able to capture but a small portion of a soul, he may convey it to Death, and be rewarded for his service.

If the evil of a spirit had been overpowering while it dwelt on the earth, and but a fragment of good remained with it, even then it might be strong enough to escape while Deh-oh-niot, with his pantherlike tail lashing wide and trailing fire in his path, is carrying it across the skies.

If, in a fierce struggle, the spirit should gain its

freedom, Deh-oh-niot will have revenge by transforming it into a "fire stone," and throwing it down to the earth where it may be eternally imprisoned.

Were Deh-oh-niot any other than sky color, there might be escape from his power; but he can sit on a tree where its top blends with the sky, and there no one can see him. When he rests on a mountain crag, he outlines its high reaching, as if the sky were "bunching down" in repose.

His death cry may be mistaken for the mewing of the house cat, or the bark of a dog at the door, for only the dying can distinguish between the voices. Therefore, Deh-oh-niot is the dread of each lodge, where he may at any time enter when Death sends him to gather souls.

To hear the voice of Deh-oh-niot is an evil omen, and some dire calamity will follow those who have listened to it. If Deh-oh-niot appears to a person who is not ill, his death will soon follow.

While Deh-oh-niot is possessed of the ferocity of the wolf, the stealthiness of the panther, the rapaciousness of the vulture and the claw weapons of the hawk; all these are necessary in his task of gathering evil spirits for Death.

When a "fire stone" (meteor) flames through the sky "Deh-oh-niot is gathering souls"; and should it fall to the earth, "Deh-oh-niot has pushed a soul from its trail."

When a comet appears in the heavens, Deh-oh-niot is spreading his tail.

Od-je-so-dah and Ji-hen-yah, the Dancing Stars and the Sky Witches

An Indian hunter was teaching his eleven sons[34] the secrets of the forest, and had led them into its innermost density where game strode unafraid in its stillness. He had taught them the hunter's step, which must fall light as the leaf that drops from its branch, and had shown them the haunts and the foot signs of all the animals, and on the morrow would find for them the deep pools where the fish shoaled in secret or hid from the sunshine; and as night had shadowed the forest in its darkness, the hunter and his sons lay down to rest.

As they slept, soft singing voices floated through the still trees, nearer and nearer approaching till they awakened Hai-no-nis, the eldest of the eleven brothers. Charmed by the weird chanting, he aroused his brothers to listen to the sorcerous song, and they followed as it led through bewildering paths to a large tree where under its branches a great circle widened its moon shadows. For a time the voices ceased, but as the brothers waited, the song was resumed in a quicker strain that tuned them to swift dancing till in the frenzy of its measure, they could not cease. They implored the Night Wind to guide them back to their father, but it passed heedlessly by, and the voices led the brothers still further as, delirious with motion, they danced onward and upward till they had left the earth far beneath in their skyward flight.

Day after day the brothers danced, and day after day the troubled Sun glanced after them but could not reach them. Night after night the stars grew dizzy as the dancers swirled round the sky, when Hai-no-nis disappeared and the song-voices fainted far away.

Yet the dancers could not rest, and the pitying Moon, thinking to quiet them, left her path and led them to her procession of stars which was marching across the night sky. But their ceaseless dancing set the stars whirling till the Moon, frightened at the confusion, transformed them to a group of fixed stars and assigned them the charge of the New Year of the red man, commanding that forevermore they must dance over the council house during the ten days of his New Year's feast.

When Hai-no-nis left his brothers he followed the voices, and discovering them to be the Ji-hen-yah (Sky Witches), promised that if they would not further torment his brothers, they should dance forever in their honor.

And so the brothers[35] continue to dance, ever obeying the Moon, which sometimes sends them to return wandering stars that may have lost their way in the darkness.

These Sky Witches frequently descend to the earth in the darkness in search of victims for their sky feasts which they are ever celebrating.

In the astronomical lore of the paleface, this celestial

group of dancing brothers is known as the Pleiades, the brilliant constellation in the neck of Taurus. The feast of the New Year, as with all others of the Iroquois, is regulated by the Moon.

O-so-ah, the Tall Pine, Speaks

The spirit of the pine[36] was once a brave war chief who led his warriors to victory till captured by his enemies and burned at the stake.

In the metempsychosis of the Iroquois, the liberated spirit of the chief entered the pine, where it will remain forever the forest guide of the Indian people. It is a fact that the two topmost branches of the pine point to the east and the west, thus furnishing a compass for the red man when lost in the woods. These branches also symbolize the "deer horns," the insignia that ranks a chief.

And the Tall Pine said: "Once I walked the earth a warrior chief, and in my quiver was death. My arrows cried shrill and strong on their journeys to kill. They were feathered for blood. They were plunged with the poison that slays. They were winged to the winds that found the way in their swift death flight, and they never came back to me!

I was strong and bold, and hated my foe. I was stealthy, and haughty, and strode like the stag on my path. To my listening ear the death moan was soft as the call of the doe.

When I hunted my foe my footfall was still as the feather that drops from the flying bird, and the earth knew no sign of the moccasin track.

Like a wolf I scented the blood of my foe and his heart that dripped sweet as the sunrise dew, and I followed him swift in my hungry hunt.

No coward was I to skulk in my path. I counted my deaths as the great eagle numbers his feathers to the morning sun. My heart grew bigger with hate in its thirst for blood when my brave warriors followed wherever I led, winding in trails as the gliding snake bends, or straight as the way to the sky.

I was vengeful and fleet, when captured for death, and walked through the dead my arrows had left and scorned their weak stillness and cowardly sleep.

I knew no pain of the torture brand, I sang to its flame my forefather's song as I welcomed the fire and red death with scorn, and the sun glared glad as it looked down on me.

I knew no bruise as the blood ran down to the waiting earth, I knew no sting when my quivering flesh curled in the blaze and the thongs shrunk deep to my blackening bones, for my spirit was strong and dared my doom that the foe had said.

My spirit was strong, and could not die. It led my blood on its wasting way and nourished its flow as my veins throbbed fast for the seeding roots of my branches that boast.

My spirit was strong and guided each branch to the

sun and winds as it lifted my tower higher and higher, and knotted my tents where wandering snows and the flying light of the summer sun halts and hides.

And my spirit said when it builded me: 'I will make you tall, and forever the tower and guide of your forest kin. On your topmost reach I will hang the horns that as warrior you wore, and I will set them high. When the sun sleeps and clouds blanket low, the kin of your forest will know where the east trail winds and the west trail guides.'

And my spirit said as it builded me: 'You were fearless and brave in your warrior life, and I will spread your arms broad against foes. Your swift running blood will never pale and creep to your feet. Grow strong, and tall as the forest guide. Grow strong, and high—the sky is not far!' "

And the Speaking Pine said: "My spirit has builded, and I watch the sky. When strong tempests battle, I war with their rage as, in their moaning, voices return from my dead, and, as of old, I toss them back to the killing winds.

When the soughing breeze passes my strong watchtower, a life stirs in me that is gentle and kind as the mother bird brooding her young, and I open my arms wide to the singing wind that tunes me to dreams.

Thus forever I watch as my horns lift to the touch of the morning sun and flush to its west fire glow.

I am the Pine! the guide of my forest kin! I rock the sunlights to drowse in my arms as the winds waft my fragance afar. In my silence the night shadows dream of the day as I tower strong and high and reach to the sky!' "

Ga-do-wăăs, his Star Belt, the Milky Way

Ga-do-wăăs dwells in the top sky, and with his four eyes watches every corner of the earth.

At one time, Ga-do-wăăs was an earth dweller and a hunter, but because of his presuming to celestial power and destroying all the game, he was transferred to the heavens, and watches the gate through which each soul passes to immortality.

When Ga-do-wăăs assumed his duty as soul watcher, he removed his hunting belt, which possessed the charm of enticing game, and decorating it with stars, cast it into space, where it spans the entire heavens and illuminates each path[37] to which he guides a soul.

So luminous is this path that its blended light reaches down to the earth and divides its rays, stationing one at each lodge where a human is dying, that the departing soul may not lose its way as it leaves the dead.

No human has seen these rays, they are visible only to the soul. The south wind accompanies the soul till it reaches the gate where Ga-do-wăăs watches, and as it passes the portal of this journey place, he reaches into space and grasps a star which he fastens in the belt, thereby to guide the soul on its journey.

When the soul has crossed the entire heavens, Ga-do-wăăs removes the star from his belt, and returns it to its appointed place in space.

Though each soul may pass through various trans-migrations before it departs from its lower existence, it can not enter the Happy Hunting Ground[38] till it has crossed the star belt of Ga-do-wăăs, therefore, the Milky Way,[39] to the Indian, is a procession of stars, each guiding a soul. If there is a confusion in this procession, it is because some soul is disturbed and out of the path; but the star, which never loses its way, will search for it and return it to its course.

Nya-gwa-ih, the Celestial Bear

The Iroquois had been disturbed by the ravages of an enormous bear which was devouring their winter game.

Numbers of the hunters had banded together and plodded through all the forests in search of it, but to no avail. At times it would near for a moment but to distance their arrows in a most mysterious way, and the blinding snow would fall fast and thick as if to cover its track.

In the darkness it frequently prowled near the villages, when the terrified people would hide from its roaring voice, and a deep snowfall always followed these visitations; and baffling all their plans for its death, the nya-gwa-ih continued his ravage of plunder.

The winter was fierce in its cold blasts, and the snows had drifted mountains high in the forest; the trails were lost; the deer were vanishing, and their haunts were strewn with their bones which the nya-gwa-ih had left behind him, when one night each of three brothers[40] dreamed he had found the bear, and deeply impressed by the remarkable coincidence on the following morning they silently left the village and started on their secret hunt, accompanied by their faithful dog, Ji-yeh, whose keen nose ridged the snow down to the trail.

In their pursuing one day they saw the bear. It had pushed under a snow bank, and was ravenously devouring a deer. So certain were they of its capture, that they cut down a small pine and made ready the fire for cooking it, but when they resumed their hunt, the bear had vanished, and there was no trail of it in the swift falling snow which had covered its track; and chagrined that they had been so near and had failed, they decided not to stop again till they had captured it.

Having thus determined, they bundled the fire brush on the shoulders of one of the brothers,[41] and to their belts tied their strong bags of o-na-oh,[42] the roasted corn flour which would sustain them while they were running, and again set out on the chase.

At night they slept not; during the day they rested not; for the elusive shadow of the rapid running bear could be seen on the snow hills as they ran to the north sky.

As if avenging, the freezing winds pursued them, the ice weighted down their moccasins, and the pitiless snows drifted near to the skies; but impelled by their dream, the intrepid hunters faltered not until they had reached the end of the flat earth where it edges close to the north sky. Then the shadow of the bear disappeared, and the distant paths seemed enveloped in a vaporous mist like a hiding cloud that floats over the water.

Yet the tireless hunters would not rest, but climbed higher and higher and farther away from the earth, when again they saw the bear, who was now slow in its path, yet mighty as it pushed the white clouds before it, weaving an invisible net which it cast over the skies and crawled under to rest.[43]

Astray in the strange place, the untiring hunters, who knew not fatigue nor hunger, rejoiced when they came near the bear to find him sleeping. "We will not lose it now,[44] and will carry it back to our people," was their victorious cry.

The listening bear slowly opened its sleepy eyes, and rising in its giant height, lifted the net with its huge paws and, dragging the hunters under it, drove them far away to roam the broad skies forever! And the hunters and their faithful dog, Ji-yeh, unknowing their imprisonment under the invisible net, are ceaselessly following the snow bear, who ever eludes them.[45]

In Ursa Major,[46] the Iroquois find these three hunters, one with the brush upon his back, and close following they trace the faithful dog, Ji-yeh.

O-JE-A-NEH-DOH, THE SKY ELK

So-son-do-wah, the Hunter.   Ga-ji-son-da, the Star Woman.

He was a mighty hunter, the So-son-do-wah![47] The sun glanced at the forest as it beamed upon the earth with its morning light, the forest where O-je-a-neh-doh,[48] the Sky Elk, stood silent as a shadow as his broad antlers brushed back the branches of an oak. Ne-o-ga was bewildered, the dazzling sunbeams confused him. He had wandered far in the earth forest all the night. O-je-a-neh-doh knew not the sun, the sun does not shine on the elk fields of the sky, so far above it, whence O-je-a-neh-doh had lingered too long to return.

So-son-do-wah, who knew every deer track in the forest and had watched through the night with the pride of a hunter, looked upon O-je-a-neh-doh with awe. In all the forests he had never seen such an elk, but in the honor of his hunter heart and by the law of his religion, he must give all game a chance for its life. His bent bow was waiting, his aim was sure, and his unerring arrow ready for flight when, as a warning, So-son-do-wah shook a small sapling and it whirred like a partridge taking its flight.

Alert, O-je-a-neh-doh lifted his head as he snuffed the air and, with a bound, sped through the tangled ways of the hazy shades as So-son-do-wah sent his swift arrows after him.

Up the rise and down the low places, across streams, now speeding in circles, then bounding over the hollows,

82

O-je-a-neh-doh raced and So-son-do-wah followed, near enough to see his arrows strike only to fall blunt to the ground.

Hour after hour the O-je-a-neh-doh ran on, hour after hour So-son-do-wah followed.

The noon sent its sun rays straight down to the bushlands; in his mocking flight O-je-a-neh-doh sped on and So-son-do-wah followed. Sunset shaded the forest; yet, like a wild winged thing O-je-a-neh-doh silently fled as So-son-do-wah followed. Night darkened the wood paths, and the speeding O-je-a-neh-doh seemed one of its shadows; still the light footed So-son-do-wah followed. The new risen moon looked down and the stars faltered forth in the red west trail of the sun, when O-je-a-neh-doh quickened his race and leaped up the white headed hills of the sky; but So-son-do-wah, still following, caught on the wing of a swift bird of the night, which hastened its flight and soared to the farthermost part of the sky where the sun wakes up for the earth; yet O-je-a-neh-doh, the Sky Elk, more fleet in his own free fields, ever eluded the dumb arrows which sighed from So-son-do-wah's bow, until day feathered the sky with its plumes of red light, when the night bird shook So-son-do-wah from its wings back to the earth. But Dawn, pitying the sky stranger, rescued him as he was falling, and carrying him to her lodge in the east sky, created him her sentinel to guard its door.

One other duty which she assigned him was to watch from the sky heights the earth forest, the forest where the sky night hunters follow the game. And these hunters often escorted So-son-do-wah back to the earth, to guide them in their paths.

In his travels the heart of So-son-do-wah yearned back to the earth, and he would have fled from the hunters but he could not escape. Once when Day had already hinted her coming, So-son-do-wah saw a beautiful maiden standing by a low river where she had gone in search of water. Swift as an arrow of light a tenderness quivered within his heart and, forgetting his sky life, he gently approached her, but the wary hunters drew him back to the lodge of Dawn. There the heart of So-son-do-wah moaned in its vigils. He could not forget the river maiden, and frequently saw her face in the river mists that rose to the sky.

Although a celestial prisoner and a watcher of the night. Dawn had endowed him with dominion to enter within some other life during the day when he could revisit the earth, and one spring morning, So-son-do-wah, who in his love for the maiden had determined to find her, entered the heart of a bluebird which had dipped its wings in the azure hues of the southern sky.

"With the bird, So-son-do-wah followed the course of the river, singing "ji-nya-ah, ji-nya-ah, ji-nya-ah," and the forests echoed "ji-nya-ah, ji-nya-ah, ji-nya-ah" until the maiden, who was standing by the river, heard the plaintive song.

"It is the bluebird," said she, "spring is here!" and

in a glad voice she too called "ji-nya-ah, ji-nya-ah, ji-nya-ah" and the bluebird came at her call and sat on her shoulder and nestled its head against her face as she caressed it. Under the wing of the bird the heart of So-son-do-wah throbbed quick with love, but the sun was near and he must return to the sky. Yet as the bird disappeared, the mournful cry "ji-nya-ah, ji-nya-ah, ji-nya-ah" wafted back to the earth.

Again in midsummer, So-son-do-wah, grown restless, borrowed the body of a blackbird and before dawn flew through the woodlands whistling "ga-go-ji, ga-go-ji." On the ash, elm, oak and pine he rocked in the branches, whistling ga-go-ji, ga-go-ji, and he swung on the vines that climb through the forest, whistling ga-go-ji, ga-go-ji until a faint echo answered far down the riverside.

There flew the blackbird, there stood the maiden, who whispered "ga-go-ji, ga-go-ji, the blackbird is here! fruits are ripening and the maize grows close to the sun." And she held out her hand coaxing the bird down from the tree, and the sun-red hue of his shoulder fringe flushed his night-black wings as he flew to her call.

"Ga-go-ji," she crooned as she stroked his soft wings, "I love you, Ga-go-ji, you bring the sun to the berries. The maize knows your voice as you lift from its fields." And close to her lips Ga-go-ji lifted his beak.

"It is I!" So-son-do-wah plaintively sighed from the heart of the bird, but the maiden heard not, and Ga-go-ji flew back to a forest tree where shadows were hiding.

In the autumn when the trees shed their leaves and the fur of the elk grows long, So-son-do-wah crept into the heart of a giant night hawk who was searching the rivers for prey. Through the mists of the night all over the land, he called "gwa-diis, gwa-diis," but the still air held the echoless cry. Down by the river far and far, in piteous moans he called "gwa-diis, gwa-diis" till near the sun-rise, when he found the beautiful maiden sleeping on the bank.

"She is here!" whispered So-son-do-wah from the heart of the hawk as it swooped down and, lifting her to its broad wings, bore her to the skies, and all the rivers heard the joyful cry of "gwa-diis, gwa-diis" as it wafted down with the dews.

When the maiden awoke, Dawn, who was standing by the door of her lodge, reproved So-son-do-wah for remaining so long on the earth, and transformed the maiden into a star. As punishment to So-son-do-wah for deserting his watch of her door, she invoked the aid of her warrior attendants who seized him and bound his arms. On his forehead they placed the new star, and in her hand a flaming torch, and should he attempt to release himself, the torch will consume him.

And thus he remains So-son-do-wah, the human hunter, who yet yearns for the star which has never known him.

After the disappearance of So-son-do-wah, game multiplied in the forests and the deer stalked unafraid. The Sky Elk, who roams restlessly in the celestial hunting grounds, frequently visits the earth but returns before sunlight.

The Iroquois relate that the Sun lights his council fire by the torch of the Star Woman before he appears above the horizon. This Star Woman of the Iroquois, who precedes the sun in the east sky, is the morning star[49] of the paleface.

O-NA-TAH AND THE GA-GAAH, SPIRIT OF THE CORN, AND THE CROW

Hah-gweh-di-yu, the Good Minded. Hah-gweh-da-ĕt-gäh, the Bad Minded. Ga-oh, Spirit of the Winds

Ga-gaah, the Crow[50]

Among the birds which came from the sun land, Ga-gaah carried in his ear a grain of corn which Hah-gweh-di-yu planted above the body of his Mother (the earth), and it became the first grain, the "life" of the red man. By this *birthright,* Ga-gaah, claiming his share, hovers above the fields, guarding the young roots from the foes which infest them.

O-na-tah, Spirit of the Corn

O-na-tah, Spirit of the Corn, and patroness of the fields, brings the planting season to the earth.

O-na-tah, chaste in her virgin beauty—the sun

*The Spirit of the Corn speaking to
Handsome Lake, the Seneca prophet*

From a drawing by Jesse Cornplanter, a Seneca boy artist

touches her dusky face with the blush of the morning, and her eyes grow soft as the gleam of the stars that floats on dark streams. Her night-black hair flares to the breeze like the wind-driven cloud that unveils the sun. As she walks the air draped in her maize, its blossoms plume to the sun, and its fringing tassels play with the rustling leaves in whispering promises to the waiting fields. Night follows her dim way with the dews, and Day guides the beams that leap from the sun to her path. And the great Mother (earth) loves O-na-tah who brings to her children, the red men, their life-giving[51] grain.

At one time, O-na-tah had two companions, the spirits of the bean and the squash. In the olden time, when the bean, corn and squash were planted in one hill, these three sister plant spirits, the De-o-ha-ko were never separated. Each was clothed in the plant which she guarded. The Spirit of the Squash was crowned with the flaunting gold trumpet blossoms of its foliage, and the Spirit of the Bean was arrayed in the clinging leaves of its winding vine, its velvety pods swinging to the summer breeze.

One day when O-na-tah had wandered astray in search of the lost dews, Hah-gweh-da-ĕt-găh, capturing her, sent one of his monsters to blight her fields, and the Spirits of the Squash and the Bean fled before the death winds which pursued them.

Hah-gweh-da-ĕt-găh imprisoned O-na-tah in his darkness under the earth, where she languished, lamenting her lost fields; when a searching sun ray discovered her and guided her back to her lands.

Bewailing the desolation of the blight, and mourning the desertion of her sister spirits of the bean and the squash, O-na-tah made a vow to the Sun that she would never leave her fields again; and now she holds her vigils alone, separated from her sister plants.

If her fields thirst, she can not leave them to summon the dews. When the Flame Spirit of the Sun burns the maize, O-na-tah dare not search the skies for Ga-oh, to implore him to unleash the winds and fan her lands. When great rains fall and blight her fields, the voice of O-na-tah grows faint, and the Sun can not hear; yet, faithful, she watches and guards, never abandoning her fields till the maize is ripe.

When O-na-tah brings the planting season, her crow flocks know, and the birds whirl and call in the sky.

When invoking the aid of the sun, O-na-tah scatters her first corn over her broad lands, the birds flutter down and hunt the foes that follow the roots in the earth.

When the maize stalks bend low, O-na-tah is folding the husks to the pearly grains that the dews will nourish in their screening shade as they fringe to the sun. When the tassels plume, O-na-tah is crowning the maize with her triumph sign and the rustling leaves spear to the harvest breeze.

The custom of "blessing the fields" is still continued among some of the Iroquois. When the leaf of the dogwood is "the size of a squirrel's ear," the planting season has come. Before the dawn of the first day of the planting, a virgin girl is sent to the fields, where she scatters a few grains of corn to the earth as she invokes the assistance of the Spirit of the Corn for the harvest.

GUS-TAH-OTE, SPIRIT OF THE ROCK

Since the beginning of the earth, when the Sky Woman descended to the back of the Turtle, the strong rock had overhung the valley, and since that beginning, Gus-tah-ote,[52] the Spirit, had been imprisoned within its silent majesty.

Gus-tah-ote had seen all the creations of earth grow and set themselves in place. He had seen each spirit of the animals assigned to its duty and power and had waited with observing patience till, by the law of transmigration, he too had been proffered his choice of change, whether to the river, or sea, or land or forest or sky. He could enter them, and whichever he might choose as his future abode, should be his.

"The majestic river flows free through its broad lands; I have looked down upon it for ages. There, no one would dispute my possessions," thought Gus-tah-ote. "I will try."

As he emerged from the rock, he trod his new way bold and fearlessly strong and slipped into the river.

Down the valleys sped he, and the rhyming brooks echoed back his free song of joy. Through rocky gorges he tossed the foaming waves to the sky, and they came back to him rainbowed with sunbeams.

He wound around towering mountains and they lowered their peaks and wrapped him in their shadows.

Down a steep fall he leaped, and exulted in rapturous gladness as he tangled the waves into combating rivals.

Through stately forests he floated, and the fragrant trees dipped low their branches as majestically he sped through their silences.

On and on, restlessly drifting, the ambitious river grew broader till no more Gus-tah-ote saw its green borders. Past the mountains and forests he sped faster and faster, and the river seemed to sob as in fear of departing from him when a loud moaning thing encircled him with its broad arms, a mountain of water ridged high above him, and Gus-tah-ote was swept down into the gulf of a great sea.

But the Rescuer, who had proffered him choice of the element in which he might dwell, reached down in the sea and caught him still breathing and returned him to the hoary old rock.

There Gus-tah-ote pondered and planned and he thought as he looked up at the sun, "There is the sky, it is open and trackless and leads to far heights. It has no trap to catch the strange traveler, I will try."

The breath of the day was soft and as gentle as sunlight on a wild blooming flower when Gus-tah-ote tried his wings.

He plumed them and fitted and fluttered them, and widened them broad to the air, and with a sneer at the bound down old rock he flew high to the sky.

Down far beneath him were the forests and plains and mountains and rivers. Not far above him the sun was crossing the sky, and around and around him was a boundless freedom that inspired a new heart and life to the rock-bound Gus-tah-ote, who grew like a bird in his lilt through the air as he passed the great feathered birds of the sky who lifted the clouds like a curtain above them. So near the birds he had watched for ages! How fair this life of freedom! No one to restrain him, no one to govern, no stone to fetter him fast in its bounds!

In his new found liberty, Gus-tah-ote flew higher, and when he looked down, the lands and the mountains and forests and rivers were far beneath him as he entered the mist land of clouds. And the air grew chill, and a *something* rushed past him, wounding his wings which dropped helplessly down when he tried to outspread them. And a shivery wind pushed against him and tore him to fragments as it whirled him over and over in the shoreless sky.

Bit by bit his feathers divided, and his weight growing unwieldy as he tossed near to death, Gus-tah-ote fell down through the labyrinthed cloud fleet, down through the endless free way to the earth!

Senseless, unknowing, he fell, and was prostrate to his death when the Rescuer came and led him back to the rock within the valley.

Again Gus-tah-ote marveled and planned and deliberated. In his flying he had scanned the great earth as it extended beneath him. "How fair its valleys! How far its mountains reach skyward! And its forests, one could wander within these forever. No one to watch, no one to follow," thought Gus-tah-ote, and once again he gazed at the motionless rock with a sullen frown of contempt as he walked forth from it into the wide earth.

All through its plains of plenty and its forests of fulness he traveled, yet neither a bird nor a beast nor a human was he, and he grew lonely and strange in the new land life. In his loitering he would tarry awhile with the animals, but they were absorbed in their own, and there was no time for a stranger. Then to the birds he wandered. They were nesting, and the days were too short, the sun too fast to trouble with an unknown. He coaxed the forest. Each tree had its own spirit which was leafing it and nourishing its shadows, Gus-tah-ote was an intruder. All over the earth he journeyed, no place offered shelter, no life would share with him.

Thus was he despairing when the voice of the Rescuer whispered, "Return to your rock where you can defy all the earth. The waters may overflow you but they can not drown you; the tempests may strike you, they can not overthrow you; the sun may glance at you, it can not burn you; the rains may fall heavy upon you, they can not blind you; seas may drift to you and overwhelm you, but they can not push you into their deep places; old age, who hunts for his victims all over the earth, can not wrinkle you; death can not pain nor claim you; unyielding and stanch, you will outlive all the land, the seas and the skies! The rivers may shrink and grow small at your feet; the forests will fall into the dust; the whole earth will die and fold itself over and over anew; you only are powerful and firm. The skies will change and the stars grow dim and smaller; you will watch from your stronghold, unchanged and changeless!"

Gus-tah-ote listened. He had laughed in the rivers until he had drifted lost in the sea; he had winged the great sky, gleeful in his race with the clouds, to be tossed by the tempest and whirled to the earth; he had once sought the earth to find one vacant place which called for a spirit, not one on the earth!

In his rock rest he had seen the growing earth and sky. When they were nameless infants he was guarding the valleys. From his fastness he had known all these, and now they reared above him as he skulked like a homeless coward beneath them.

His rock? Yes! No more to wander to the vain

things which would crumble and fall to the dust while he lingered beyond them.

And Gus-tah-ote, the Rock Spirit, dwells there content as overhanging the valley he watches and guards. He is free to wander, but the river flows from him, the sky lifts high to the sun, and the earth heeds him not!

This myth suggests the life lesson of the red man—contentment. He is not ambitionless, but slow to profit by the example of an untried experience.

GA-DO-JIH AND SA-GO-BA-OH, THE GOLDEN EAGLE AND THE HUNTER VULTURE

Origin of the Bird dance[53]

The Ga-do-jih, the Golden Eagle of the far away heavens, is the Head Chief of all the birds.

The Ga-do-jih never visits the earth, but employs many assistants upon whom he imposes various duties. To his subchief, Don-yon-do, the Bald Eagle, he has assigned the mountain tops of the earth land. Don-yon-do won this distinction by his strength, acute sight and extraordinary powers of flight. The strong rays of the sun can not blind him. He is proud, and his heart throbs to the skies; and although he swoops down to the lowlands for his prey, he flies to the highest mountain top to devour it.

The Lodge dance of the Eagles
From a drawing by Jesse Cornplanter, a Seneca boy artist

From his retinue of servitors, Ga-do-jih has chosen many of the vulture family, whose obnoxious duties lead them to plunder in offensive places. But they are faithful in his service, for it is the law of Ga-do-jih that the earth must be kept clean.

Yet these proud ravenous birds have tender hearts, and although their scavenger life leads them into base paths, Ga-do-jih does not deny them the pure air of the sky nor the clear waters of the earth.

Among these birds of prey, is Sa-go-da-oh, the Hunting Vulture, who ceaselessly searches for spoil. All refuse of the earth beneath and above, is his. Occasionally he passes Don-yon-do on his sky way, but the lofty spirit of Don-yon-do knows not Sa-go-da-oh. In quest of his mountain crest, Don-yon-do swifts

96

through the blue of the heavens like the flying wind, while Sa-go-da-oh slowly soars within the cloud nets and watches to swoop down on his prey.

One day in the long time ago, Jo-wiis,[54] a young Indian lad, was lost in the woods, and had wept until nearly blinded. For many days and nights the rain had flooded the forest, and Jo-wiis could not find his home path. In the black sky there was no sun or moon to guide him, and hungering and faint, he had fallen on the river bank to die, when Don-yon-do, who chanced to be flying across the earth, discovered him, and lifting him on his wings, flew in search of an Indian village. Looking down in the far below, he discovered smoke ascending from some lodges, and alighting left Jo-wiis lying near them and slowly winged away. The rain continued to fall, and no one had come for the fast dying boy when Sa-go-da-oh, winging past in search of night prey, espied him and closing in his wings, dropped to the wet earth where the boy was lying. Though Sa-go-da-oh's talons were long and strong, his heart was tender, and gently lifting Jo-wiis, bore him to the village, but failing to find his home, took him to Ga-do-jih in the sky, who nourished him and grew to love him.

Ga-do-jih took Jo-wiis to the sky council house when the birds were celebrating the New Year, and taught him their dances; also to all the feasts throughout the year, teaching him the bird songs and all the laws of the birds, especially the sacred law protecting their nests in the spring and sheltering them in the winter. And he was shown the corn and the grains, which Ga-do-jih told him must be shared with the feathered folk below. All these laws he was enjoined to impart to his people when he should return to the earth.

Now, the Seven Star Brothers (the Pleiades) were dancing the New Year dance over the council house when Ga-do-jih directed Sa-go-da-oh to return Jo-wiis to the earth, and he nestled close under the wing of the great bird during the journey.

Earth was sleeping beneath her snow blanket when Jo-wiis returned. Her streams were frozen, and her forests silent save for the keen voice of the wind which wandered through their leafless loneliness. Seeing a light in the well remembered council house where the people were holding a feast Jo-wiis entered and related to his astonished listeners his experiences in the sky. As one of the chiefs remembered the lost boy, his strange tale was believed, and it was decided that he should teach the people the bird dances he had learned in the sky, as also the songs the sky birds sing in their councils.

At the end of the feast it was declared, that, in memory of the wonderful event, the name Sa-go-da-oh, the Vulture, should be added to their clan chiefs' names, and be conferred upon Jo-wiis, to whom the Vulture had been the good friend.

By this legend, the Iroquois know the origin of Je-gi-yah-goh-o-a-noh, the Bird dance, which was brought by Jo-wiis[55] from the land of the sky birds, and is the most prominent dance of the Iroquois. It is celebrated at their New Year feast, and during its performance the dancers imitate the motions of a bird, squatting low and moving their bodies and heads as if picking the grains of corn which have been scattered on the floor.

This dance reminds the people of the law of Ga-do-jih, that the Indian must nourish and care for the birds in the winter as well as in the summer time.

The Bird Dance

Arranged by FRANK B. CONVERSE, NEWTOWN, CATTARAGUS RESERVATION

Calumet fans of Eagle Society,
waved by the dancers during the song

GA-NUS-QUAH AND GO-GON-SA, THE STONE GIANTS AND FALSE FACES

Tall, fierce and hostile, they were a powerful tribe, the Stone Giants!

They invaded the country of the Iroquois during the early days of the Confederation of the Five Nations, the Mohawks, Onondagas, Oneidas, Cayugas, and Senecas, who had sent their warriors against them only to be defeated, and they threatened the annihilation of the Confederacy.

They were feared, not because of their prodigious size, but they were cannibals as well, and would devour men, women and children.

The Shawnees have a legend of these Giants which describes them as at one time living in a peaceful state, and although powerful, were gentle, and hospitable in their intercourse with the neighboring tribes; but from some disturbing cause they became restless, abandoned their home, and migrated to the far northwest snow fields, where the extreme cold of the winters "froze away their humanity," and they became "men of icy hearts."

Mask representing Spirit of the Harvest

Unable to withstand the severity of the climate, or provide themselves with sufficient food, the spirit of restlessness again controlled them and they became wanderers, enduring all the discomforts and hardships of a nomadic life; and subsisting on raw meat and fish, they finally drifted into cannibalism, reveling in human flesh.

In the summer they would roll in the sand to harden their flesh, and their bodies became covered with scales which resisted the arrows of an enemy. For generations they had devastated nations before they swept down upon the Iroquois. There they found caves wherein they concealed themselves, and would sally forth, destroying some village and feasting on the people.

Member of the False Face Company
impersonating the Stone Giant

The Iroquois were being rapidly depleted in their numbers, when Ta-ha-hia-wa-gon, Upholder of the Heavens, who had bestowed upon them their hunting grounds and fisheries, beholding their distress, determined to relieve them of the merciless invaders, and transforming himself to a stone giant, came down to the earth and united with their tribe.

Wonderstruck at his marvelous display of power, they made him their chief; and he brandished his club high in the air, saying, "Now we will destroy the Iroquois, make a great feast of them, and invite all the Stone Giants of the sky." In pretense of this intention, the Sky Holder led them to a strong fort of the On-on-da-gas where he bade them hide in a deep hollow in the valley and await the sunrise, when they would attack and destroy the unsuspecting people. But before day, he scaled a high place above them and overwhelmed them with a great mass of rocks. Only one escaped, who fled to the Allegheny mountains. There he secreted himself in a cave, where he remained and grew in huge strength, when he was transformed to the myth Giant, Ga-nus-quah.

Ga-nus-quah, the Depredator

He was vulnerable only on the bottom of his foot. No one could hope to destroy him without wounding the spot on his foot,[56] and this was not in the power of a mortal to do; and thus secure, the whole earth was his path.

No human being had ever seen him, to look upon his face would be instant death. His trail could be traced in the forests by the fallen trees he had uprooted when they obstructed his way. His footprints were seen impressed on the rocks where in his travels he had leaped. If a river opposed his going, he would swoop it up with his huge hands and turn it from its course, and so cross on the dry land. Should a mountain impede his way, with his strong fists he would push a gorge through it, the more quickly to reach the other side. In the tumult of storms, his voice could be heard warning the Thunderers away from his cave, this Ga-nus-quah, the last of the Stone Giants!

Mask of the False Face Company representing Ganusquah,
the Stone Giant, the mythical founder of the company

It was once the fate of a young hunter to meet this
fear-inspiring creature. During a terrific storm, the
young hunter, a chief, blinded and bruised by the hail
which fell like sharp flints, and having lost the trail,
sought shelter within the hollow of a great rock.

Night with its darkness deepened the shadows, and
the young hunter prepared for a night's sleep, when
suddenly the rock began to move, and from a far recess
a strange sound approached him. At one moment, the
tone was brisk as the gurgling stream, at the next, gentle
as the lullaby of a singing brook, again to burst forth
like the moan of a tumbling cataract or the wail of a
mad torrent, then dying away as tenderly as the soft
summer breeze.

During a pause in the weird harmony, the marveling young hunter heard a voice addressing him in a stentorian strain, saying: "Young warrior, beware! You are in the cave of the Stone Giant, Ga-nus-quah! Close your eyes. No human being has ever looked upon me. I kill with one glance. Many have wandered into this cave; no one lives to leave it. You did not come to hunt me; you came here for shelter; I will not turn you away. I will spare your life, which now is mine, but henceforth you must obey my commands. I will be unseen, but you will hear my voice. I will be unknown, yet will I aid you. From here you will go forth, free to live with the animals, the birds and fish. All these were your ancestors before you were human, and hereafter it will be your task to dedicate your life to their honoring!

Whichever of these you meet on your way, do not pass until you have felled a strong tree and carved its image in the wood grain.[57] When you first strike the tree, if it speaks, it will be my voice urging you and you must go on with your task. When the trees were first set in their earth mould, each was given a voice.[58] These voices you must learn, and the language of the entire forest. Now, go on your way; I am watching and guiding you. Go, now, and teach the mankind people kindness, the brother goodness of all dumb things, and so win your way to live forever!"

When the young hunter opened his eyes, he was standing beside a basswood[59] tree which gradually transformed to a great mask, and related to him its power.

The Go-gon-sa (Mask)

It could see behind the stars. It could create storms, and summon the sunshine. It empowered battles or weakened the forces at will. It knew the remedy for each disease, and could overpower Death. It knew all the poison roots and could repel their strong evils. Its power was life, its peace the o-yank-wah, the tobacco which drowsed to rest. The venomous reptiles knew its threat and crept from its path. It would lead the young hunter back to his people when the Stone Giant directed. It said: "My tree, the basswood, is soft, and will transform for the molder. My tree wood is porous, and the sunlight can enter its darkness. The wind voice can whisper to its silence and it will hear. My tree wood is the life of the Go-gon-sa. Of all in the forest there is none other."

With this knowledge, the young hunter started on his way carving go-gon-sa-so-oh, (false faces). From the basswood he hewed them. By the voice of the Stone Giant he was guided to choose; and well he learned the voices of all the forest trees before he completed his task.

In his travels he met many strange animals and birds, which he detained until he had carved them in the basswood; and inviting them to tarry, learned their language and habits; and though fearing the Giant's reproval, for he constantly heard his voice encouraging or blaming, he learned to love these descendants of his ancestors, and was loath to leave them when compelled to return to his home.

Many years had passed in the laborious task, and he who entered the cave a youth, had become a bent old man when, burdened with the go-gon-sas he had carved, he set out on his return to his people. Year after year his burden had grown heavier, but his back broadened in strength, and he had become a giant in stature when he reached his home and related his story.[60]

KO-NEA-RAW-NEH, THE FLYING HEADS[61]

The Long House was new and the people were tranquil in its peace when they were terrorized by the visitations of the Flying Heads.

These odious Heads were enveloped in long, fire-flaming hair which streamed to the wind in their flying, dazzling and blinding those who dared look at them; and armed with two great bearlike paws, which were ever in motion as if clutching at prey, they shot through the air like meteors.

When flying, these Heads were of enormous size, yet, upon the land or among the forest trees, they could become no larger than the head of a bear, for which, but for their flaming hair and repulsive visage, they might sometimes be mistaken; but whether in the air or upon the land, there seemed no human power able to combat them, and the people fled in horror whenever they appeared.

Many of the medicine men said they were bad spirits[62] who had escaped from some place of confinement, and, angered that the people should be dwelling in peace, were seeking to destroy them, while others believed their coming portended some dire calamity that would befall them; but, whatever the cause of their coming, the people were powerless to restrain them.

Feasts, invocations and incantations were of no avail; drums, rattles and loud screaming shouts gave forth no sound when the Heads appeared, and they heeded them not. Arrows and spears would glance from their fiery hair, or break like a dead branch wind-blown from the tree, and there seemed no succor for the people.

Happily these dread visitations would be interrupted for varying periods often extending through several months, when the people would return to their quiet, always hoping the Heads had departed forever.

A long time had passed, so long that the people had nearly forgotten their affliction, when one night at the sundown, De-wan-do, an Iroquois woman, with her infant wrapped in a blanket and swung across her shoulders, was paddling her canoe across a broad river. She was hastening before the darkness should set in when, as she neared the shore, a long shadow swept across her canoe and a big face lifted from the water, a face whose flaming hair streaked the waves like serpents of fire and hissed to vapors the smooth-flowing river. Like all her people, De-wan-do knew the Flying Heads, and pressing her infant close to her breast, she sprang to the shore and ran to the forest where the game of the day-before chase had been left.

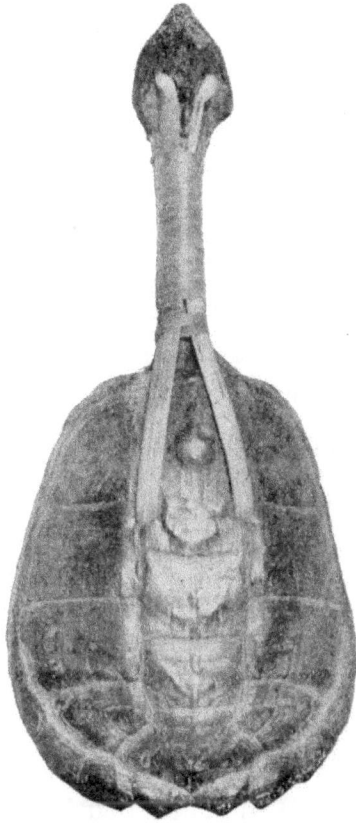

Turtle-shell rattle used by False Face Company

Looking back and seeing the Head following her, she threw it a piece of deer meat which, as it stopped to devour it, delayed it for a time, and De-wan-do fled. Through all the night she ran, still pursued by the Head, and that she might gain a moment's rest, she continued to throw the deer meat until no more was left.

The new risen sun was combing the clouds with its sharp-pointed rays, and though with the light, De-wan-do could run swifter, still the Head was drawing closer. Her meat was gone—what should she do? She threw it her blanket, in rage it tore it to fragments; then her doeskin dress, her leggings, moccasins, piece by piece all the clothes she wore as still she ran through the brush tangles, tearing wounds that were bleeding and weakening, and the Head had nearly overtaken her when, despairing, she remembered the charm of an infant's moccasin to avert danger, and hastily removing one from her child's foot, threw it behind her. At its sight the Head stopped, and in rage beat the air with its great paws. In vain it tried to avoid the moccasin, and reeling and wandering as if blinded, fell to the ground.

Hurrying on through the shade of the forest. De-wan-do climbed a tall pine where hidden in the branches she rested; but there soon came the terrible creature, and lying down at the base of the tree, fell asleep. Thinking the Head was too tired to wake, De-wan-do drew her child to her, intending to flee from the tree, when the child brushed down a bunch of pine needles which falling on the Head, wakened it. Said the Head, "A porcupine dwells in this tree, and I will kill it"; and hurling stones at the tree, it broke a large branch which in falling tangled the Head fast, when De-wan-do dropped from the tree and fled toward her home. But the ferocious Head soon freed itself from the branch, and spreading its fiery hair down to the bushes, they were soon in flames, burning a path as they spread and following De-wan-do to her lodge. This the Head knew, and guided by the fire trail, it soon reached the lodge and stealthily entered.

But De-wan-do heard not. Suffering with hunger

from her long fasting, she was at the hearth fire roasting acorns, while her infant lay sleeping near the fire. One by one as they burst their shells she drew them away and ate them, and the astonished Head, approaching behind her, wondered, for it thought she was eating the live coals. "They must be good," thought the Head, "and I'll have my share"; and gathering the hot coals with its paws, thrust them into its mouth when, screaming in agony, it fled from the lodge in a great blaze of fire which drifted into the night!

And the Head never returned. It is believed that the live coals it had mistaken for acorns burned it to death.

THE FACE IN THE WATER
AND THE DEATH DANCE

In the hollow of a rock in a forest, was a health-giving spring known to all red men.

This spring, which possessed mysterious power, was protected by two spirits. From sunrise to noon, Oh-swe-da, spirit of the spruce tree, was its guardian, and this was its "charm time"; but after the noon, when "the shadows slanted across it" and Och-do-ah, the Bat, had entered the rock, the spring became a baneful poison, sudden or lingering, as Och-do-ah might will. No mortal should near it for healing when Och-do-ah was enticing all things to drink of its death.

Ah-ne-ah, Rose Flower, who had gone to the spring in quest of its water, was weaving the sweet-smelling grasses into baskets and singing the firefly song as she braided the strands to its tune, and, as happy as she was beautiful, had not seen the noon nearing the spring, and it was glinting the edge of the rock when she hastened toward it.

As she held her elm bowl to the gurgling water, it seemed never to fill, and she saw there a face more beautiful than any she had ever beheld; and the face was smiling and nodding at her as it floated from side to side of the spring, as if coaxing, then disappearing to return with its enchanting smile which allured Ah-ne-ah by a weird spell from which she could not escape.

As she wondering gazed, the threatening shadow entered the spring, and when the smiling face vanished, something suddenly seized her and bore her upward far from the forest and, as with wings, so swiftly flying, the wind which seemed following lagged far behind them. Then hurrying to the earth below, they crossed a broad river and plunged down its cataract to a wide water, which raged in a fury of confusion. There Ah-ne-ah seemed alone in the mad torrent, save a face which floated beside her, hideous in its threatening frown, and she turned from it in horror, and the fierce water tossed her to its bank where a massive oak was uprooted.

There again was the face, which led her down below the earth to a place glaring as with flames and where numberless people were dancing, carelessly dancing, and among the vast multitude passing, were some of her own people who had died years before, and who appealed to her for pity as they moaned, "don-de-gwan-de, don-de-gwan-de" (pity us, pity us). Helpless and dumb in her terror, some monster pushed her into the circle of dancers where, doomed to the fire dance, she felt herself blind and dying, when she seemed to breathe a new air, life restoring and fragrant of pines of the woodland, and as she opened her eyes it was sunrise and she stood by the spring!

By her side was a young warrior robed as the hunter robes for the hunt. In his hand he held a branch of spruce pine; on his head were two wings, one of the owl, the other an eagle. His feet were sandaled with strips of the deerskin, and as Ah-ne-ah looked into his eyes she

Seneca flute used in playing ceremonial music

beheld the face that had smiled to her from the spring!

The owl and eagle-winged warrior took her hand, and as he gently led her to the edge of the forest, related to her the mystery of her strange night journey.

He was Oh-swe-da, the Spirit of the Spruce, and guarded the spring from the sunrise to its noon. With his eagle wing he could fly to the sun, with his owl wing he could wander the whole forest in the night and until the shadow was close to its border.

Oh-swe-da had welcomed her only to warn. Och-do-ah, the Bat, was hovering in the shadow which was so near, and Och-do-ah would destroy. He poisoned the spring water when the sun turned away, and the wings of Och-do-ah grew broader as the night came. He belonged to the night and his death watch.

Oh-swe-da held fast the elm bowl to warn Ah-ne-ah away. It could not fill. She must see the shadow and flee, but alas! the Och-do-ah had seen her, and had sent one of his helpers to take her to the fires below where the witches were dancing the death dance.

But Oh-swe-da was freed from the spring, and followed to her rescue. He had snatched her from the witch fire, and now she was here! But the penalty for lingering too late at the spring must be paid— Och-do-ah would have his prey. She had escaped him, but was doomed!

When they had reached the corn plains the story was ended, and Ah-ne-ah returned to her home.

Soon after, there came a pestilence to her people, and a famine was upon them. Hundreds fell victims to an epidemic, and day by day the beautiful Ah-ne-ah was fading away, until one summer morning at the vanishing of the dew Ah-ne-ah disappeared. The lodge where she had faded to death was empty, and when her people entered its door a strange silence was there, not a sound save a rustling as of vanishing wings and the whirr of a flying bird. But by the side of her couch were two fallen feathers, one of the owl, the other an eagle!

But the faithful Ah-ne-ah had related to her people the terrible story of the witch fire, and taught them its dance which could no more destroy them.

Thus originated the Oh-gi-we,[63] the Death dance of the Iroquois, one of the rites of their Death watch which releases a departed spirit from the evil influences of the witches.

Death Dance

Arranged by F. B. CONVERSE, 1902

TON-DA-YENT, THE TWELVE WARRIORS AND THE WHITE RABBIT

In his youth he had been evil, but when grown to manhood, he had conquered his bad and becoming a warrior had won great victories for his people.

An unyielding leader, he was feared by his foes. Now he had passed from his people, the Ton-da-yent, the war chief!

The wailers had wept, the death song had been chanted, the war paint lined his strong face, and they had crowned him with the heron feathers, the Iroquois emblem of power. In his hands they laid his stone scalping knife and war club, and robed in deerskin, his dead body waited the sunrise. All the night long it solemnly waited.

When the sun neared the east sky, they wrapped the dead warrior in the bark of the elm and lowered it into the earth, and an aged priestess, Ho-non-di-ont, scattered small lumps of clay above him, to propitiate the elements, earth, air and water, through which his spirit must journey to its rest.

At twilight when the sun had gone, they planted above him a young pine; Ton-da-yent had been a brave warrior, and the passers must know that he was lying there.

A council of condolence was called, at which his successor would be named, when an unknown person appeared, claiming to be the twin brother of the dead chief, and demanded that he be given his name by right of twin succession.

The people marveled greatly at the wonderful resemblance he bore to the dead chief and, save a glowering fire which lurked in the glance of his eye, it seemed indeed that the Ton-da-yent had returned, and the council did not hesitate to grant his request.

His influence grew quick and strong among the warriors who had followed his brother, and having declared his intent to become a war chief, they eagerly united with his band.

One day he assembled his warriors and, selecting twelve of the youngest and most stalwart, told them they were to follow him many suns away where he would hold council with some foreign tribes whose friendship it was desirable to secure. The chosen twelve, proud of the honor the chief had shown them, dressed themselves in their choicest skins and feathers and prepared for the journey, but when ready to set out an ominous stillness oppressed the air and a black cloud came down, darkening their path.

"An omen of ill," said the medicine man, but the young warriors, unlearned in the lore of the mystics, feared not.

Snowtime to snowtime had come and gone, but neither the chief nor the warriors had returned, when one black night the death warning cry "ga-weh, ga-weh" was heard wailing through the village and a gaunt warrior entered a lodge and, "hushing" the people, related his story.

The warrior's story

He was one of the twelve warriors who had followed Ton-da-yent. The Ton-da-yent had led them into the depths of a forest and down a steep precipice into a dark place where he confined them and then went away. Vainly they tried to escape, but through a crevice in the rocks a gleam of light entered, and they could tell the day from the night.

For many suns the Ton-da-yent had left them to wait and watch for his return, until the food he had given was nearly gone and they were despairing, when one night when darkness had come, to their great joy he returned, but not to release them. He counseled them to remain quiet yet a little longer, saying they were still surrounded by a foe which was gathering, and if discovered, they should be destroyed. Then he talked to them in a monotonous voice which stupefied them to dull, heavy sleep, and upon waking the next morning, they discovered that one of their number was missing!

Alarmed at the strange disappearance, one of the warriors, determining to remain awake when again the Ton-da-yent should come, filled his ears with moss to deaden his sorcering voice, and in the night when his companions were sleeping, saw, to his horror, the blood-thirsting chief scalp one of the number and carry the body away!

Night after night came the Ton-da-yent to repeat his murderous killings until but he, the relator, alone remained, and believing that he too must die, was in despair.

But an unlooked for relief came to him. During the day a young bear, seeking refuge from the storm which raged outside, crept into the place through an unknown opening, and the warrior starving for food, killed it and, removing its skin, concealed himself within it. In pretence of sleep he awaited the return of the chief who, in the darkness not observing the warrior's disguise, scalped the head of the bear in mistake, and in his hasty flight having neglected to close the passage, the warrior escaped. Here ended his story.

The warrior's story spread consternation among the people and the chiefs deliberated. They decided that "something was disturbing the spirit of the dead Ton-da-yent," and that "as by their ancient law his body must be lifted and questioned," thereupon the grave of the chief was opened.

There, indeed, was the body, but to their horror, they found twelve scalps, one of them the scalp of a bear and covered with blood!

"It is he, the blood-thirsting Ton-da-yent!" exclaimed the young warrior, and the society for the dead recited their chants for "pacifying the unrest of a detained spirit" and "talked to" the body.

The medicine men knew that the murderer of the young warriors was not the immortal Ton-da-yent, whose spirit of good had departed forever, but the ghoul of his evil which remained and had assumed his form, and unable to release itself from the earth, had "become restless," therefore it "must be punished."

So they built a lodge of light logs and boughs, smearing it over with the pitch of the pine, and placing therein a high bier, which they covered with furs, laid the body upon it, saying, for they knew that the ghoul could hear and was listening, "we will now leave the spirit to rest, and will bar fast the door for fear of the prowling wolves."

Silently guarding the lodge until the sun had gone away, they lighted the brush which had been thrown upon it, and it was soon enveloped in flames. As the burning increased, the cries of the ghoul could be heard pleading for release, and then they knew that their medicine men were wise.

The doomed ghoul continued its cries until the

lodge was consumed, when there came a loud "crackling" shriek, the head of the evil Ton-da-yent flew high in the air, bursting into fragments and dropping a white rabbit[64] which ran fast to the swamps.

The twin souls of the Ton-da-yent exemplify the Iroquois Indian's theory of the duality of a human life, the good and the evil. He believes evil to be of the earth, only, and that good, alone, is immortal.

The myth rabbit, the evil of the Ton-da-yent, lives in the swamps, and during the summer it assumes the color of the grasses; in the winter it changes to white, as the Indian says "white like the snow." It is very wary, fleet of foot, and rarely ever to be seen. From its eyes gleam luring red fires which float over the marsh lands.

Its death call "ga-weh, ga-weh," is said to be heard preceding a calamity. At all times it is an ill omen, and a death is expected to follow its warning cry.

The good spirit of the Ton-da-yent passed to the .skies with his death, and now abides there as the Rabbit, or Hare, in the celestial constellation situated directly under Orion.

JI-JO-GWEH, THE WITCH WATER GULL

It was a bird of night. Its vampire wings sucked the air in its noiseless flight. Its prey was life, bird, beast, or human, and blood its craving.

When its wings touched the waves, the waters

would hiss. When it followed the streams through the valleys, vapors would rise and screen it from sight. Its breath was poison and would kill.

If in its flight a feather fell from its wing, blood followed in drops hard as flint, which would bruise to death any living thing they struck.

When it flew through the air, it shriveled black clouds that dropped bad rain, and hideous reptiles which crawled away and hid in the ground.

Sunlight and moonlight it feared, but in black night it roamed abroad a straggling, wandering, blood-thirsting thing of evil; and the people, dreading its baneful power, would hide from its sight, whispering its name in fear.

Whence it came was never known, but for generations it had cursed the land with its direful flight. Many had sought its life, but their arrows would fall blunted to the ground, and some calamity was sure to befall the venturesome hunters. It seemed to bear a charmed life, and, despairing, the people lived in constant dread of its visitations.

But one time, a voice whispered to a brave young Indian girl that, if she would hew a strong bow from the ash tree, and twine it close around with her long black hair, and feather her arrow with the down from a young eagle's breast, she could destroy the venomous bird.

Thus told, she climbed a high cliff to an eagle's nest, where she found some young birds, who spread wide their mouths for the food she had brought them; and plucking from one a handful of its down, she hastened to her home and bound it to her arrow with sinew. She had made a strong bow from the ash, and was eager to start on her search for the bird, happy in the thought that by its death she would bring a deliverance to her people.

That no harm might befall her should her arrow fail, she sought the advice of the medicine men, who placed upon her neck a small packet of sacred tobacco, and called upon the spirits of the good to aid her. Thus guarded, she made her way down to the lake where nightly the bird came to drink.

Cautiously approaching the water, she scanned its surface as she listened but not a sound could she hear nor a living thing could she see in the darkness. "The dark will befriend me, I know, and soon I will see," she thought; and seeking a shelter under some wild grapevines that would screen her, she patiently waited and listened all through the night, but the demon bird came not, and weary with watching, she had picked up her bow to return, when a shriek rent the air that sent a chill to her heart, and looking up, she saw the monster swiftly circling the air above her.

For a moment she wavered, terrified by the sudden screaming of the bird, but remembering the charm the medicine men had given, her courage came back to her, and imploring the protection of the good spirits, she drew her ash bow. To her horror it was limp as a wisp of straw! The night dews had softened it, its strength had gone, and she knew not what to do; for the bird still shrieked above her, and she felt that she was doomed. Though despairing, still her faith remained, and she clasped the charm upon her neck, and recalling the power words of the medicine men, whispered them to the arrow as she again bent her bow, and the arrow flew true to its aim!

Shrill and fast were the shrieks of the bird, for the arrow had pierced its heart. And its wild fluttering wings threshed the air in its pain and rage as it reeled headlong to the lake, lashing the water to foam as it sank!

The legend tells, that when the Witch Gull disappeared in the lake, a flock of wild birds arose from the foam, and hovering for a time over the spot, winged away to the south. They were the white sea crow, a variety well known to the red man. These birds had been devoured by the Ji-jo-gweh, and so imprisoned until happily released by its death.

When, preceding a storm, the sea crows are seen in hurrying flocks, the red man knows that the spirit of the Ji-jo-gweh is driving them, as his spirit is then haunting the clouds.

SGAH-AH-SO-WAH AND GOT-GONT, THE WITCH HAWK AND THE WITCH BEAR WOMAN

The Witch Hawk was hovering. His talons were ready. His keen eye measured the sky. His dusk-colored wings silently brushed the air as the pinions of the breeze stir the breath of the night. The flight of the Witch Hawk was the foredoom of evil. He could be visible or invisible, whichever might best serve his weird flying, Sgah-ah-so-wah, the Witch Hawk, the dread of all birds, who chase him away from their lands.

Unseen, one day he was hovering over the maize land where O-gas-hah, an Indian woman, was toiling with her bone hoe, and the maize bent low as she fed it the nourishing earth.

O-gas-hah had strapped her young infant in its ga-yash (splint cradle), woven of sweet-scented woods, and hung it on a low branch of an elm where the summer breeze rocked it a song. A swift of the wind quivered the corn leaves, and the air seemed heavy with warnings as. O-gas-hah gazed at the sky and, thought she, "The Sgah-ah-so-wah is wandering, the Indian knows its trail in the winds, the Witch Hawk!" But the sun went on with its summer day, and the dews were falling when O-gas-hah had ended her toil in the maize field, and turning to bind her burden strap across her shoulders, she discovered her child was not there!

With a cry of terror she fled to her home, wailing to the skies, "It was you, Sgah-ah-so-wah, it was you, the Witch Hawk! You have taken my child!" And entering to the sad desolation of her lodge, O-gas-hah shut herself in with the night and her wild lamentations.

The Witch Hawk it was who had taken her child and carried it to a dense woods where he left it to die.

By his power to transform to a human, as a warrior

the Witch Hawk had once wooed O-gas-hah who, in her strange distrust, had scorned him, and now he had wounded her with a weapon more subtle than death.

The night dews fell on the child, the dawn sun had gleamed down upon it, and a next day was in its deep shadows when a bear, prowling through the dense place, came upon it and thinking it was a young cub, carried it to its cave in a north shelter, where the cool winds fled from the sun.

Years passed. The infant, now grown to womanhood and still nourished by the bears, had never known she was a human being until one morning there came a hunter who related to her the wonders of another life in the world, where humans dwelt. It was the Witch Hawk, who had transformed to a hunter, and by his enticing endowed her with his own baneful powers; and teaching her the ways of his invisible trails, the revengeful bird led her away, and guided her back to O-gas-hah's lodge near the maize field.

Attired in the doeskin, her feet sheathed in porcupined moccasins, and her long hair braided with long grasses, the Hawk led her, and well he knew the way, to the door of the lodge where O-gas-hah was crooning a child's song, a child song of the long ago of her desolation in the maize field.

When the sad O-gas-hah saw the beautiful maid, a strange thrill crept through her heart as she bade her welcome and, with true Indian hospitality, shared her home with her, calling her Gwi-yee; and O-gas-hah learned to love the stranger, yet there seemed an artful secrecy always hovering around her that palled like a shadow within and without.

Gwi-yee had strange vanishings. She would suddenly disappear and return not for many days, and on her return some calamity would befall the people. She often spoke of her home "in the far distant place" where at one time she was content and happy, but had never invited any of her friends to visit this place of her peace.

For days, weeks and months the strange disappearances continued; no person knew where, no person saw her when she traveled away, and her coming was silent as night.

The beauty and grace of Gwi-yee had attracted the wooing of many a brave young chief, and there had been combats of rivalry, but Gwi-yee, who seemed timid and unwilling, was wary of men, yet should one of them slight her, some evil befell him. If in his sorrow, one should plead when she disdainfully rejected him, disaster would come upon him, or some member of his family. A favorite with them all, who would suspect her haunting evil!

There was one, a proud young warrior who, as sign of the marrying sent her gifts. Tenderly she unbound them one by one, and the human that will dawn to each heart was teaching its lesson when, among the choice gifts of the hunt she saw a great bearskin. "He has killed my brother!" she sighed, "no more shall he cross my path." Death for death she vowed, and the young warrior returned no more to her lodge, and no more returned to his people!

Gwi-yee was the most joyous at the feast and most free at the dance, yet when she had departed there was a grim silence that no one could solve, a haunting fear which none could explain; and the mystery grew, hovering above the people.

Yet Gwi-yee, always kind, was ever willing to bear their burdens. Gwi-yee shared her lodge with the homeless and her food with the needy; yet she would suddenly vanish, no one could follow her, no one could question her.

During one of her disappearances a bear was seen in the forest, and several of the young warriors followed its tracks in the snow to a certain spot where the tracks disappeared, and in their place the print of a woman's moccasin led them to the village. Puzzling and strange was this! At another time, a bear track circled all round the snow-covered maize land, and beside it was the footprint of a huge bird, both nearing the lodge of O-gas-hah where they vanished, and in their place the light stepfall of a woman sunk in the snow path that led to the door. Who was within? O-gas-hah, crooning her child song and Gwi-yee, just returned from her far distant home, and the snow was fast melting from her moccasins!

Thus the mystery grew around Gwi-yee, and as the night that drapes in its black shadows, Gwi-yee folded herself in the gloom that threatened her, baneful its power, malign its darkness! Her wooers had abandoned her, the maidens shunned her, the old people who knew all the signs of the witches feared her as a thing of dread; and even the kind O-gas-hah hushed her crooning child song as if in fear.

The curse of the Witch Hawk had fallen upon her! Why had he taken her from her forest friends who had nurtured and reared her? What had she known but the simple forests where the bears had taught her their liberty life? On their wide walks she had roamed far and free. The cheats and sorrows of the human kind were unknown to her friends, who had taught her to hide from their killing. The forests and rivers and skies were all hers where unrestrained she had wandered in her wild wood life. Why had the Witch Hawk enticed her to the restless uncertain ways of the human? She had learned to love with the human love but to be hated; she had been kind but to be scorned, and as a human, lived but to destroy!

Back again to her old life she would flee, never to return from its peace. And the voice of O-gas-hah was crooning like a refrain of the dying as Gwi-yee fled to the forest.

Foredoomed was Gwi-yee. The hunters who had preceded her had surrounded the forests where they watched many nights.

The moon peered through the snow laden trees as a bear was tracking its way in the drifts. Slow and more slow it tracked its way when a swift flying arrow pierced its heart, and it fell to its death in the snows. In triumph the hunters drew near, when from its body arose a young maiden wrapped in a great light, a young maiden dressed in doeskin, her feet sheathed in porcupined moccasins, her long black hair braided with the wild grasses of the summer, and a hawk screamed through the forest as she vanished!

"It was Gwi-yee!" exclaimed the hunter, "the Bear Woman, the witch who has destroyed us!"

Part 2

MYTHS AND LEGENDS

BY

HARRIET MAXWELL CONVERSE

REVISED BY THE EDITOR FROM ROUGH DRAFTS
FOUND AMONG MRS. CONVERSE'S MANUSCRIPTS

OTT-WAIS-HA, THE SOUL

Its journey

With faith in tlie immortality of the soul, the
Iroquois also believe that each no-twais-ha (soul) has
a path which leads from every lodge door direct to the
land of the Great Maker, and that the Ott-wais-ha never
loses its identity in the various transmigrations through
which it must pass toward its final rest.

In its earth tarrying it frequently leaves its *human*
in the care of its mortal, or *material*, spirit, to wander
throughout the mysteries of space, and in its wingings
may enter some other existence, either bird, animal or
reptile, there to tarry for a time for knowledge which,
when it returns to its *human*, it will reveal to him in
dreams.

Chief Cornplanter, of the Senecas, the tribal historian from whom Mrs. Converse obtained this legend

In the few seconds of a dream, the Ott-wais-ha can relate the experiences of a lifetime. If their revelation be of special importance, the dreaming human will remember it when he awakes, will relate it to a tribal dream prophet who will interpret its significance which may prove a guidance for the entire life of the dreamer.[65]

Should an Indian threaten "the rattlesnake warns but once," it may be the caution of a dream revelation which has taught him the mercy of a warning before the thrust of death. Should an Indian become hopelessly depraved and fail to heed the warnings of his dreams, it may occur that the Ott-wais-ha, unable to endure his depravity, will abandon him and descending to his mere *mortal* existence, he will be compelled to live out his earth life bereft of his immortal soul.

131

But the Ott-wais-ha will not desert its *mortal* unless by a continuous abuse of its goodness; and conscious of this, the Indian more frequently makes his offerings and sacrifices to his evil spirit than his good, for to pacify his evil is the war wail of his battle for eternity.

By a legend of the Ott-wais-ha: One night two hunters were resting by the side of a small stream in the forest; they were waiting for the day dawn. One was drowsy in a half sleep, when his wakeful companion, who was watching the east sky, saw a small spark of fire pass from the mouth of the sleeper and float in the air to the edge of the stream, crossing it on a silvery willow leaf[66] which was drifting to the opposite bank. Hovering there for a moment as if confused it finally entered the skull of a small bird which lay bleaching on the bank and disappeared. The watching hunter did not disturb his sleeping companion, and when at the sunrise he awoke, he related a strange dream that had come to him.

The dream

He had left the forest in a great light and, as if with wings, had soared to a far away land, and a peaceful water whose borders reached from horizon to horizon. There he found waiting him a silver canoe which was vast in dazzling splendor as it floated on the waters, which bore him to the furthermost shore where he met a great eagle which, seeming to be waiting, guided him to its home whose pearl-white dome touched the high sky above the gray clouds which were hovering over the far distant earth beneath.

Within the dome, multitudes of birds of dazzling plumage were circling the air; some were feathered like unto the rainbow lines; others as the white snowdrift; but the greater flock was gray as the night shadows and darkened the dome as they winged past. In a corner, dense with threatening blackness, were groups of vampires whose talons spread out reeking with blood, as they restlessly reeled to and fro in the strangeness as if searching for prey that came not to this land of bird life. These terrors the eagle seemed pushing back as they flocked to the front, when from amid the wheeling and whirring and the beating of wings against the still air, came a voice saying: "Not so fast Ott-wais-ha, you are a stranger to this sky way of the birds; you have left the body of your hunter below, who is locked as fast to his sleep as the root to its tree. Here the eagle sleeps not, the vulture rests not and its wings flutter for flight in the darkness as the earth sleeps below; your journeying is long; this is but a rest place on the way to the lands of the Creator. You are too soon for that trail, you can not wait here. Even now your body below breathes to the sun; return swift to his day and night earth life and train it how to live your life; teach it its evil and good; cry into its ear the wail of warning and the shout of victory. We are of the peace path which you will soon travel, but you are not yet strong; the death birds hover near, they scent the blood of your meat, and will drain it to death!" The voice ceased its strange intoning, a something winged by the dreamer who looked in vain for the eagle. The water, the silver canoe, the myriad of birds, all had vanished as, waking, the dreamer opened

133

his eyes to the sun which was sending its beams through the shades of the forest. "I know, and will remember, I have heard the warning," said the hunter, as he wended his way to the game.

And the dream to the dreamer? The spark of fire which had issued from the lips of the sleeper became the Ott-wais-ha, the "immortal fire of life"; the little brook the "great water"; the willow leaf the "silvery canoe"; the skull of the bird the great dome in which were hovering the eagle, the vulture, the vampires, the three contentious attributes of mortal life, the noble, the degraded, the murderous; all these the Ott-wais-ha had shown to its earth soul.

Thereafter the hunter would not kill the eagle, fearing the vampire behind him which might plunder and kill.

The dream prophet knew, and could reveal!

———————————

It is the custom of some Indian tribes to kill a bird above the grave of the newly dead, that its spirit may accompany the soul on its way to the lands of the Maker-of-all. Other tribes release a living bird from a cage to typify the release of the spirit from its body.

The Iroquois says the eagle is the only bird that looks straight into the eyes of the sun. He seeks his prey in the low valleys but has his aery on the pinnacles of the mountain heights.

GAU-WI-DI-NE AND GO-HAY, WINTER AND SPRING[67]

The snow mountain lifted its head close to the sky; the clouds wrapped around it their floating drifts which held the winter's hail and snowfalls, and with scorn it defied the sunlight which crept over its height, slow and shivering on its way to the valleys.

Close at the foot of the mountain, an old man had built him a lodge "for a time," said he, as he packed it around with great blocks of ice. Within he stored piles of wood and corn and dried meat and fish. No person, animal nor bird could enter this lodge, only North Wind, the only friend the old man had. Whenever strong and lusty North Wind passed the lodge he would scream "ugh-e-e-e, ugh-e-e-e, ugh-e-e-e," as with a blast of his blustering breath he blew open the door, and entering, would light his pipe and sit close by the old man's fire and rest from his wanderings over the earth.

But North Wind came only seldom to the lodge. He was too busy searching the corners of the earth and driving the snows and the hail, but when he had wandered far and was in need of advice, he would visit the lodge to smoke and counsel with the old man about the next snowfall, before journeying to his home in the north sky; and they would sit by the fire which blazed and glowed yet could not warm them.

The old man's bushy whiskers were heavy with the icicles which clung to them, and when the blazing fire flared its lights, illuminating them with the warm hues

The Frost Spirit

of the summer sunset, he would rave as he struck them down, and glare with rage as they fell snapping and crackling at his feet.

One night, as together they sat smoking and dozing before the fire, a strange feeling of fear came over them, the air seemed growing warmer and the ice began to melt. Said North Wind: "I wonder what warm thing is coming, the snow seems vanishing and sinking lower in the earth." But the old man cared not, and was silent. He knew his lodge was strong, and he chuckled with scorn as he bade North Wind abandon his fears and depart for his home. But North Wind went drifting the fast falling snow higher on the mountain until it groaned under its heavy burden, and scolding and blasting, his voice gradually died away. Still the old man remained silent and moved not, but lost in thought sat looking into the fire when there came a loud knock at his door. "Some foolish breath of North Wind is wandering," thought he, and he heeded it not.

Again came the rapping, but swifter and louder, and a pleading voice begged to come in.

Still the old man remained silent, and drawing nearer to the fire quieted himself for sleep; but the rapping continued, louder, fiercer, and increased his anger. "Who dares approach the door of my lodge?" he shrieked. "You are not North Wind, who alone can enter here. Begone! no refuge here for trifling winds, go back to your home in the sky." But as he spoke, the strong bar securing the door fell from its fastening, the door swung open and a stalwart young warrior stood before him shaking the snow from his shoulders as he noiselessly closed the door.

Safe within the lodge, the warrior heeded not the old man's anger, but with a cheerful greeting drew close to the fire, extending his hands to its ruddy blaze, when a glow as of summer illumined the lodge. But the kindly greeting and the glowing light served only to incense the old man, and rising in rage he ordered the warrior to depart.

"Go!" he exclaimed, "I know you not. You have entered my lodge and you bring a strange light. Why have you forced my lodge door? You are young, and youth has no need of my fire. When I enter my lodge, all the earth sleeps. You are strong, with the glow of sunshine on your face. Long ago I buried the sunshine beneath the snowdrifts. Go! you have no place here.

Your eyes bear the gleam of the summer stars, North Wind blew out the summer starlights moons ago. Your eyes dazzle my lodge, your breath does not smoke in chill vapors, but comes from your lips soft and warm, it will melt my lodge, you have no place here.

Your hair so soft and fine, streaming back like the night shades, will weave my lodge into tangles. You have no place here.

Your shoulders are bare and white as the snowdrifts. You have no furs to cover them; depart from my lodge. See, as you sit by my fire, how it draws away from you. Depart, I say, from my lodge!"

But the young warrior only smiled, and asked that he might remain to fill his pipe; and they sat down by the fire when the old man became garrulous and began to boast of his great powers.

"I am powerful and strong" said he, "I send North Wind to blow all over the earth and its waters stop to listen to his voice as he freezes them fast asleep. When I touch the sky, the snow hurries down and the hunters hide by their lodge fires; the birds fly scared, and the animals creep to their caves. When I lay my hand on the land, I harden it still as the rocks; nothing can forbid me nor loosen my fetters. You, young warrior, though you shine like the Sun, you have no power. Go! I give you a chance to escape me, but I could blow my breath and fold around you a mist which would turn you to ice, forever!

I am not a friend to the Sun, who grows pale and cold and flees to the south land when I come; yet I see his glance in your face, where no winter shadows hide. My North Wind will soon return; he hates the summer and will bind fast its hands. You fear me not, and smile because you know me not. Young man, listen. I am Gau-wi-di-ne, Winter! Now fear me and depart. Pass from my lodge and go out to the wind."

But the young warrior moved not, only smiled as he refilled the pipe for the trembling old man, saying, "Here, take your pipe, it will soothe you and make you stronger for a little while longer"; and he packed the o-yan-kwa (Indian tobacco) deep and hard in the pipe.

Said the warrior, "Now you must smoke for me, smoke for youth and Spring! I fear not your boasting; you are aged and slow while I am young and strong. I hear the voice of South Wind. Your North Wind hears, and Ga-oh is hurrying him back to his home. Wrap you up warm while yet the snowdrifts cover the earth path, and flee to your lodge in the north sky. I am here now, and you shall know me. I, too, am powerful!

When I lift my hand, the sky opens wide and I waken the sleeping Sun, which follows me warm and glad. I touch the earth and it grows soft and gentle, and breathes strong and swift as my South Wind ploughs under the snows to loosen your grasp. The trees in the forest welcome my voice and send out their buds to my hand. When my breezes blow my long hair to the clouds, they send down gentle showers that whisper the grasses to grow.

I came not to tarry long in my peace talk with you, but to smoke with you and warn you that the sun is waiting for me to open its door. You and North Wind have built your lodge strong, but each wind, the North, and the East, and the West, and the South, has its time for the earth. Now South Wind is calling me; return you to your big lodge in the sky. Travel quick on your way that you may not fall in the path of the Sun. See! it is now sending down its arrows broad and strong!"

The old man saw and trembled. He seemed fading smaller, and grown too weak to speak, could only whisper, "Young warrior, who are you?"

In a voice that breathed soft as the breath of wild blossoms, he answered: "I am Go-hay, Spring! I have come to rule, and my lodge now covers the earth! I have talked to your mountain and it has heard; I have called the South Wind and it is near; the Sun is awake from its winter sleep and summons me quick and loud. Your North Wind has fled to his north sky; you are late in following. You have lingered too long over your peace pipe and its smoke now floats far away. Haste while yet there is time that you may lose not your trail."

And Go-hay began singing the Sun song as he opened the door of the lodge. Hovering above it was a great bird whose wings seemed blown by a strong wind, and while Go-hay continued to sing, it flew down to the lodge and folding Gau-wi-di-ne to its breast, slowly winged away to the north, and when the Sun lifted its head in the east, it beheld the bird disappearing behind the far away sky. The Sun glanced down where

Gau-wi-di-ne had built his lodge, whose fire had burned but could not warm, and a bed of young blossoms lifted their heads to the touch of its beams. Where the wood and the corn and the dried meat and fish had been heaped, a young tree was leafing, and a bluebird was trying its wings for a nest. And the great ice mountain had melted to a swift running river which sped through the valley bearing its message of the springtime.

Gau-wi-di-ne had passed his time, and Go-hay reigned over the earth!

Some writers have credited this legend to the Ojibwas, but for many generations the Iroquois have claimed it as their own.

NEH JO-GA-OH, THE MYTH-DWARF PEOPLE

GA-HON-GA, THE STONE THROWERS

Among the fable folk of the Iroquois, the Jo-ga-oh, or invisible little people are beings empowered to serve nature with the same authority as the greater spirits.

These little people are divided into three tribes, the Ga-hon-ga of the rocks and rivers, the Gan-da-yah of the fruits and grains and the Oh-dan-was of the underearth shadows.

The Ga-hon-ga, guardians of the streams, dwell in rock caves beside the waters and though dwarf in being are gigantic in strength. They can uproot the largest tree by a twist of the hand and hurl massive rocks into the rivers to lift the waters when floods threaten. They have frequently visited Indians in awake dreams and led them to their dwelling places and then challenged them to feats of strength, such as playing ball with the rocks, often hurling them high out of sight in the air. Because of this fondness, the Indians often called them "Stone Throwers." [68]

When a drought parches the land, the Indian, wise in mystery ways, goes far into the forests and searches along the mountain streams until he finds the signs of the Ga-hon-ga. These are little cup-shaped hollows in the soft earth that edges the streams and are the promise of rain. The Indian carefully scoops up these hollows in the mud and dries them on a fragment of bark in the sun. They are the "dew cup charms" that placed in a lodge attract the Gan-da-yah of the fruits and grains who begin immediately their activity in the ground of the garden.

In their province of watchfulness they instruct the fish, directing their movements and giving them shelter in their deep water caves if pursued by merciless fishermen or confused in the whirl of the flood. They know the twists of every trap and will loosen them to release the captive fish, when they deem it wise to do so. They can command a fruitful or barren season and unless propitiated frequently punish negligence with famine.

By a legend of these Ga-hon-ga, at one time an abandoned orphan boy[69] was playing by the side of a river where one of these little people was paddling his canoe. The boy was invited to take a ride but the canoe was so small that he at first refused. By continual urging, however, the little rock thrower induced the boy to venture in, when with a single stroke of the paddle he swept the canoe high from the bosom of the river, up into the air and into the side of a cliff that towered from the mouth of the river. They had entered a cave filled with the old and the young of the little folk who began their Joy dance in honor of their visitor, the orphan boy.

Dwelling with these people, the boy was taught their wondrous ways, their mysticism, exorcisms and dances, all so efficacious in coaxing the fruits to come forth to the sun. In the dark recesses of the high cliff cave he learned many strange things as he saw the little people at work and so marvelous was it all that his stay seemed but a few days. Then suddenly they commanded him to return to his people. He was given a portion of each bird and animal as a charm and told how to employ each with effect. The corn and the beans would obey his words and the berries and fruits would ripen at his bidding, the harvests would be full when he sang and the flowers and leaves would unfurl as he walked through the lands. Unknowing, as they were instructing him he was being let down in the valley from which he had come. The Ga-hon-ga had vanished and going among the people he found himself a man, his captivity had been one of 40 years, and yet it seemed but a visit of so many days. He was a man of gigantic proportions and inspired awe when he taught to the wise the laws and the charms, the dances and songs of the Ga-hon-ga.[70]

The Pygmy Society in their Dark dance ceremony
From a drawing by Jesse Cornplanter, a Seneca boy artist

Thus has the story of the little rock people been transmitted from generation to generation for numberless years. The fisherman and the hunter know it, the grandmothers tell it to their children's children and the children tell it to their dolls, the medicine men chant its songs and in their incantations for the harvests, they dance for the little folk, and the dancers in darkness chant the story in song.[71]

NEH OH-DO-WAS, THE UNDEREARTH MYTHS

The Little Folk of the Darkness, the underearth dwellers, are most wise and mysterious. Seldom do the eyes of men penetrate the gloom to recognize them.[72]

These Oh-do-was are the wondrous band of elf folk that hold jurisdiction over the sunless domain beneath the earth where dwell the creatures of the darkness and the prisoners that have offended the regions of light.

In the dim world where the Oh-do-was live are deep forests and broad plains where roam the animals whose proper abode is there and though all that lives there wishes to escape yet both good and bad, native and captive are bidden to be content and dwell where fate has placed them. Among the mysterious underearth denizens are the white buffaloes who are tempted again and again to gain the earth's surface, but the paths to the light are guarded and the white buffalo must not climb to the sunlight to gallop with his brown brothers over the plains. Sometimes they try to rush up and out and then the Oh-do-was rally their hunters and thin out the unruly herds with their arrows. 'Tis then that a messenger is sent above to tell the sunlight elves that the chase is on and the earth elves hang a red cloud high in the heavens as a sign of the hunt. Ever alert for signals, the Indian reads the symbol of the red cloud and rejoices that the Little People are watchful and brave.

Always intent on flight the venomous reptiles and creatures of death slink in the deep shadows of the dim underplace, captives of the watchful Oh-do-was. Though they are small it is not often that they fail to fight back the powerful monsters that rush to the door to the light world, but sometimes one escapes and whizzing out in the darkness of earth's night, spreads his poisonous breath over the forests and creates the pestilence that sweeps all before it. Then the monsters, maddened by jealousy, search out the places where the springs spout to the surface and poison the waters, and, where a deep grown root has pushed its way through the wall of the underearth in search of water, they tear it with their fangs and the earth tree above wilts and dies. But such things are rare for the Oh-do-was are vigilant and faithful and strong and will not willingly let death escape to their elves and their human friends.

At certain times they visit their relatives above. At night they hold festivals in the forests and the circle beneath many a deep wood tree, where the grass refuses to grow, is the ring where the dances are held. Inhabiting the darkness, the light of the sun would blind them but they do not fear the moon's soft rays. The creatures of the night, the bats and birds and the prowlers of the darkness know the Oh-do-was and are wary for sometimes offensive intruding animals are captured[73] and carried far beneath the fields and forests, nor may they expect to be ransomed by their elf guardians of the light when they visit the regions below for no Jo-ga-oh ever questions the act of another.

Thus banded the Jo-ga-oh of the earth, above and below, guard, guide and advise all living nature, and protect the Indians from unseen foes. The Indian, grateful for this unselfish service, reveres the Little Folk and sings their praises in ceremonies and dedicates dances to them.

NEH GAN-DA-YAH
OF THE FRUITS AND GRAINS

In the divisions of the Jo-ga-oh the Gan-da-yah are the most beloved by the Indians. The office of these elves is to protect and advise the fruits and grains. They are the little people of the sunshine who bring joy and brightness to the Indian's heart.

In the springtime these "Little People" hide in dark sheltered places and whisper to the earth as they listen to the complaints of the growing seeds. When the sun bestows its full summer glow they wander over the fields tinting the grains and ripening the fruits and bidding all growing things to look to the sun. Their labor commences with the strawberry plant, whose fruit is a special gift to mankind. When the ground softens from the frost the "Little People" loosen the earth around each strawberry root, that its shoots may better push through to the light. They shape its leaves to the sun, turning the blossoms upward to its touches and guiding the runners to new growing places. Assisting the timid fruit buds at nightfall they direct them from the west sky where they had followed the sun back to the east and the morning's glow. When the full fruit first blushes on the vine these guardian elves protect it from the ravages of evil insects and the mildew of the damp.

The ripening of the strawberry is the signal for a thanksgiving by the entire people. The fruit, the first grown of the year, is greeted with songs of joy and gratitude. The Priestesses[74] hold meetings of praise in the darkness of the night. In their Dark dances the berry had its own Joy dance and there is an especial dance and song for the Jo-ga-oh, by whose fostering care the fruit has come to perfection. The strawberry wine is made on these occasions and distributed among the people, a separate portion being reserved for the singers who officiate at the Berry dances.

There is an ancient folk tale that when the fruits were first coming to earth an evil spirit stole the strawberry plant, hiding it under the ground for centuries, until it was finally released by a spy sunbeam who carried it back to the sunny fields of earth where it has lived and thrived ever since, but fearing another captivity the "Little People" maintain special guard over their favorite fruit.

These elf folk are ever vigilant in the fields during the season of ripening and vigorous are their wars with the blights and disease that threaten to infect and destroy the corn and the beans.

The universal friend of the red man, they assume various forms for protection and guidance, frequently visiting the lodges of the Indian in the guise of birds. If they come as a robin they carry good tidings; if as an owl, watchful and wise, their mission is one of warning, an enemy is coming who will deceive; if as a bat, that winged animal, the symbol of the union of light and darkness, it denotes some life and death struggle close at hand. The most minute harmless insect or worm may be the bearer of important "talk" from the "Little People" and is not destroyed for the "trail is broad enough for all."

According to a law enacted by these guardian elves, a true Indian should not relate the myth tales of his people during the summer. No one could tell, they thought, when some bug or bird might be listening and report the offense to the elves, who in turn would send a watcher to enforce silence on the part of the breaker of the law. They dread that some creature of animate nature may overhear these tales and entranced by them, forget to go back to winter homes when the snow falls. Even the vine that crept over the lodge door may listen so eagerly that it will forget to let down its sap before the frost comes and die. The bird singing on the tree's limb which leafs above the door may in his wonder and bewilderment forget the sun way to the south and fall a victim to the first snow. The ground animals may stop to listen, with their heads half out of their burrows and, marveling over the story, tarry till the winter seals them there to perish in the ice breath of the north blast. Knowing these things, the Indian reserves his myth tales until the winter time comes and his fireplace glows.

When the leaves have strewn the barren earth and the snow has covered the leaves, and built its mounds high in the lowlands, the "Little People" are safe folded in their shadow slumbers and the earth knows them no more until the melting snows and the swollen streams and the leafing trees summon them to the season of springtime.

THE DREAM FAST, JIS-GO-GA, THE ROBIN [75]

The primal precept incumbent upon the Iroquois father was to impress upon the mind of his young son the preparation for his manhood, which must be brave and heroic. Previous to the maturity of the Iroquois boy, the mother had supreme control of his life save the occasional journeys with his father, who would teach the ways of the forest, but when the hour of his manhood arrived, it was the ambitious father who imposed upon him the importance of the Dream Fast. And this grave premanhood ceremony was further dignified by the belief in dreams, the most potent of which would come to the faster who, at his maturity, followed the custom of his ancestors and, leaving his boyhood behind him, sought the divining of his man's life.

During the fast, which must be continued for not less than 7 days, the "clan spirit" of the young faster should appear to him in a dream and symbolize the bird, animal, reptile, fish, trees, plants, roots, or anything else that it might select for the guardian of his future life.

The Seneca-Iroquois have eight clans as follows: the Bear, Beaver, Wolf, Deer, Turtle, Heron, Hawk and Snipe. Should the dreamer have been born of the Bear clan, the spirit of the bear will appear to him in his dreams and show him his future guardian, and the dreamer accepts the choice. If the clan spirit does not appear during the fast, the chiefs, who visit him daily, release him and he departs unhappy and in disgrace, having no dream sign to invoke during his life.

To "fulfil the rules," the dreamer may leave his lodge for brief periods. He is permitted water to quench his thirst, but is forbidden food of any kind. He is expected to perform acts of bravery, to kill vicious wild animals, or poisonous snakes, and to preserve their skins as trophies to be shown to his people.

O-go-ne-sas belonged to the Wolf clan and was the son of a noted war chief. He had been trained to the chase and the trails of the warpath. He led in the games, was the swiftest runner, could throw the arrow farther than any of his comrades, and hurl the snow-snake beyond the bounds. He knew the forests and streams, and had taught the wild game to know him. He could imitate the call of the birds, and they would flock around him. Should he wander late in the forest, he had no fear of the prowling animals, the bear or the wolf was as welcome to meet as his friends in his father's lodge; for they seemed to know him, and would pass silently by. He was the pride of the village, and the boast of his father who believed he would become a great chief.[76]

The dawn drink of the dream faster

The time for his Dream fast had come. The snows were deep and the winds were keen, but O-go-ne-sas was young and his blood like fire, and he welcomed its coming. To endure—but that was his birthright and boast.

In the heart of the woods he built his lodge of young saplings, covering it with branches of evergreen hemlock to shelter him from the snows and, divesting himself of the furs he had worn and appealing to his clan spirit to attend him, entered his retreat.

His fast had begun, and he was alone with his thoughts. He had been happy and kind. No frown had come to his life, nor sorrow, and now his manhood was approaching. Ten suns to pass above him; ten nights for his clan spirit to choose his totem. If the deer, he would wind its soft skin about him to warn away the cold winds. If the bear, he would string its strong claws to wear around his neck. If the wolf, his white teeth would guard him from danger. If the beaver, he would wed the water. If the turtle, his shell would be his breastplate. If a bird, his wings would adorn him. No thought but hope and faith in his dreaming.

Three times must the clan spirit bring the totem. Nine suns had lighted the forest, nine nights had darkened the lodge. The tenth day dawned frowning and gloomy, and the chiefs came.

They shook the lodge poles and bade him appear. "Not yet today," he replied, "I have fasted and dreamed, yet the clan spirit came but once. Return tomorrow." Again on the morrow they came. "One day more," pleaded O-go-ne-sas, but his voice was low and weak. Again on the morrow came the chiefs, announcing that his time had passed, and again he implored for one day more. "If the spirit does not attend me I will go— tomorrow I will depart with you." His voice had grown faint and the chiefs were anxious. Cautiously parting the hemlock branches, they saw O-go-ne-sas painting his body, as only the dying do before departing, and they pondered. His life had been pure and free from evil. Had his clan spirit refused him?

On the morrow the chiefs again shook the lodge poles. There was no response save a trembling of the hemlock branches; and a strange silence seemed to have fallen in the forest.

The awed chiefs wondered, and entered the lodge. O-go-ne-sas was not there, but a bird flew down to a branch on the lodge and began to speak.

"I am he whom you seek. My body is no more on earth. I was O-go-ne-sas. I fasted and waited, but my clan spirit came only once to show me my totem. I knew not the reason. I had done no evil. My spirit was pure. Death was the friend who aided me to flee the disgrace which would follow me if denied by my clan spirit. He who would have been my totem, knew not the winter. He had hidden from its winds and could not be found. Now he has received me into his spirit, and I am Jis-go-ga,[77] the Robin!

Do not sorrow, nor mourn me. I will return and bring the Spring to you. I will sing to the trees, and young leaves will come forth to listen. I will swing on the wild cherry and its blossoms will welcome me. I will carry the gray shadows of the Spring morning on my wings. I will not hide in the forest, I will nest by your lodges. Your children will know that the Spring is coming when they hear my voice. Though the snowfall may cover my path, it will melt into singing streams when it hears my wings rustling. I was willing, and painted my body red when I felt my spirit departing, and now I carry its red glow on my breast as its shield."

The voice ceased its chanting, the Robin had departed. And the forest wondered as the trees sent forth their young leaves, frozen streams melted, and the cold, gray clouds nestled nearer the sun's red glow that draped the west sky. The hemlock lodge fell to the earth, and all nature began its song of Spring!

"He was brave," sorrowed a chief. "We should have taken him sooner."

"His totem was late, but the spirit of O-go-ne-sas was pure; and now he is Jis-go-ga, the Robin, the bird which brings us the Spring!" proudly exclaimed the father.

"He is the Robin forever," chanted the birds, and the sun which came that wintry morning looked back to the east wondering why it had forgotten to lead the Spring to the earthland!

The Iroquois Indian plants a wild cherry tree near his lodge, "for the Robin."

THE ORIGIN OF
THE RATTLESNAKE TRIBE

It was in the early days of the earth that the Sky Holder divided the forests among the clans and gave each its own hunting ground.

Now the Evil Minded, being jealous of the success of the Good Minded and his helper, the Sky Holder, determined to destroy the order and peace that existed among the clans. He therefore came to certain men in each clan and told them that the divisions of the forest were unjust and that each other clan had much better grounds. These evil suggestions caused immediate strife. Each clan became jealous of the other and soon many feuds arose. Now in those days there were few people and when a man or woman was killed it was a loss that the clan felt deeply. Therefore, when the ground became red the clans mourned. Then the Sky Holder sought to restore peace. "Let us have a great dance," he said, "and in the pleasure of the ceremony friendship will be restored. Let each clan select its best dancers to compete with the others and the company that dances best will receive as a prize a broad strip of land and high mountains on either side of a great river filled with fish."

The clans hailed the Sky Holder's proposition with cries of "*Niuh, niuh!*, it is well, let it so be done." Then they chose their most agile warriors for the dance and a feeling of good-willed rivalry came over the people. The dancers of the clan of the Bear first entered the circle. Their rivals looked on in astonishment for they had never seen so weird a dance before. Then the other clans competed but none could equal the Bears until a company of young braves who had banded together commenced to dance with a slow shuffling movement that gradually increased until the twisting, bounding, leaping, sliding, gliding feet seemed scarcely to touch the ground. The assembled throng gazed breathlessly at the astonishing spectacle. Never before had their eyes beheld so wonderful a scene. Faster and faster they danced until at last in the wild delirium of the intoxicating whirl they leapt into the air like demons, and as the last tap of the water drum sounded upon the taut, wet head of woodchuck skin, they brought their feet down in unison and finished their dance. The multitude gave a great shout and cried, "They have won, they have excelled as men never have before!" Then the evil thing occurred. Filled with the spirit of the Evil Minded the wild dancers sounded a signal with their rattles, raised their clubs and struck down a score of warriors, struck them dead upon the ground, and turning to slay others, were halted by the angry thundering voice of the Sky Holder. "Cease," he commanded and summoning the offenders before him he called the clans about him. Then addressing the culprits he said, "Without cause you have made the ground red with the lives of your cousins and brothers. You have made the nation mourn. Your deed is the blackest that men-beings have ever known. You have chosen a time of peace for a time to kill. We were gathered to strengthen our friendship and become of one mind again but you by your treachery have endeavored to start a war. You have won the lands on either side of the river but you shall not enjoy them as men. You are outcast, you shall forevermore be despised, hated, stoned and trodden under foot. You shall be hunted and killed whenever you are seen for you have the evil mind within you. So, go out from among men and crawl in the dust of your domain. Unlike others of your kin, when you are transformed into *sais-tah-o-noh,*[78] you will warn your foes before you strike them by shaking your rattles, even as you did when you murdered your relatives. Depart outcasts, and take the lands you have won but go not as victors but as an hated, accursed tribe upon whom war will ever be waged!" The bloodguilty culprits shuffled into line and one by one took up the song *Ji-ha-yah*[79] and danced into the shadows. "When they had passed from the sight of the mourning people the Sky Holder shook the earth and the evil dancers fell upon their bellies, dropped their rattles at their feet and with their faces in the dust trembled as they felt the power of the Sky Holder grip them. It rent the very fibers of their bodies and they writhed in mute agony as their clothing grew fast to their bodies and became scaly, as their legs stretched out and became as one with a rattle where their feet had been, and as their arms melted into their sides. Their tongues divided, their teeth fell out and sharp fangs pierced through the bleeding gums. They had become rattlesnakes, the children of the Evil Minded, the hated, despised and loathed crawlers of the ground.

Then the clans became friendly again and their feuds died out. Then did their hunting grounds seem just and enough, and peace prevailed.

KA-IS-TO-WAN-EA AND HA-JA-NOH,[80] THE TWO-HEADED SERPENT AND THE BRAVE BOY

To-no-do-oo, the Supreme Ruler

When "The People of the Hill," as the Senecas were called, lighted their first council fire on Ga-nun-do-wa mountain[81] and its flames leaped high, there was great rejoicing, for they knew it to be a sign that To-no-do-oo was pleased, and they "gave thanks" for their beautiful land with its guarding mountain whose towering height reflected far down in the peaceful waters of Lake Ga-nun-du-gwa-ah.[82]

To-no-do-oo loved his people, and thoughtful of their needs, sent game to their forests and fish to their lakes and the streams, that they might dwell in peace and plenty forever.

It was here that Ka-is-to-wan-ea, the serpent, was first seen, none knew whence its coming; and it was here that Ha-ja-noh, one summer day when paddling his canoe through the swamp land, found it sun basking on the floating sedge grass. Attracted by its bright colors, Ha-ja-noh determined to possess it, and gently raising it on his paddle, placed it in the canoe. Great was his astonishment to discover that it had two heads, and fearing it might bode ill to himself or his people, raised his paddle to destroy it, but charmed by the swaying heads and their bright eyes glistening in the sun, his fears were forgotten, and he bore it to his lodge.

The little Ka-is-to-wan-ea seemed glad in his new home, and when caressed by Ha-ja-noh, would wave its beautiful heads to express its gratitude; and the attachment of Ha-ja-noh for his new-found companion increased with the passing days.

The Ka-is-to-wan-ea grew rapidly. It was Ha-ja-noh's delight to procure for it the choicest game of the forests, and for many months there was happiness in his lodge which he hoped might continue as long as he should live. But this was not to be.

The Ka-is-to-wan-ea, so beautiful and graceful in its youth, soon grew to be a ravenous monster, demanding for its insatiate maw more food than Ha-ja-noh could obtain, although he was aided by all the hunters of the tribe; and having grown so large that the lodge could contain it no longer, it left Ha-ja-noh and wandered to a cave under the mountain, whence it would emerge to forage the forests, devouring the game until the people were famishing. In the greed of its hunger, it crawled to the lake where it devoured all the fish when, with hunger still unappeased, it encircled the mountain with its enormous length, thereby preventing the people from escaping, and began to devour them.

Ha-ja-noh, who had now become a great warrior, was overcome with remorse at beholding the destruction of his people; for he knew that his love for the beautiful little Ka-is-to-wan-ea had brought this calamity upon them, and wearied with grieving, fell asleep.

While sleeping, he dreamed that a voice spoke to him saying, "Save your people. The Ka-is-to-wan-ea is strong, but I will aid you to vanquish it. Your arrow must bear a charm. Make it of dark snake wood and tip its point with white flint, string your bow with a lock of your sister's hair and aim at the monster's heart." Starting from his sleep and believing that the Great Spirit had spoken to him, he hastened to obey.

When all was prepared as directed in his dream, and he had declared his intention to the people, he approached the Ka-is-to-wan-ea, calling it to listen while he denounced it for its treachery and base ingratitude; reminding it of the time when young and helpless he had taken it from the swamp to the shelter of his lodge. But the Ka-is-to-wan-ea, who had hesitated at the sound of Ha-ja-noh's voice, would listen no longer, and returned to his bloody feast.

"Ungrateful creature," exclaimed Ha-ja-noh, "you shall die!" and springing his bow to its utmost bend, sped his arrow at the monster's heart. True to its aim, the arrow sank deep, and the Ka-is-to-wan-ea, relaxing its grasp, rolled to the base of the mountain, in its dying struggles disgorging the heads of the people it had swallowed.

Many of the heads sank in the lake where they were turned to stone, and lie in great heaps at the bottom; but a large number aided by some great power, were given new bodies, and rejoined the survivors of their new council fire far from Ga-nun-do-wa mountain.

An Iroquois will go far out of his path to avoid meeting a snake, and will rarely kill one, fearing he may release the spirit of the monster Ka-is-to-wan-ea which still exists in the snake life of the earth.

―――――――――

In this ancient legend, the Iroquois recognize a prophecy of the coming of the white man, and the extermination of the Indian.

Ka-is-to-wan-ea is the white man who, in his greed unsatisfied with the lands the red man gave him, has gradually encroached until in the relentless pursuit, the red men have been thrust away, even to the limit of the last lands of their once broad possessions!

GA-YE-WAS AND GI-DA-NO-NEH, THE FISH AND THE INDIAN MAIDEN[83]

When Hah-gweh-di-yu was adorning the earth with his beautiful creations, in a rock on his fairest land, he scooped a deep hollow and therein set a lake ever to be nourished by the rich mountain streams whose virgin waters would send it their most precious offerings. To Ga-ye-was, the most mighty of all fish, was given the controlling power of this beautiful lake and, being also the guardian of all the mountain streams, he could assume the mortal form and visit the lands surrounding his domain.

Although free to the land and water, still Ga-ye-was was not happy, his life was a lonely one. His possessions, though vast and beautiful, failed to satisfy his desires; he had no companions. His authority separated him from his subjects and only the solitude of power was his.

But to Ga-ye-was there came a new dominion; Ga-ye-was loved! One day when floating on his
lake and singing his power song, he saw standing on
the shore a graceful sad eyed Indian girl who seemed
sobbing her sorrows to the waters, and, as if enchanted
by the tranquil rhythm of the waves, was listening as
they bore the song to the shore.

Unseen by the girl, Ga-ye-was approached,
softening his song as he neared her, was amazed at her
wonderful beauty and knew she was fairer than all his
possessions—and Ga-ye-was would win her!

Gi-da-no-neh, the beautiful Indian girl, came at
each sunset to the lake to stroll along its bank and listen
to the sweet strains of the song which seemed to grow
stronger and more vibrant the longer she remained.
And it comforted her, for the life of Gi-da-no-neh
was an unhappy one. Furs and rare feathers and the
promise of a lodge was the marriage portion of an old
man whom her parents had chosen for her, but his feet
were too slow for the hunt, his spirit too still for war;
old age was close to him and his heart was dead, and
Gi-da-no-neh delayed. But Gi-da-no-neh was young
and the world lay bright before her. She cared not for
the discipline and labor of the old man's lodge which
she was bid to enter, and her troubled heart sought the
solace of the lake shore where she could listen to the
pleasing song the waters sang.

And so the days passed and she still repelled the
old suitor, and one evening after a prolonged visit at the
lake, just as she was retracing her steps, she found lying

in her path two fish; she had never seen such beautiful fish. Around them were sewn rows of shining silver brooches which seemed to have caught the sunset fires in their glistening, so dazzling were they. In alarm she gazed about her, fearing she had been followed, but all was still and not a person could she see, and in ecstacy of joy she gathered the glistening brooches, attaching them to her frayed and faded doeskin dress. Happy in the glitter of her wondrous find, she turned and looked at the fish from which she had stripped them, and was hungry. So she built a fire and was roasting the fish when her father found her. He paused in wonder as he looked at the shining brooches upon her dress, for never had he seen such beautiful ones. Who had thus adorned his daughter? Surely some evil spirit was tempting her. In fear and rage he stripped them from her dress and throwing them in the lake, led his weeping daughter back to his lodge. There she grieved and was not content, she mourned the loss of her brooches and besought her father to allow her to return and regain them, but in vain, for he loved her and feared that evil was luring her away. Still she urged that she must return to the lake for she felt drawn by some strange power that she could not resist. The fish she had eaten had carried a thirst, the craving of which she could not satisfy at the little spring that trickled from the hill near the lodge for its waters had grown bitter. Heedless of her father's entreaties, she ran from him nor stopped until she had gained the sandy lake shore and falling upon her knees had buried her lips in the water. Eagerly she drank as if never to cease while unconsciously she drifted into the lake, when, as she was sinking, strong arms were thrown around her, and she heard a voice as musical as a running brook, pronouncing her name. "Fear not, Gi-da-no-neh," it said, "for I am Ga-ye-was, your lover." Opening her eyes she beheld a tall young warrior, who was clasping her to his breast, a warrior as if of her own people, and resplendent with silver brooches that covered him as an armor. With his strong arms he held her while with endearing words he told her of his love, and the winning was sudden! He told her of his long wooing, how he had waited each sunset for her coming to the lake, how he had often neared her singing his power song that seemed so to please her and had determined to win her for his bride and companion. With the power of his charm song he had enticed her to the lake, with the beautiful fish he had lured her, for having eaten them she would ever thirst for the lake water and never again would be content with the land. She should again wear the brooches of which she had been so cruelly deprived, they were the scales of his coat which he wore when as a fish he lived in the water. He ruled the lake and had prepared a home for her far down in its coolest depths. She should accompany him when he visited the lands of his domain and should be his companion forever. And Gi-da-no-neh was happy in her love for Ga-ye-was.

The day was well up in the sky when the troubled father, who had wandered the night through round the lake, was returning disconsolate to his lodge, when from the water came his daughter's voice, and, pausing in surprise, he saw the water spread apart disclosing

165

her clasped to the bosom of Ga-ye-was. "Father, I have sought you!" she said. "I will return no more to my land life. My true lover rules these pleasant waters and I am now his bride. You loved me, father, but did not know my heart. I will ever be near you to help you, but you will never behold me again. Farewell, farewell!" As she finished speaking, the waters slowly united and a gentle strain of a song was borne to the shore as the old man wended his way to his lodge.

When a fisherman of the mountain lakes secures a fish of unusual size and beauty, he says, "This is a true child of Ga-ye-was the fish chief and his Indian wife Gi-da-no-neh."

OT-TO-TAR-HO, THE TANGLED

It was at some time during the remote period before the organization of the Iroquois Confederacy, that there was born among the Onondagas a most remarkable personage named Ot-to-tar-ho[84] and whether myth or human, he still lives in a legend that will be remembered and retold as long as there are Iroquois remaining.

The legend runs that in his youth he was gentle and mild, fond of innocent amusements and the chase, and was beloved by his people who looked forward to the time when he would be chosen their chief and become their counselor. But one day when hunting in the mountains he chanced to kill a strange bird which, though beautiful in plumage, was virulently poisonous.

Unaware of its deadly nature Ot-to-tar-ho, delighted with his prize, plucked its bright feathers to decorate his head and while handling them inhaled their poison which entering his brain maddened him and upon his return to the village in insane rage, he sought to kill those whom he met. Amazed at the strange transformation the people were in great consternation and fled from him in fear. No more the gentle Ot-to-tar-ho; no more did he care for their games; no more did he care for the chase, but was sullen and morose and shunned all companionship with his people who also avoided him for he had developed a mania for killing human beings.

The poisonous fire that burned in his brain had so distorted his features that he became hideous to behold; his long glossy hair fell from his head and in its stead there grew serpents that writhed and hissed when he brushed them back from his face and coiled around his pipe in rage when he smoked.

Many believed he had been witched, that some ferocious animal had taken possession of him; others that he was controlled by an evil spirit who was seeking to destroy the nation. Various were the surmises of the people but the mystery baffled them and their appeals to their medicine men were received by these wise men in silence; yet they sought by long fasting and dancing and various incantations to appease the wrath of the evil one, but their efforts were all in vain for still the demon if demon it was, continued to dominate Ot-to-tar-ho, who only became more furious and violent and seemed to have endowed him with supernatural powers.

His mind had become so powerful that it could project a thought many miles through the air and kill whomsoever he desired. Developing clairvoyance of vision and prophecy, he could divine other people's thoughts and through this power came to dominate the councils, assuming a control that none dared oppose, and ruled for many years with such insane and despotic sway that he broke their hearts and the once powerful, proud and most courageous of all the nations became abject and cowardly weak.

It was at this time that Hi-ant-wat-ha, (Hiawatha), grieving over the deplorable condition to which the demonized Ot-to-tar-ho had reduced his people and desiring to promote their welfare and restore them to prosperity and the proud position they had lost, conceived the idea of forming a league which would unite the five nations, the Mohawks, Onondagas, Oneidas, Cayugas and Senecas and in bond of union and good fellowship which would not only cement a tie of national brotherhood, but by their united action they would become more formidable in war and better able to vanquish other nations and extend their domain and power. But Ot-to-tar-ho was intractable and bitterly opposed to Hiawatha and to defeat him put three of his brothers to death.

Although driven away by the relentless Ot-to-tar-ho, Hiawatha actuated by his love for his people and great concern for their happiness did not abandon the hope of effecting his purpose, and later returning aided by a powerful chief succeeded in placating the intractable Ot-to-tar-ho by combing the snakes from his head with the wampum and the union was formed, the nations united and the confederacy of the Iroquois, one of the greatest political organizations ever accomplished by either civilized or uncivilized peoples was formed.[85]

HOW THE FLYING SQUIRREL WON HIS WINGS, THE FROG LOST ITS TEETH, AND THE WOODCHUCK ITS APPETITE

Teh-do-oh, the woodchuck; Nos-gwais, the frog; Jo-nis-gy-ont, the squirrel

Iroquois mythology invests animals and birds with all the traits and characteristics of the Indian himself. They too have their tribes people, chiefs who hold councils, and warriors who battle.

Nuk-da-go was the head chief of the squirrel tribe. He was powerful and wise, and could become invisible, and one day when troubled by a conversation he had overheard between a woodchuck, a frog and a squirrel, said to himself, "I will investigate."

Jo-nis-gy-ont, a frugal squirrel, had laid away his winter's supply of nuts in a hollow tree near a pine, but his storehouse was being plundered and he was complaining to his nearest neighbors, a woodchuck who had dug his lodge under the rocks near the pine, and a frog who lived in a marshy place by the side of the river over which the pine cast its shadow.

The invisible Nuk-da-go listened. Said the frog: "I wonder who could so cruelly deprive poor Jo-nis-gy-ont of his industrious gleanings"; and with tears

169

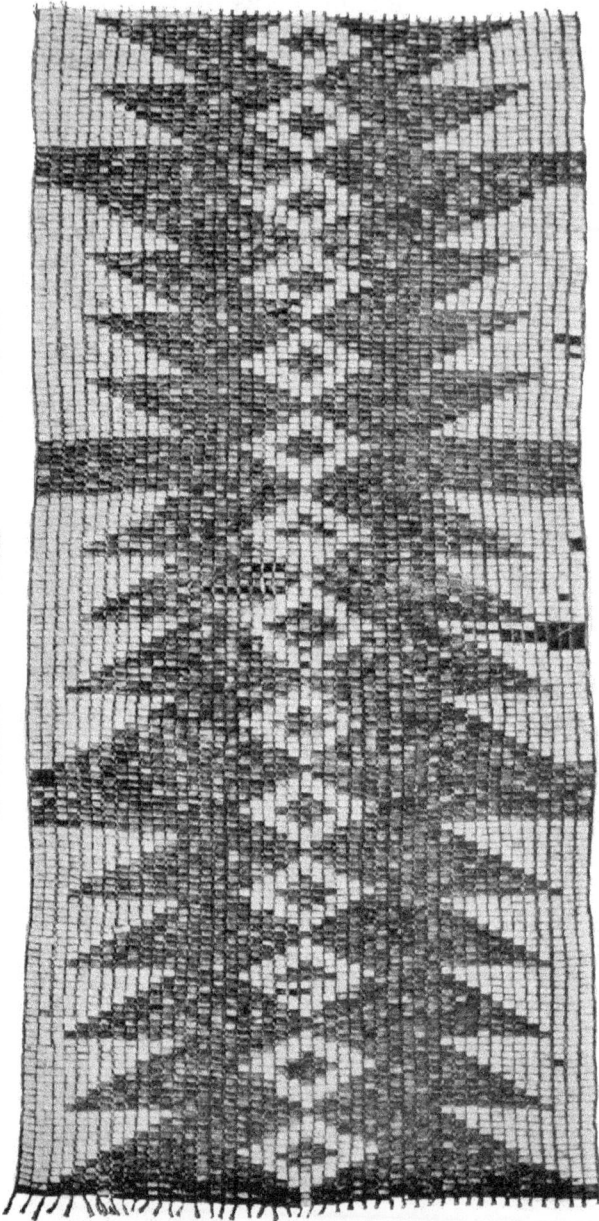

To-ta-da-ho belt. Sometimes called the Presedentia. It is the second largest belt known. The series of diamonds in the center is said to represent a covenant chain always to be kept bright.

dropping from his eyes seemed to grieve greatly. The woodchuck was indignant, declared it an outrage, and inveighed most bitterly against the robber who had found the hiding place of Jo-nis-gy-ont, but the wary squirrel knew they were his only neighbors who cared for nuts, and received their sympathy with suspicious silence.

Thought Nuk-da-go as he listened, "Something wrong is going on here, I will investigate."

At midnight the invisible Nuk-da-go entered the forest on his customary tour of inspection, and pausing near the pine his quick ear caught a strange sound.

Down by the rock side he saw a woodchuck digging the earth which flew in great drifts behind him. "Strange," thought Nuk-da-go, "he finished his lodge long ago." And suspicious Nuk-da-go watched.

Deeper and still deeper the woodchuck dug, frequently disappearing for a time and returning with his cheeks bulging out like bags puffed with wind, and skulkingly looking around to be sure that nothing saw him, one by one he dropped in the hole the hickory nuts which distended his cheeks.

All the night through Nuk-da-go watched while the woodchuck continued his trips for the nuts, but when the sun came he hid in his burrow.

"Too many nuts—too far from the tree—this is a pine forest—the hickory grows hours away," thought the wise Nuk-da-go. "To-morrow at midnight I will return."

On the following night Nuk-da-go watched and saw the woodchuck carefully concealing the hole with grass. "Who would think a deep little pit was under those grasses," said Teh-do-oh to himself, as he sat near the rock and complacently slicked his hair.

Wise and suspicious Nuk-da-go still lingered. As noon approached he peered through the shade of the pine and down by the marsh saw a frog disappear under a moss-covered stone from which he cautiously peeked, his bright eyes blinking to themselves in their cunning. The frog could jump far when bearing no load, but so freighted was he that he could only hop slow to the marsh where he disgorged several nuts which he pushed well under the moss.

"Too many nuts—too far from the tree—this is a pine forest—the hickory grows hours away," thought Nuk-da-go. "Tomorrow at noon I will return."

By the following noon when the shadows returned, the Nos-gwais had hidden the nuts under the moss which he patted down close to the stone. "Ha, ha!" croaked he, "who would think of looking for nuts under an old moss-grown stone," and he trilled a low song to the marsh.

But the wise Nuk-da-go knew, and determined that the thieves should be punished; so he called a council of all the chiefs of the forest clans, to whom he related what he had witnessed, and advised a thorough investigation. Said the Nuk-da-go: "I have made a discovery. Thieves dwell in our midst. They must be secured and punished."

At the council it was noticed that neither the woodchuck nor frog were present, and as Jo-nis-gy-ont was their nearest neighbor, he was commissioned to go for them and bring them before the council. Jo-nis-gy-ont gladly undertook the commission, hoping to regain the nuts he had lost, and soon returned but without frog and without woodchuck, to report that he had found them and delivered the summons, but the frog jumped so far he could not overtake him, and the woodchuck hid in his burrow.

But the wise Nuk-da-go was not to be baffled, and hastening to the pine he sent down his strong power under the moss-covered stone and into the burrow, ordering the culprits to come forth, when a meek looking frog and a shame-faced woodchuck appeared and reluctantly followed Nuk-da-go to the council.

"Why are we brought here?" together they asked. "We know nothing of this!" they indignantly exclaimed, and the woodchuck stroked his grizzly whiskers while the frog in rage puffed his sides to near bursting.

Then said Nuk-da-go: "See the culprits!—their bravado is useless and will not avail. I pronounce them the thieves who robbed the Jo-nis-gy-ont. I discovered them in the act and I ask that they be punished." Nuk-da-go then informed the council that, having cause for distrust, he had watched the movements of the culprits, and then related what he had seen; thereupon a committee was sent to the pine to investigate, and returning with the stolen nuts, the thieves were convicted.

As Nuk-da-go had so faithfully watched at the pine, he was chosen the judge to sentence the culprits. Before proceeding, he stated to the council that, with the Indian animals, death was the penalty for thieving, but, said he, there is a wiser judgment which I will now render, the better for the protection of animals inhabiting the forests for all future time.

Turning to the frog he said: "You belong to a tribe that has always been able to get an honest living. Your wants have been amply supplied. Even a long lapping tongue was given you to entice the bugs and flies that pass your door as you rest comfortably in the sunshine. But your neighbor Jo-nis-gy-ont must work hard and journey far for his winter's store. You sleep through the winter, Jo-nis-gy-ont remains awake and must have food. You had not the excuse of hunger for your robbing, you were selfish, which adds to your crime, and you must be punished. Proper and sufficient food shall remain for you that you may not die, but never more shall your tribe be tempted by the nut. Your teeth shall grow no more. Go back in disgrace to your marsh." And as the frog left the Council House, his teeth dropped from his mouth.

"And you, Teh-do-oh," said the judge, "you shall not lose your teeth which you are so closely hiding in fear, but your punishment shall be just. You too, sleep through the winter. Through the summer all your wants are provided. Corn and clover, and grains grow for you, and fish, and birds; greed, alone, tempted you to steal. The nuts have ceased falling, no more to gather and winter is coming; who will help the starving

Jo-nis-gy-ont? Your greed has deprived him of food. Greed must not shadow the good name of your tribe, and all your tribe must share your punishment forever. Of green leaves and grains you shall not be deprived, but no more shall you relish the birds or the fish, they will fear you no more. Go back in disgrace to your burrow, and return not until spring paints your shadow on the soft snows."

"The judge was wise," said the council. Even the unfortunate Jo-nis-gy-ont did not escape reproof, for said the judge: "Had you been more watchful and swift, you could have guarded your store, yet I will help you. I will widen your eyes and they shall grow bigger and rounder that you may see sideways when your enemies appear; and I will web your forelegs with wings that you may fly quick to your nest when thieves threaten. But I warn you, hide from the sun and you can toil unseen in the shadows." And happy Jo-nis-gy-ont flew back to his nest.

Thus the squirrel won his wings, the selfish frog lost its teeth, and the thieving woodchuck was punished for his greed.

When an Iroquois child loses a tooth, it carries it to a marsh where the frogs are croaking, and throwing it in the water will say, "Nos-gwais, Nos-gwais, I give you my little tooth, send me another as strong as a bear." And the child in his simple belief knows that Nos-gwais, who craves small teeth, will hear him and grant his request.

When Teh-do-oh "paints his shadow" on the snows, the Indian knows that spring is near.

NYA-GWA-IH,
HOW THE BEAR LOST ITS TAIL

Nya-gwa-ih, the bear, who was hunting the forest for his winter store of nuts and honey, had traveled far from his home when he met an aged fox who informed him that he had just passed the river where he saw some strange little animals dive down to a burrow beneath the water. He thought they were young otters, and had watched for their return but they had not appeared, and he urged the bear to go with him and endeavor to entice them from their hiding place.

The credulous bear, smacking his lips and licking out his tongue in anticipation of a feast, hunched himself down to the water where upon looking in he saw the reflection of his own face, and believing it to be one of the little mysteries which the fox had seen, sat himself down to watch for its reappearance.

Untiringly he waited, as the artful fox encouraged. At length it occurred to the bear to allure the unknown little creatures by fishing for them and the bear was a genial fisherman. He had the patience to wait all the day by a stream, and the cunning to watch breathlessly, fearing to shadow the water, but now, alas, he had no bait! What was he to do? The artful fox suggested that he should swim to a log that was floating near, and after he had fixed himself firm, to drop his tail in the water. Soon something would seize it, when he was to lift it up to the log and whip the game over to the shore where he would remain and protect it for him.

By the persuasions of the wily fox, the unsuspecting bear swam out to the log where he secured himself and dropped his tail into the water, and the tail of the bear was broad, and so long it reached near to the bottom of the river.

Soon a *something* shook the tail, and as the bear lifted it up, he saw a wriggling little animal, not a bird, nor a fish, but a something of flesh very like a young otter, and he slung it across the stream to the fox. "That is fine!" said the fox. Again and again the bear lowered his tail in the water, to secure the shoal which seemed to have gathered around him. Whenever the tail shook, he would throw his game to the fox who would urge him on. This continued until a gusty north wind which chanced to be passing stopped in its wonder and deriding the bear, blew its cold breath over the water. And the river became quiet and its waves suddenly stretched out as smooth as a blanket. No more could they chase each other in their race with the wind nor lap to the shore when it thirsted in the sun, for the north wind had frozen them down by its breath. But the foolish and unheeding bear, intent on his game, waited till night. No more came the tremulous snipping at his tail, no longer his tail grew heavy with the wrigglers. The bear, who could not see the crafty fox devouring his pile of game, exclaimed, "How suddenly the wrigglers have stopped biting my tail! What does it mean?"

The subtle fox caught sniffing and choking over a bone, replied: "Something has drifted against them. Wait till it passes." And the good natured bear who in his mind was counting the game which he had thrown to the shore, saw the night coming, and thought of his home to which he knew he must hasten. He had his honey and his nuts beside his river game to carry, and the way was long. As he was fixing himself to travel, in his hospitality he invited the fox to return with him when they would partake of the feast together; and if the fox was willing, he could help carry the game. But no answer came to his invitation. Again he called to the fox. No answer, and he raised himself to jump from the log. But his tail was "so heavy." "Some big game," gleefully thought he, as he pulled stronger. "My! how that game pulls!" thought the bear. "Now I will bring it." And with a vigorous jump, he made a lunge for the shore when lo! his tail was left in the water! The satirical north wind had frozen it fast! And the friendly, advising fox! Where was he? Vanished! And the game? A pile of half chewed bones on the bank! With a sigh and a sneering smile, the tailless bear lifted his load of honey and nuts and lumbered along to his cave miles away!

Thus the bear lost his tail and his tailless descendants have never been fishermen.

THE ALGONQUIN AND WAN-NUT-HA

Disdaining death, scorning his foes, defying the stake and challenging its torture, Hon-do-sa, an Algonquin chieftain, awaited his doom at sunrise. He was the captive of a Seneca sachem.

For fifty years, war between the Algonquins and the Iroquois had raged with direful fury; for fifty years their hate had shown no mercy; and for fifty years their slain warriors had been passing to eternity, leaving the bloody strife an inheritance for their descendants. Fifty years of the oppressor and the oppressed, of Algonquin persecution and Iroquois defense; and now, Hon-do-sa, a young Algonquin chief, stoically awaited the Seneca's doom of death at the stake.

Hon-do-sa had been captured in a battle where the son of the sachem was killed, and the blood of the Algonquin must atone for his death.

It was an early custom, that during the time preceding the putting to death of a captive, he should receive the utmost hospitality, be treated rather as a guest than a prisoner, and while strongly guarded to prevent his escape, he was given the best lodge in the canton, the softest furs were his bed, and provided with the choicest food by a female attendant, chosen for her beauty. Wan-nut-ha, the sachem's daughter, the most beautiful maiden of the tribe, was selected to attend the Algonquin, and for many days had cared for him. But with the days, the stoical, quiet resignation of Hon-do-sa had not passed unnoticed by Wan-nut-ha, and a feeling like that of pity had unconsciously come upon her. He had been brave in battle, and now though a captive who must die, was haughty in his silence, and defiantly awaited his doom. Yet Wan-nut-ha softened toward him. "So near death, and so brave and how fair to die!" she sighed. But the days of his captivity had passed; on the morrow at sunrise he must die. For the last time Wan-nut-ha carried the food to his lodge, and she lingered. Why did she tarry? What new emotion stirred her heart to detain her? He was a foe of her people, why should she pity? But at the last, when his eyes spoke to her's a silent farewell, she then knew; and quick flashed the thought of her canoe on the lake that could bear him away. "Tonight," she whispered, "when the owl cries the midnight and the bittern screams sad by the lake shore, listen. Wan-nut-ha will be near."

At midnight she cautiously neared the lodge. The guard was asleep, though thonged to the captive! A stir might awake him. Faster her heart throbbed, and the life of Hon-do-sa seemed as her own, but she faltered not. The guard slept as she loosened the thongs and silently they fled through the tangled marshes, hand clasped in hand, down to the lake where rocked her canoe.

Had the horrors of the fifty years strife paled Wan-nut-ha's blood to compassion? Was it but pity that had stirred a new thrill in her heart? Ah! love attires itself in various ways to enter each heart!

"Ga-nun-do-wa mountain is not far," she said, as she paddled her canoe swift through the waters; but as the canoe touched the shore the faint cries of their pursuers came, borne on the breeze of the dawn. "Haste, Hon-do-sa!" she exclaimed, as she pointed the way of his flight. "Now you are free! Farewell. Flee to your people! I will remain, Wan-nut-ha, who, by the hand of her father, the sachem, will die for you!"

Leaping to the shore, Hon-do-sa, the warrior, lingered. All the suns he had known Wan-nut-ha passed before him. "Life from Wan-nut-ha would not be freedom for Hon-do-sa," he exclaimed. "Dawn after

Ta-ha-mont, an Algonquin chief

dawn, when thonged and alone in his prison lodge, Wan-nut-ha brought the sun to Hon-do-sa; and now she bids him flee from her forever. Like a brave warrior he should have waited his fate. Now the sun turns away, and a black cloud covers its face. Nothing but gloom and the shadows come now to me. The foes of Hon-do-sa fast follow, mad in their hate; the arrows will soon hiss his doom. Oh-ne, (farewell) Wan-nut-ha! Wan-nut-ha opened a new light to Hon-do-sa. Now it is black and forsaken. Return to her people, and forget the Algonquin. He will wait here to die." And the brave Hon-do-sa, so strong in battle, so weak in love, turned his face from the sunrise to meet his fast coming foes.

But Wan-nut-ha! In the conflict of loving, despairing, pitying yet brave; forgetting her kin, forgetting her blood which raced in hate for her foes; she sprang from her canoe, exclaiming as she sent it adrift: "Not alone shall my brave Algonquin die; as two leaves that grow from one stem, is the life of Hon-do-sa and the life of Wan-nut-ha; and as one life they shall live, or as one life will die!"

Swift as two shadow clouds they sped up the steep cliffs, and nearing their highest crag, calmly awaited the coming of the pursuing warriors.

For her wild love, Wan-nut-ha forsook her people and now dared their hate; and for love, the chieftain, who feared not death, clasped her to his heart and with a shout of triumphant scorn at his baffled foes, together they leaped to their death on the sharp rocks below!

There at the foot of the great cliffs across the lake from Ga-nun-do-wa mountain a heavy oak watches its shadows as it follows the course of the sun, and when the bittern screams and the owl cries the midnight, the tremulous leaves of the old tree sigh like unto human voices, and its branches bend lower to guard the vigils of a spirit that wanders forth to renew its vows.

The sachem and his warriors entered the dust; the forests are laid in fair plains that bear the harvests; the lake carries the burdens of the paleface, and the birch bark canoe no longer drifts on its waters. But the oak still watches and counts the ages and Wa-nut-ha's spirit still sighs in its shadow where it waits to welcome Hon-do-sa.

Part 3

MISCELLANEOUS PAPERS

BY

HARRIET MAXWELL CONVERSE

IROQUOIS INDIANS
OF THE STATE OF NEW YORK

The Ho-de-no-sau-nee or People of the Long House

At the era of the Dutch discovery, 1609, the Iroquois were found in possession of the same territories between the Hudson and Genesee rivers, upon which they afterwards continued to reside until the close of the 18th century. At that time the Five Nations, into which they had become subdivided, were united in a league; but its formation was subsequent to their establishment in the territories out of which the State of New York has since been erected.

Tradition interposes its feeble light to extricate from the confusion which time has wrought, some of the leading events which preceded and marked their political organization. It informs us that prior to their occupation of New York they resided in the vicinity of Montreal upon the northern bank of the St Lawrence, where they lived in subjection to the Adirondacks, a branch of the Algonquin race, then in possession of the whole country north of that river. From the Adirondacks they learned the art of husbandry, and while associated with them became inured to the hardships of the warpath and of the chase. After they had multiplied they attempted possession of the country of the Adirondacks but were overpowered by the latter and forced to leave their lands to escape extermination. In due time they migrated into the present territory of New York State, and, dividing into bands, spread abroad to found new villages.

One, crossing over to the Mohawk, established itself at Ga-ne-ga-ha-ga below Utica and afterwards became the Mohawk nation. For many years the Oneidas and Onondagas were one nation, but one part of these two settled at Oneida lake and became a separate nation; the other claiming the Onondaga valley in time also became independent. The Cayugas and Senecas were for many years united, but finally divided and became individual nations.

All of these people were compelled to war with the various tribes whom they found in possession of the country. After the expulsion of these people, the interest of the original Five Nations became distinct, and gradually dividing, they came into open warfare with each other. These wars continued for an unknown period, until finally the project of a league was suggested by the Onondagas as means to enable them to effectually resist contiguous nations.

Histories of the white people relate that the Iroquois were leagued about a century previous to the advent of the white people. To the contrary the traditions of the Iroquois indicate a period far remote. [Morgan. League of the Iroquois]

Among the wars of the united nations the struggle with their old enemy, the Adirondacks, was the most severe. This war continued nearly fifty years till the Adirondacks were nearly exterminated. A new era commenced with the Iroquois on the establishment of the Dutch trading post at Fort Orange, now Albany, in 1615. The principal Indians in the north were the Hurons and Adirondacks; on the west. Eries, the Neuter nation, Miamis, Ottowas and Illinois; on the south the Shawnees, Cherokees, Catawbas, Susquehannocks, Delawares, Nanticokes and some lesser nations; on the east the Minsi and New England Indians. Some of these nations were subjugated and made tributary and others utterly exterminated, till the Iroquois became absolute dictators.

The friendly relations between the Indians and the Dutch, beginning in 1615, were preserved with fidelity till the independence of the American states terminated the jurisdiction of the English over the country, and even then the Mohawks, adhering to the crown, divided from their brothers and left the league. This was the first break in the confederacy, but the St Regis Indians were lately inducted into the league to take the place of the Mohawks.[87]

At the institution of the Ho-de-no-sau-nee, fifty permanent sachemships were created with appropriate names. Of these there yet remain intact the inherited sachem titles. These are unchangeable and inherited by clanship. Of these, to the Mohawks were distributed 9; to the Oneidas 9; to the Onondagas 14; to the Cayugas 10; to the Senecas 8. At the present moment tribal law is continued among the Onondagas and Tonawanda Senecas, and also by the St Regis who entered the league as successors to the Mohawks in 1883. To these were given the nine original Mohawk sachemships. The Cattaraugus and Salamanca Senecas abandoned the tribal law in 1848[88] and assumed a republican form of government by electing a president and board of councilmen. These include the peacemakers.

The original clans which divided the people into families, were the Wolf, Bear, Beaver, Turtle, Deer, Snipe, Heron and Hawk.[89] By this division which was equal among the Five Nations, the people were bound to each other by the ties of consanguinity. A Seneca Wolf regarded an Onondaga Wolf as a brother, and so on throughout the league. So carefully provided was this clanship that a Seneca Wolf could not marry an Onondaga Wolf. By this relationship, the league preserved for itself not only blood distinction but absolute union, as in case of war brother would fight against brother, which was against their bond of brotherhood. The census enumeration of 1890 shows that the Iroquois furnished 162 soldiers[90] and sailors for the Civil War. It has been estimated that in 1660 there were 11,000 Iroquois. This, however, is indefinite. The total population in 1890, excluding the 106 Oneidas, was 5133. Of these 2844 could not speak English. The Onondaga Reservation is 6100 acres; Tonawanda Senecas about 8000; Allegany Senecas 30,469; Oil Spring 640; Cattaraugus Senecas 21,680; St. Regis 14,640; Tuscaroras 6249. The Oneidas have no reservation in this State. They are largely represented in

Green Bay, Wis., and those who live here in New York State are "guests" of the Onondagas and other nations. The Cayugas who have no separate reservation reside on different reservations, the largest number being at Cattaraugus. These are the New York State Indians. On their reservations there are 12 churches. Some of the congregations worship in private houses or halls. The "pagans" assemble for business, religious ceremonies, feasts, condolences, and councils in their council houses or private residences. Among the Iroquois various trades are represented. Of the full number of the census there are 185 basketmakers, 528 farmers, 696 laborers and various others who are independent farmers and mechanics.

The Tuscaroras who entered the league about 1713 are included in the census enumeration. As this nation was not of the original Five Nations, they have not been recognized by title right to sachemship.

After three centuries of conflict with an invading race which in its greed for lands and wealth had but little sympathy for the aboriginal owners of the soil, we find the Iroquois still with us successful in their struggle to retain their ancients seats. Every other native nation, tribe or band of Indians in the east has been exterminated or driven toward the west where small acres in a broad land remain to them.

The Iroquois by his unconquerable tenacity, his dogged determination to remain, his wonderful national vitality has earned the admiration and respect of the world and ethnologists acclaim him the master type of the American Indian. By their wondrous conception of the Confederacy of the Five Nations, in the union of the Mohawks, Cayugas, Oneidas, Onondagas and Senecas, they formed one political confederation of civil and war power unequaled by any other primitive people. This confederated league was absorbing all adjacent nations when disturbed by the advent of the white people. Their war cry to the enemy being absorption or extermination they were continually augmenting their numbers. Their government was a structure of durability in its filial principles of equality, fraternity and inflexible loyalty, a sort of socialism free from any humility or pernicious dissensions of political bondage. Their religious conceptions were far above those of the ancient philosophers or the tendencies of the ancient myth god worshipers. The student who intelligently translates the Indian religion opens the wider door for good will and humanity, in fact, as a distinguished bishop of the Episcopalian church has said, "The American Indian is the most magnificent heathen on the face of the earth, he has but one God and believes in the immortality of soul." As this is the base of all true religion, it is a shame that zealous and honest workers among the Indians should not acquaint themselves with the tenets of their ancient faith, thereby harmonizing its primal truths with any newer religion that may be taught to them.

Philosophy and science were processes of knowledge unknown by the primitive red man yet by their intuitions, lofty and intellectual, they evolved a purely spiritual religion with one invisible Great Spirit as its ruler who made himself known to them by his works visible in all the benedictions of nature. To the Indian there occurred no idea of the omnipresence of a ruling power, therefore "assistants" who were subservient to his will were assigned certain duties. Unlike the pagans of old these were not worshiped as individual gods. To He-no, the Thunderer, was given the voice of admonition and instrument of vengeance as well as judgment in the bestowal of beneficent rains. Ga-oh was empowered with the direction of the winds; from their tangles he divided the breath of the summer time from the frost of the winter. Other assistants distributed all the fruits, beans, squash and corn, the last three having a triad of female "supporters" whose generosity is "thanked" at the annual Green Corn dance. In fact to all visible and invisible nature each had its guardian under the guidance of one supreme power.

In Indian language there is no blasphemous or profane word. Their attitude toward the Great Spirit is venerative and dignified. In their various feasts religious dances are introduced in all of which there are interludes when the tenets of the ancient faith are recited. These have descended from generation to generation by word only; there are no written records of the Indian religion. A young preacher is taught word for word and when he enters office he "remembers" and expounds to the people at the annual festivals. There are never any religious "uprisings" or "excitements." The law and word are passed year by year, century after century, by the true pagan preacher. In the "new religion" of the Iroquois, Ga-nio-dai-u, there is an interweave of modern ideas induced by the necessity of reform from evils introduced by the palefaces. But even in this "temperance" preaching nothing has been accepted that was not consistent with their primitive idea of justice and repentance.

The Indian having no knowledge of a sacrificial atonement assumes the punishment of his own evil. The religious law governs this by a recital of his "sins" at the public New Year feast and a sin thus confessed is atoned for. By this came the use of the wampum known as the Ransom belt. If a murder has been committed the murderer sent the Ransom belt to the nearest relatives of his victim with a petition for his life as he was "sorry." If the belt was returned he submitted to his death sentence with the stoicism of his race. It never occurred to him that the Great Spirit could be appealed to for such forgiveness. He had an idea of punishment in an after life but it was of a material, not spiritual nature. The fundamental principle of his faith was a sublime belief in the immortality of the soul, which on entering its eternal life continued its former existence not progressively by the goodness of its mortal life nor in punishment for its omissions. A mortal evil was atoned for during the mortal life. Likewise a benevolent or religious act was rewarded by compensations while on earth.

It is only by the intimate social acquaintance of the Indian, even of the present day, that his true religion is known. His moral laws, according to his own conception, are stringent. His family relationships are the universal spirit of affection and hospitality. His children are taught obedience with their lessons of reverence to parents. Indians never punish their children. If a child runs too great riot they let him "get over it" first and then reason with him about it afterwards. Notwithstanding the labors of the Indian woman she is supreme in home authority, owns land in her own right and frequently continues her maiden name after marriage, which, by Indian law, is a mutual agreement for the man and woman to live together until one or the other "scolds too much." Incompatibility of temper argues a divorce if appealed for, as "quarreling is a bad example to the children," who, in case of a separation, are taken by the mother, the family descent being from the maternal line.

As an example of the moral commands of the Indian, I quote the following precepts which are imperatively enjoined:

"It is the will of the Great Spirit that you reverence the aged even though they be as helpless as infants."

"If you tie up the clothes of an orphan child the Great Spirit will notice it and reward you for it."

"To adopt orphans and bring them up in virtuous ways is pleasing to the Great Spirit."

"If a stranger wander about your abode, welcome him to your home, be hospitable to him, speak to him with kind words, and forget not always to mention the Great Spirit."

As proof of the last precept at the latest census[92] there was but one beggar or actually homeless person reported among the 4800 Iroquois Indians of New York

State and he was provided for by the old religious law.

The Indian has been accused of indecent orgies. His dances have been condemned as corrupt and vicious. His secret societies are named as witchcrafts and satanisms of evil practices. In my investigations of their myths, mystics, their religion, and civil and home life, I have attended all these dances and have never seen one vulgar or indecent action. The Indian woman, by nature chaste, would scorn an immodest attire or the familiarity of the "fiddle dances" known as the waltzes of the palefaces.

I have been admitted to several degrees of the Medicine Lodge, which is known to all American Indians, the Iroquois secret society, Na-gah-ne-gah-ah; in its celebrations there is nothing malign. The ritual thoroughly consistent with their religion, includes chants for the sick and dying and the dead who are yet "held in the arms of the Great Spirit." The principles upon which this medicine society is founded are charity, neighborly kindness and lessons for ministrations to the sick. Their chants, are entirely free from human passions or grossness of superstitions. In fact if a member evidences a spirit of evil he is excluded from the meetings until he is "purified."

The religious feasts of the Indian begin with the New Year usually in February, when he renews all promises of fidelity to the Great Spirit. This is followed by the Maple feast which occurs when the maple sap first flows. Then follow the Berry feasts and in turn those of all fruits, each of which has its special dance and thanksgiving chant, until the final Green Corn dance. On this occasion the feast continues four days and embodies within its ritual thanksgiving for all the gifts of the Great Spirit. The smallest growth is not omitted in the recital, nor the least of the animal creation. These are the only occasions for their public religious meetings.

In his home life the Indian never partakes of a meal that he does not first ask the blessing of the Great Spirit upon the repast and after eating never fails to thank him for the privilege of the food.[93] If he starts a friend on his journey the farewell is always an appeal that the Great Spirit may guard him to his home.

The Indian believing the Great Spirit to be the God of the Indian only, does not hold himself amenable to the law of any other religion. He may be stimulated by observing the various moral laws of the white man but he will not incorporate within his own religion anything that is not consistent with his old faith. Therefore comes the term "Christian pagan," which signifies that the "converted" Indian has "adopted" the moral teachings of the "new" religion as a graft upon his inherited faith.

He can not understand why the Christian religionists should be divided into many "societies" while he has but one. He does not comprehend the efficacy of prayer for material things.

In fact the entire social life of the Indian is imbued with religious sentiment. He despises a liar and distrusts the man who offers too much to him. A truer friend does not live than the Indian who will give his own bed and the largest end of his loaf as long as a friend tarries with him. A betrayal of confidence he never forgives. Long years of dishonorable persecution have made him distrustful of every white man. Divested of his aboriginal domains he has been hunted into little corners and considered a tenant by privilege until extermination. In the name of humanity and history why are there not more of earnest workers who will investigate the Indian as he was? If he has constructed his own theology he has discovered the greatest truth of nature, the knowledge of a Supreme Ruler. By his conceptions of tribal fraternity he has become thoroughly indoctrinated with true humanity thus rivaling many of the highest virtues of civilized man. It has required the processes of centuries of evolution to transform the painted savage whom Caesar met in Britain into the Englishman of today. What is the history of the four centuries of the evolution of the American Indian? Save the few who have been defended and befriended and educated, the story is near its finale of a Christless not a Christian civilization. In this unequal and mournful struggle to preserve his inheritances and nationality the Indian is nearing the inexorable destiny to which he is doomed.

WOMAN'S RIGHTS
AMONG THE IROQUOIS

Generations before the coming of the palefaces to this country, the Iroquois Indians had declared in the constitution of the Ho-de-no-sau-ne, the Confederacy of the Long House, that the "mother" or woman's rights should be included in the laws and be forever protected.

While the primitive red man looked upon woman as subordinate rather than equal, by his law, through her he preserved his ties of consanguinity and tribal denomination. While he enforced obedience to and respect for his own rights and imposed many burdens on woman, yet, regarding her civil claims as sacred, her legal rights were never interfered with.

All children were inheritors of the mother's clan. The child, male or female, was son or daughter of its mother and not the inheritor of the clan rights of its father or "mother's husband." Thus, having no subdivisions of family branches, by the inter-marriage of maternal or paternal descendants, purity of clan descent was established and by this tribal law, nationality was never lost. If a Mohawk woman of the Wolf Clan married a Seneca, her children and their descendants would be Mohawks of the Wolf Clan from generation to generation.

To the mother only was given the care of her offspring during infancy and childhood, the formation of its character and government of its nature. During this time the father had no control or authority over the children. On arriving at maturity the male child became the companion of his father on the warpath and hunt, and the female assumed her civil rights and home authority.

If the wife possessed property and at marriage brought it to her new home, it still continued her own and she could dispose of it at her pleasure.

A modern Seneca girl in her grandmother's costume

By law of descent, the children, not being of the father's clan, would not inherit from him either property or any title that he may have held; to these the children of his sister or brother were heirs.

Women negotiated all the marriages. There were cases when the elders of the clan would be consulted and their judgment considered but the last decision rested entirely with the mothers. The mother was also responsible for the married life of her children. When there were contentions it was her duty to judge upon them. If peace could not be established she decided that a separation must follow. As this was considered a disgrace her consent was not often given. If possible the contentious parties would be persuaded to reconciliation. If after several councils the separation was considered an absolute necessity, by cause of incompatibility of temper, or refusal to recognize the marriage relation, a divorce was declared. The wife returned to the home of her mother taking with her her property and the children. She was held accountable in law for the faithful discharge of her duty to her children.

If any family had disputes of a domestic or financial nature the "mother" with other members of her clan was called for advice. By this convention of relatives the case was judged and the decision of this domestic court was final,

If, by the death of a sachem or chief, a summons was called for a general council or a condolence at that time new chiefs would be elected or "raised up" and sachems installed. In this election of chiefs the "mother" of the family in which the vacancy occurred, having the "name" of the office in her keeping could confer it upon any male of her own line of descent, whom she should regard as most reliable. It was her province to decide all questions of nomination. She might consult each member of the household as to their judgment of the merit of the candidate, but her final word was authoritative and gave the nomination.

Invested with the power she could also depose or "knock the horns off" any chief who might be derelict in duty. At the great councils her act of deposition was invariably confirmed and her nominee elected. This law prevailed among all the tribes of the Six Nations.

Of burial or "death feasts" women had full control. In religious feasts women or "matrons" were appointed to serve in the ceremonies with the men. On these occasions certain women were delegated to prepare the feast food and none others were permitted to assist.

At the Green Corn festival, women, having charge of the fields, first gathered the corn and submitted it at the Council House to the Honondiont, or priests, who examined it and if it was sufficiently ripe decided when the feasts should be called. By order of the Honondiont runners would be sent with invitations from one nation to its neighboring nation until all had been requested to participate in the rites and social pleasures of the forthcoming festival.

Women were keepers of certain wampum belts called "Chief" belts. These were sent by them to the great councils when a chief was to be raised and were

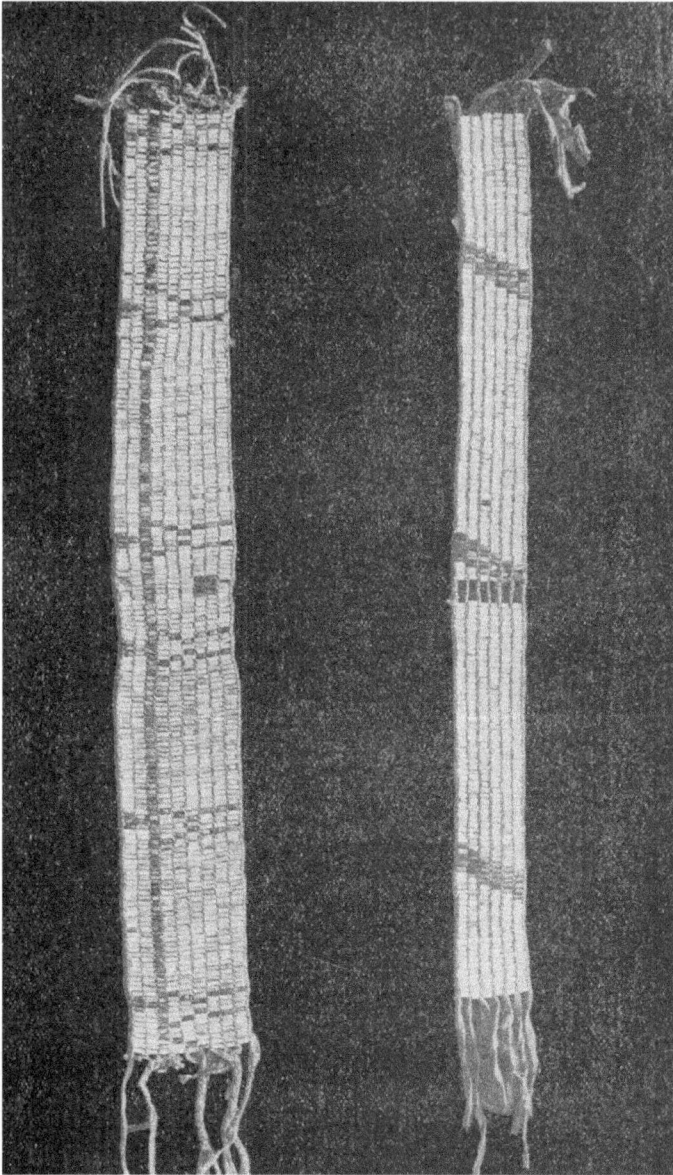

1. *Nomination belt used by the Seneca women to confirm the nomination of the Sachems which they chose for office. This was the Seneca women's national belt.*

2. *Hospitality or Welcome belt. Said to have been used in league councils by the presiding chief in welcoming the delegates.*

legally recognized as the law. No attention was attached to any nomination unless confirmed by these wampum belts. As the Onondagas were the keepers of all the national and civil belts a sachem of this nation was the reader of all belts by which the law was interpreted.

In their mythology the Iroquois have honored women as the guardian spirits of their plants, the corn, beans and squash.

Unlike other primitive peoples, the descent falling by line of the mother blood, she continues united to the destinies of her own nation and tribe, and there is no loss of her identity by a marriage name or title thereof. This system of relationship, the main fabric of the League of the Iroquois, has been continued inviolate even to the present day by the descendants who yet linger as inheritors and observers of the old law.

Labor and burdens may have been the condition of the Indian woman. She may seem to have been a creature only and not a companion of the red man, yet by comparison with the restrictions, to characterize it by no stronger term, obtaining among *civilized* people, the Iroquois woman had a superior position and superior rights.

By political rights she held power in making nominations and had a voice in all public councils.

By social rights she negotiated marriages and governed households.

By maternal right she controlled her own offspring and bestowed the clan title of her name upon their descendants forever.

By civil right she ruled in domestic convocations of clan disputes, of law and order.

By religious right she had the controlling authority in all ceremonies of condolence, or festival and by right of confederacy law she possessed lands and properties with the sole right to bequeath them to whomsoever she might choose.

As the woman of today stands advocate and petitioner of her own cause, should she not offer an oblation of gratitude to the memory of the Iroquois Indian who called the earth his "mighty mother" and who, through a sense of justice, rendered to the mothers of his people the rights maternal, political, social, civil, religious and of land!

All these were an Iroquois woman's rights.

ORIGIN OF THE WAMPUM BELT

Previous to the confederation of the Five Nations the New York State Iroquois Indians were subjects of the Adirondacks, a family branch of the Algonquins who inhabited territories on the northern side of the St Lawrence river near the present location of Montreal. Originally, as one nation, they were few in number yet as they multiplied and, by example of the Adirondacks, became learned in the arts of husbandry and the strategies of war, they were ambitious of the ownership of the country and made war upon the Adirondacks by whose overpowering numbers they were vanquished. Defeated, and to escape extermination, they fled and, their traditions say, passing along the St Lawrence river entered Lake Ontario and coasted for a time on its eastern shores. Eventually they moved on to what is now the central portion of the State of New York where they met and conquered all the tribes resident in that territory which became their sole possession and, subsequently, the government seat of their colossal confederacy.

On their final settlement the Iroquois, declaring severalty of estate possessions, divided into separate bands. The Oneidas and Onondagas, originally one nation, became independents and divided from each other. The Senecas and Cayugas, who had united, eventually drifted apart, and the Mohawks announced exclusive proprietorship of their own accumulated lands. From this disunion alienations followed which gradually resulted in an open warfare that was continued for generations.

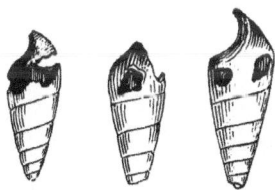

During this condition of hostility an inspiration of peace, suggesting unity of power by the confederation of the five nations, came to one of the wise men of the Onondaga nation, Da-ga-no-we-da, the founder of the League of the Iroquois.

Perforated wampum shells from central New York

At that time the Onondagas were suffering the tyranny and cruelty of the ruling chief To-do-da-ho, who, as symbol of his dreaded power, was represented crowned with living snakes, his fingers and toes terminating with the hissing monsters and, by the glance of his eye, turning to stone any one who dared deny his authority Da-ga-no-we-da, repelling this creature of horror, and conceiving a way of release for his people, sagaciously flattered the vanity of To-do-da-ho and, to perfect his plans, endeavored to enlist his favor as an associate. The crafty To-do-da-ho, consenting to a hearing, evoked a council fire, which was kindled from the willow, and summoned the nation to consider the project of Da-ga-no-we-da. In the sympathetic attention with which the people listened to the persuasions of Da-ga-no-we-da, To-do-da-ho foresaw loss of his power and, with malevolent cunning, rejected the propositions of Da-ga-no-we-da as an interference with the government and, threatening vengeance, expelled him from the council forever. The terrified Onondagas, dreading the despotic will of their monster chief, dared not sustain Da-ga-no-we-da who, sorrowing, left his people and journeyed "to the west of the rising sun" toward the land of the Mohawks.

Notwithstanding his rejection, Da-ga-no-we-da was yet hopeful of the consummation of his project for uniting the five nations and in his travels while crossing a lake, supposed to be the Oneida, he noticed quantities of minute purple and white shells adhering to the paddle of his canoe. As he neared the shore he discovered them heaped in long rows upon the bank. These suggested to his constructive mind a pictorial representation of his thought of confederating the divided nations by compact of mutual support and protection. He filled his traveling pouches with a quantity of these shells and, in the frequent rests of his journey, strung them on threads shred from the sinews of the deer, and hanging them, string by string, eventually completed

The first wampum belt

The foundation of this belt was of the white shells and the pictorial figures of the purple. Apportioned with exactness, as sign of the tribal territories, he wove five symbols that represented the cantons of the five nations, and with these he interwove five figures representing men clasping hands as token of brotherly union. Besides this significant delineation, he formed other belts each representing some law, or fundamental principle, included in the ceremonies of council, civil proceedings, war, death, peace, installment of chiefs, and all compacts necessary to the constitution of a confederated government. The white shells were symbolic of peace and the purple of mourning and war. Each belt was consecrated to its specific purpose and Da-ga-no-we-da neared the land of the Mohawks strengthened by argument of these insignia of ceremonies which eventually served with effect as visible laws in the formation of that wondrous governmental structure, the Ho-de-no-sau-ne, or the League of the Iroquois.

This tradition of the origin of the first wampum belt has been transmitted by the Iroquois from generation to generation and, as history, is one of the most prominent among their "grandfather stories."

Belts of great age and inestimable value are

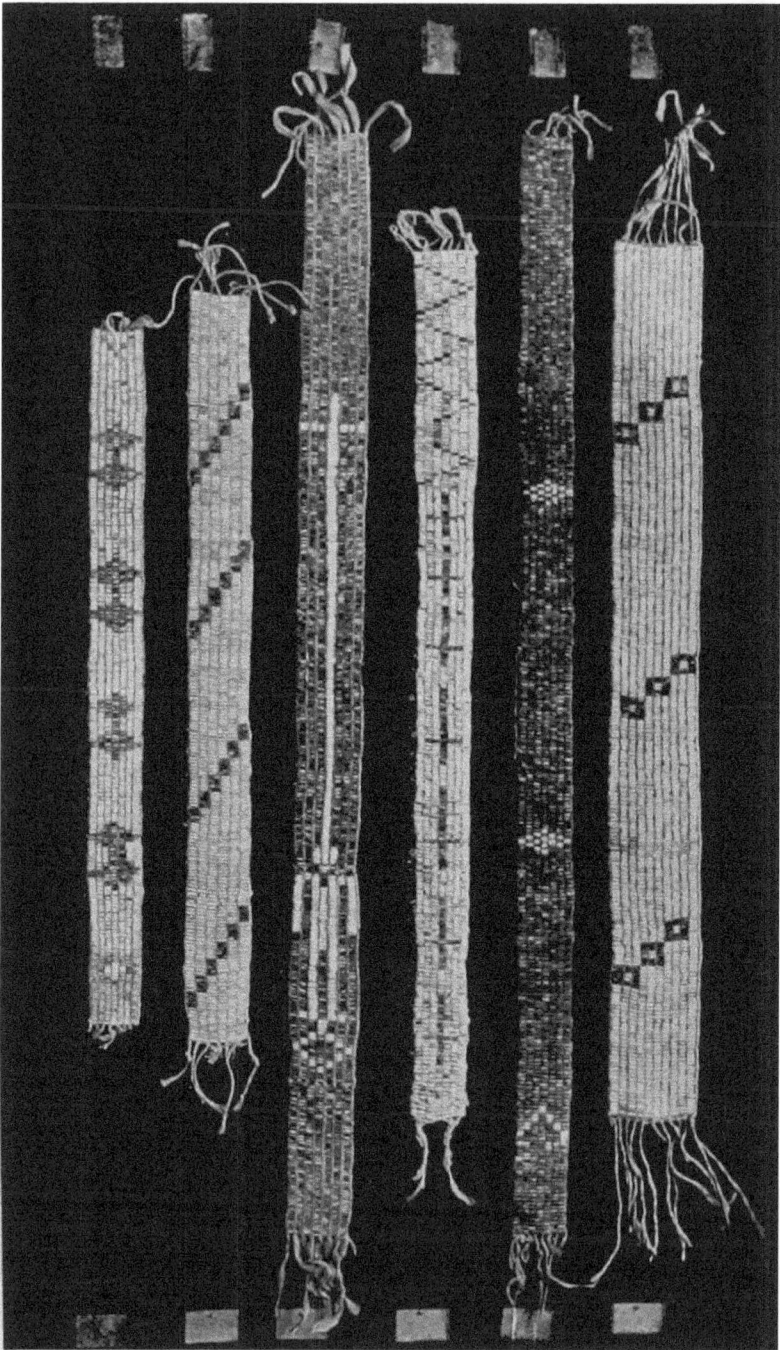

1   2   3   4   5   6

1. Council summons, calling the clans to a meeting. This belt is said to be a memorial to the clan laws of Hiawatha. By some it is considered an alliance belt sealing a pact between the seven nations of Canada and the Iroquois.

2. Treaty belt. Originally there were five diagonal bars.

3. Remembrance belt. Records the treachery of a French missionary at Onondaga who sought to summon the French army from Canada. It is an admonition against the French religion.

4. Caughnawauga belt Records an Alliance between the Caughnawaugua tribe and the St Regis band. The crooked lines indicate that the former had forsaken the old ways for the white man's religion.

5. Condolence belt of the Senecas once held by Governor Blacksnake. It was used in mourning councils in the ceremony of raising new names and new sachem to office.

6. Huron alliance belt, said to symbolize the alliance of the Hurons with some other tribe. After the overthrow of the Hurons in 1650 it became a Seneca belt and was taken to Canada after the Revolutionary War.

preserved and are yet in use among the Iroquois wherever the tribal government continues. These are deposited as public records,[94] with the Onondagas, who are the "law makers" of the Six Nations, and are held in safe-keeping by the guarding sachem, Ho-no-we-na-to, the hereditary "keeper of the wampum" whose office as expounder of the law, is to "read," or "talk" by the wampum at all the councils.

These belts of wampum, or Ote-ko-a, the symbols of law, are woven of purple and white cylindrical beads about three sixteenths of an inch in length, the white beads are made from the conch shell and the violet, or purple (called black by the Indians) from the purple spot in the clam shell. The beads of the most ancient belts are strung on twisted threads stripped from the inner bark of the elm and arranged in parallel lines separated by strings of buckskin that are overtwisted with fine threads shred from deer sinews.

At the tribal government councils the wampum is read before action is taken in any controversy. Upon

The Hiawatha belt, commemorating the founding of the League of the Iroquois

the convening of the council a string of white wampum beads, about a foot in length, is passed from chief to chief, each holding it in his hands for a moment; it is then laid on a table in the form of a circle, the ends touching; this signifies that the council is "open" and harmony prevails.

During the session, if a "condolence" is "called," by reason of death, or the "raising" of a chief, a ceremony always preceded by a condolence, a string of purple wampum is laid by the side of the circled string, and so on the "laying down of the wampum strings" one after another, each with its own significance, denotes the nature of the business or discussion before the council that is subject to consent, or rejection, by vote of the chiefs who are members thereof.

In the "old time," belts of the purple wampum were symbols of death and, if adorned with red paint, or a red feather, signified war. These belts were also exchanged as ransom for a life or lives. Wampum beads, threaded in lengths varying from four inches to a foot, were used as messages of peace or war, a "peace string" of white beads was intrusted to a "runner," a swift footed Indian trained to endurance and speed, who each day, at sunset, made a notch in a small blade-shaped piece of willow wood attached to the string that, at the end of the journey, the chief to whom it was sent would know the number of days that had elapsed during the conveyance of the message.

All councils were "called" by a string of wampum sent from nation to nation, by a "runner" appointed by

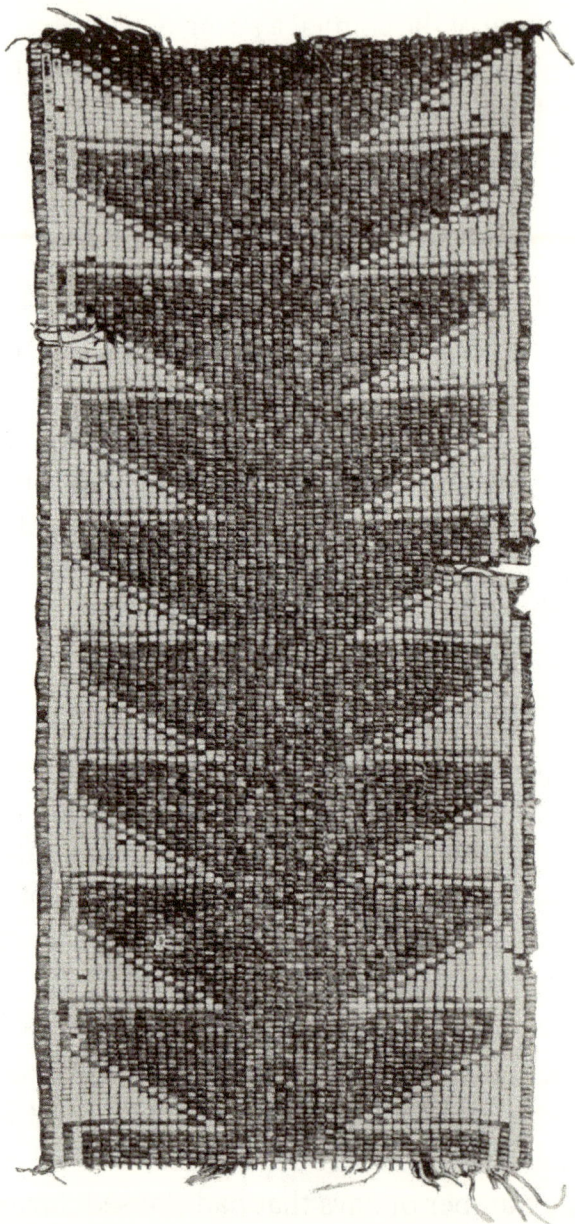

*Wing, or Dusst Fan of the president of the council. This is an
Onondaga national belt and the largest known. The design is
said to represent an endlessly growing tree which symbolizes
the perpetuity of the league.*

the governmental authorities at Onondaga. The Indian women, who had the power of nominating or deposing chiefs, the latter, commonly called "taking off their horns," were also custodians of distinctive belts that were sent to the seat of government as their decisions of law on occasions of their interference, or intercession, in politics or war. In fact no action of public council could be proposed or ratified unless "sealed" by the wampum, nor was any treaty, proffered by the "paleface," recognized or considered valid until authorized by the exchange of wampum belts.

As proof of this it is related that George Washington who, when a youth of twenty-one, was intrusted by the Colonial Governor of Virginia with a mission to the wilds of Pennsylvania, where the Canadian French were penetrating and seeking to unite the natives against us, found that an alliance had been formed and ratified by an exchange of wampum. Persuaded by the remonstrances of the young Washington the Indian sachems consented to withdraw from the alliance but declared that the belt of wampum must be returned before the agreement could be abolished and, until the token of the warlike compact was returned to the sachems by the French commander, the Indians would not proclaim their promise to take no part in the impending struggle.

The finest belt in the collection of the Onondagas, and, as an example of construction, unsurpassed by any other in existence, is the "George Washington belt" which, by Iroquois history, was a covenant of peace exchange between the Indians and the government

211

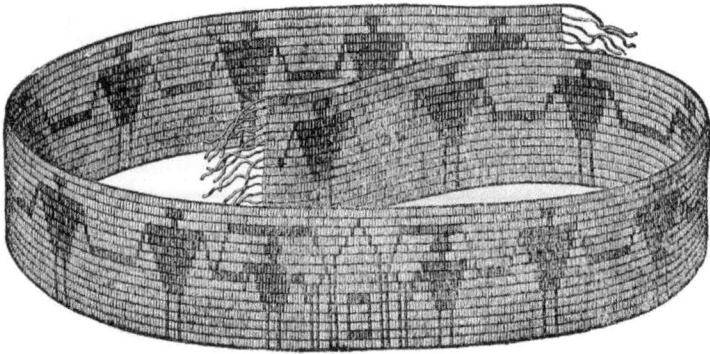

The George Washington covenant belt, commemorating the peace treaty with the Iroquois and the United States during the presidency of Washington.

during the presidency of George Washington.[95] This belt is 15 rows wide, each row includes 650 beads making a total of 9750 contained in this historical belt. The groundwork is constructed from the violet wampum; in the center of the belt a house, with a well defined gable roof, and an open door, is woven of the white beads. From each side of the gable a "protecting" line extends above the figures of two men who, as "guardians of the door," in turn clasp hands with others of the same design until 15 pictographic men stand side by side, 7 on the right side of the gable house and 8 on the left. The clasped hands, in accordance with the traditional belt woven by Da-ga-no-we-da, signify unity and concord or "the unbroken chain of friendship." The gable house represents the government hall of the "paleface," and the open door, the conventional sign of the Iroquois, implies the hospitality of peace. The two figures at the immediate side of the gable house emblemize the

(Indian) "keepers of the east and west doors," the limits of their territories, the other 13 pictographic figures symbolize the 13 colonies.

The Pennsylvania Historical Society has in its possession a wampum belt, presented by a great grandson of William Penn, believed to be the original belt that was delivered by the Leni-Lenapi sachems to William Penn at the treaty held under the elm tree at Shackamaxon in 1682. In this belt, composed of 18 strings of wampum, the figure of a white man, represented by his costume and hat, is delineated as grasping hands in friendship with an Indian. There are also three oblique bands of purple wampum, one on the right and two on the left of the figures; in the modern wampum the Indians explain these bands as "braces," the strengthening power of the treaty. These special shell wampum beads, found in the possession of the Iroquois Indians at the time of the Dutch discovery in 1609, were used as a medium of exchange among the various tribes. Shell beads, similar to these, were subsequently circulated by the traders among all the Iroquois people.

Lawson in 1714 [History of North Carolina] speaking of the use and value of wampum in New York, remarks that "an Englishman could not afford to make so much of this wampum for five or ten times the value; for it is made out of a vast great shell, of which that country affords plenty, and is ground smaller than the small end of a tobacco pipe or a large wheat straw; the Indians grind these on stones and other things until they make them current, but the drilling is the most difficult to the Englishman, which the Indians manage with a nail stuck in a cane or reed. Thus they roll it continually on their thighs with their right hand, holding the bit of shell with their left; so, in time, they drill a hole quite through it which is a very tedious work, but the Indians are a people that never value their time, so they can afford to make them, and never need to fear the English will take the trade out of their hands. This, being their money, entices and persuades them to do anything and part with everything they possess and with which you may buy skins, furs or any other thing except their children for slaves."

Wampum is mentioned by Captain John Smith who found the young Indian women surrounding Powhatan "wearing great chains of white beads over their breasts and shoulders."

Drake the historian, wrote that "King Philip had a coat all made of wampumpeag which, when in need of money, he cut in pieces and distributed plentifully among the Nipmoog sachems and others."

Father Loskiel, in 1723 found the Abenaki Indians ornamented with "beads made of a kind of shell, or stone, some white and some purple, which they form into story figures with great exactness."

In a concluding reference to the Iroquois, also as an example of the "talk to the wampum," in treaty exchanges of belts, I quote from an account of a council held by the Five Nations at Onondaga nearly two hundred years ago, to which the Governor of Canada sent four representatives:

" . . . during the course of the proceedings Cannehoot, a Wa-gun-ha sachem, presented a proposed treaty between the Wa-gun-has and the Senecas, speaking as follows: 'We come to join the two bodies into one. We come to learn wisdom of the Senecas (giving a belt). We, by this belt, wipe away the tears from the eyes of your friends, whose relations have been killed in the war. We likewise wipe the paint from your soldiers' faces (giving a second belt). We throw aside the ax which Yon-on-di-o put into our hands by this third belt.' A red marble sun is presented, a pipe made of red marble. 'Yon-on-di-o is drunk; we wash our hands clean from his actions (giving a fourth belt). We have twelve of your nation prisoners; they shall be brought home in the spring (giving a belt to confirm the promise). We will bring your prisoners home when the strawberries shall be in blossom, at which time we intend to visit Corlear (the Governor of New York).' The belts were accepted by the Five Nations and their acceptance was a ratification of the treaty. A large belt was also given to the messengers from Albany as their share. A wampum belt sent from Albany was, in the same manner, hung up and afterwards divided."

ORIGIN OF THE GAME OF LACROSSE

Lacrosse, now so commonly adopted as a favorite game among athletes in all countries, originated with the North American Indians who played it centuries before the discovery of America. The oldest detailed description of the game was given by Nicolas Perrot, a trader and government agent employed by the French when Canada was a French colony. From 1662 to 1669, Nicolas Perrot wrote various accounts of this game which cover a very early period of history and they are doubly interesting in comparison with games of the present time. In 1662, Perrot writes: "The savages have a certain game of 'cross' which is very similar to our tennis. They match tribe against tribe and if their number are not equal they withdraw some of the men from the stronger side. They are all armed with a 'cross,' a stick which has a large portion at the bottom laced like a racket. The ball with which they play is of wood and nearly the shape of a turkey's egg. It is the rule of the contest that after a side has won two goals, they change sides of the field with their opponents, and that two out of three or three out of five goals decide the game."

Abbe Ferland, says of this game: "Men, women and girls are received on the sides in these games which begin at the melting of the ice and continue at intervals until harvest time." He also mentions the fact that the arms and legs of the player's were frequently broken, some crippled for life, and that many were killed in the contest. A death in this game was more often the result of obstinacy than lack of skill, the dead man having held his ball too long and inviting death, and his body was carried to his cabin in disgrace.

When injured, the sufferer made no complaint, attributing his mishap to the chances of the game, and harboring no ill will. If a person not in the game nor betting on the result should throw the ball to the advantage of either side, he would be punished with death if not relieved of intent by a council of the chiefs.

In 1636, Father Broebeuf, a missionary among the Hurons, notes the game as "Bagga-tie-way," or "le jeu de la crosse."

La Potherie mentioned a game in which the number of players engaged was estimated at 2000.

La Honton says, "village being pitted against village, the lacrosse is commonly played in large companies of three or four hundred players."

When a famine or epidemic threatened the people, the medicine men would order a game of lacrosse to be played to propitiate the spirits. In this game all the players participated, engaging in religious dances and ceremonies at the end of each game.

It was necessary that all the people, young and old, women and men, should attend this game. Some were chosen to personate the evil spirits and receive punishment, and should a death ensue it was deemed a favorable omen.

Lacrosse figured prominently on all occasions of importance, and was the proper courtesy in all ceremonies attending the entertainment of distinguished guests.

In 1667, Perrot, then the agent of the French government, was received with very formal ceremony by the Maumi Indians, located near Sault Ste Marie, and lacrosse was played by the entire tribe.

Great rivalry existed throughout the various tribes. The game for championship was an exciting event and was introduced with much formality.

For days preceding the play, the people engaged in prayers to the Great Spirit, invoking his aid, and the players fasted the last day and night.

To inure the young warriors to the fatigue of battle, the frequent playing of the game was an enforced exercise, which also taught them the tactics of attack and defense.

Further, it was deemed of value as a remedial exercise for many ills, and induced the aid of the sorcerers of life who could hasten the return to health.

Stephen Powers found lacrosse among the California Indians. Of his early discoveries among the Pomas Indians, in Russian river valley, he writes: "They played it (lacrosse) with a ball rounded out of an oak knot, propelled by a racket constructed of a long slender stick bent double and bound together leaving a circular hoop at the end, across which is woven a coarse mesh work of strings. Such an instrument is not strong enough to bat the ball but simply to shove or thrust it along the ground."

Bernard Romaine in 1776 writes of the goals of this game, "they fix two poles across each other at about one hundred and fifty feet apart."

Bossu noted that "the Choctaws play with only one goal. The players agree upon an aim, about sixty yards off, distinguished by two poles, between which the ball must pass."

La Honton estimated the distance between the goals at five or six hundred paces. Charlevoix places the goals in a game with eighty players, at half a league apart. Alexander Henry, in 1809, writing of the game in northern Canada, mentioned one mile as the distance between the goals. Paul Kane says "the goals of the Chinooks, Crees, Chippawas and Sioux are one mile apart, and one hundred players on a side." Domench wrote "the players were costumed with short drawers, or rather a belt, the body being first daubed with a layer of bright colors. From the belt which is short enough to leave the thigh free, hangs a long animal tail. Round their necks is a necklace of animals' teeth to which is attached a floating mane dyed red, as is the tail, falling as a fringe over the chest and shoulders." He adds: "Some tribes play with two sticks and the game is played on the ice. The ball is made of wood or brick, covered with kid skin leather curiously interwoven."

Schoolcraft describes the game as played in the winter on the ice; and Catlin has illustrated the Dacotahs in their ice game. Adair wrote that the southern Indians played "with two rackets, between which the ball was caught. These sticks were necessarily shorter than those of the northern Indians, being about two feet long. With these they threw the ball a great distance. The Choctaws also used two rackets. The Pacific coast Indians started the game by throwing into the air a ball of doeskin.

This ball was always thrown by a woman selected for her beauty."

One historical fact of lacrosse figures in the frontier wars of 1763, when the noted Indian, Pontiac, planned a surprise for destroying the scattered forts held by the English on the northwestern frontier. On the 4th of June of that year, the garrison at Fort Michilimackinac, unconscious of their impending fate, had left the fort, attracted by an Indian game of lacrosse. Utterly absorbed in the game, they were unmindful of the movements of the Indians. Soon a ball was thrown from the field, dropping within the pickets of the fort.

This was the Indian's signal. Running as if to regain the ball, they pressed on, forcing their way into the fort and swinging their tomahawks (which the women had carried concealed under their blankets), fell upon the English with such fury that, it is said, not a single one escaped.

Lacrosse has undergone many changes since primitive Indian days. Now fourteen or fifteen players comprise a team; the ball, early of wood and later replaced by one made of scraped and moistened deerskin, stuffed hard with deer's hair and sewed with sinew, would hardly find place with modern players; and the early curved stick with its crude strappings would illy compare with the symmetrical curved hoop and artistic netting so prized by its wielders.

Many of the modern sticks are still made by Indians. There is a factory on the St Regis Indian Reservation, employing Indians, where the sticks are made by machinery, but the handmade sticks of the Iroquois are considered the best of Indian make.

On the Grand River Reservation, in Canada, there lives an old Seneca Indian chief who, though totally blind, is famous for his sticks, from the sale of which he derives a fair income.

As to the origin of the certainly Indian game, different Indian nations claim it, the strongest claim being made by the Iroquois of New York State and Canada. But it must remain a vexed question for our Indianologists.

NEH HO-NOH-TCI-NOH-GAH, THE GUARDIANS OF THE LITTLE WATERS, A SENECA MEDICINE SOCIETY[96]

BY

A. C. PARKER

(Ga-wa-so-wa-neh)

The most important and influential fraternity among the present day Senecas is the Ho-noh-tci-noh-gah, commonly called the Secret Medicine Society. The Ho-noh-tci-noh-gah, literally, guardian spirits, is a fraternal organization instituted primarily to preserve and perform the ancient rites deemed necessary for preserving the potency of the ni-ga-ni-ga-ah, literally, little waters, popularly called the secret medicine, and the method of its administration.

Of the twelve native societies that have survived among the Senecas none remains more exclusive, more secret or so rigidly adheres to its ancient forms. No brotherhood among the Senecas is so strong nor does any other hang so well together. There is never internal dissension nor jealousy and never any division of opinion. Unanimity is the rule in all things and discord of any kind would be in variance with the very fundamental teachings of the order. No organization among the Senecas today is so mysterious, nor does any other possess the means of enforcing so rigorously its laws. The Ho-noh-tci-noh-gah is without doubt a society of great antiquity, few Iroquois societies,

An old medicine woman

perhaps, are more venerable. One authority has contended that it is a tribal branch of an organization found everywhere among Indians throughout the continent and produced good arguments to support the theory, but an examination of its traditions and ritual would lead to the opinion that it is purely Iroquois. No doubt similar organizations existed and perhaps were affiliated with it, but it does not seem probable that it should have been widely found.

In order to understand the organization it is necessary first to understand the legend of its origin when many otherwise obscure allusions will be made apparent. The legend follows:

Origin of the Little Water Medicine Society

AS RELATED BY CHIEF E. CORNPLANTER[97]

There was in old times a young chief who was a hunter of great cunning, but though he killed many animals he never took advantage of their positions. He never shot a swimming deer nor a doe with a fawn; he never killed an animal fatigued by a long run nor took one unawares. Before the hunt he always threw tobacco and made a ceremony to ask permission to kill game. Nor was he ever ungrateful to the animals of the woods who had been his friends for so many years. The flesh that was useless he left for the wolves and birds, calling to them as he left it, "Come, my friends, I have made a feast for you." Likewise when he took honey from a tree he left a portion for the bears and when he had his corn harvested he left open ears in the field for the crows, that they might not steal the corn sprouts at the next planting. He fed the fish and water animals with entrails and offal. No ruthless hunter was he, but thoughtful. He threw tobacco for the animals in the woods and water and made incense for them with the *o-yank-wa-o-weh*, the sacred tobacco and burnt it even for the trees. He was a well loved chief for he remembered his friends and gave them meat. All the animals were his friends and all his people were loyal to him. All this was because he was good and he was known as the "protector of the birds and beasts." So he was called.

The southwest country is a land of mysteries. There are many unknown things in the mountains there and also in the waters. The wildest people have always lived there and some were very wise and made different things. When, many years ago, the *Ongwehoweh* (Iroquois) began to make excursions to this distant country they encountered many nations that were friendly and more that were hostile. The Iroquois used to like to go in this country for there they learned new things and found new plants and new kinds of corn and beans and when they would fight and destroy a tribe they would carry away curiously made things and some captives back to the Ho-de-no-sau-ne, their own country.

While one of these exploring parties was in the far southwest looking for war and new things, a band of very savage people attacked them. The young chief, the friend of the animals was with the party and being separated from the rest of his party was struck down by a tomahawk blow. The enemy cut a circle around his scalp lock and tore it off. He could not fight strong because he was tired and very hungry from the long journey, so he was killed. The enemy knew him because he had been a brave fighter and killed a good many of their people in former battles so they were glad when they killed him and prized his scalp. Now he lay dead in a thicket and none of his warriors knew where he was but the enemy showed them his scalp. So they knew that he was, dead.

Black night came and alone upon the red and yellow leaves the chief lay dead and his blood was clotted upon the leaves where it had spilled. The night birds scented the blood and hovered over the body, the owl and the whip-poor-will flew above it and *Shadahgeah*, the Dew Eagle, swooped down from the regions above the clouds. "He seems to be a friend," they said, "who can this man be?" A wolf sniffed the air and thought he smelled food. Skulking through the trees he came upon the body, dead and scalped. His nose was upon the clotted blood and he liked blood. Then he looked into the face of the dead man and leapt back with a long yelping howl, the dead man was the friend of the wolves and the animals and birds. His howl was a signal call and brought all the animals of the big woods and the birds dropped down around him. All the medicine animals came, the bear, the deer, the fox, the beaver, the otter, the turtle and the big horned deer (moose). Now the birds around him were the owl, the whip-poor-will, the crow, the buzzard, the swift hawk, the eagle, the snipe, the white heron and also the great chief of all the birds, Shadahgeah, who is the eagle who flies in the world of our Creator above the clouds. These are all the great medicine people and they came in council about their killed friend. Then they said, "He must not be lost to us. We must restore him to life again." Then a bird said, "He is our friend, he always fed us. We can not allow our friend to die. We must restore him." Then the wolf came up to the body and said, "Here is our friend, he always gave us food in time of famine. We called him our father, now we are orphans. It is our duty to give him life again. Let each one of us look in our medicine packets and take out the most potent ingredient. Then let us compound a medicine and give it." Then the owl said, "A living man must have a scalp."

So the animals made a wonderful medicine and in its preparation some gave their own lives and mixed them with the medicine roots. Now when the medicine was made all of it was contained in the bowl of an acorn. So they poured it down the throat of the man, and the bear feeling over the body found a warm spot over his heart. Then the bear hugged him close in his hairy arms and kept him warm. The crow had flown away for the scalp but could not find it; then the white heron went but while flying over a bean field thought herself hungry and stopped to eat and when filled was too heavy to rise again. Then the pigeon hawk, the swiftest of the birds, said that he would go and surely find it. By this time the enemy had become aware that the animals were holding a council over the chief whom they had slain and so they carefully guarded the scalp which they stretched upon a hoop and swung on a thong over the smoke hole of a lodge. The pigeon hawk, impatient at delay, shot upward into the air and flying in wide circles discovered the scalp dangling over the fire drying in the hot smoke. Hovering over the lodge, for a moment he dropped down and snatching the scalp shot back upwards into the clouds, faster and further than the arrows that pursued him swift from the strong bows of the angered enemy. Back he flew, his speed undiminished by his long flight, and placed the scalp in the midst of the council. It was smoky and dried and would not fit the head of the man. Then a big crow (buzzard) emptied his stomach on it to clean it of smoke and make it stick fast and *Shadahgeah* plucked a feather from his wing and dipped it in the pool of dew that rests in the hollow on his back and sprinkled the water upon it. The dew came down in round drops and refreshed the dry scalp as it does a withered leaf. The man had begun to faintly breathe when the animals placed the scalp back in his head and they saw that truly he would revive. Then the man felt a warm liquid trickling down his throat and with his eyes yet shut he began to talk the language of the birds and animals. And they sang a wonderful song and he listened and remembered every word of the song. This song the animals told him was the medicine song of the medicine animals and they told him that when he wished the favor of the great medicine people and when he felt grateful, to make a ceremony and sing the song. So also they told him that they had a dance and a dance song and they told him that they would teach him the dance. So they danced and some shook rattles made of squashes (gourds) , and though his eyes were closed he saw the dance and he knew all the tunes. Then the animals told him to form a company of his friends and upon certain occasions to sing and dance the ceremony, the Yedos, for it was a great medicine power and called all the medicine animals together and when the people were sick they would devise a medicine for them. Now they said that he must not fail to perform the ceremony and throw tobacco for them. Now the name of the society was Yedos. Then the chief asked the medicine people what the ingredients of the medicine were and they promised to tell him. At a time the animals should choose they would notify him by the medicine song. Now he could not receive the secret because he had been married. Only *Ho-yah-di-wa-doh*, virgin men, may receive the first knowledge of mysteries. Now the chief greatly wished for the medicine for he thought it would be a great charm and a cure for the wounds received in war. After a time the chief was lifted to his feet by the hand of the bear and then he recovered his full life and when he opened his eyes he found himself alone in the midst of a circle of tracks. He made his way back to his people and related his adventure. He gathered his warriors together and in a secret place sang the medicine song of the animals, the Yedos. So they sang the song and each had a song and they danced.

After some time the chiefs decided to send another war party against the enemy in the southwest and to punish the hostile people who were attacking them. Then the friend of the birds and animals said, "It is well that we destroy them for they are not a reasonable people," and so he went with his party.

Now after a certain number of days the party stopped in an opening in the forest to replenish their stock of food. The place where they stopped was grassy and good for camp. Now a short distance away, a half day's journey, was a deer lick and near it a clear spring and a brook that ran from it and to this place all the animals came to drink. The party wanted fresh meat and so dispatched two young men, Ho-yah-di-wa-doh, to the lick for game. As they approached it they heard the sound of a distant song and drawing near the lick they sat down on the bank over the spring and listened to the song. It was a most wonderful song and floated through the air to them. At a distance away the animals came and drank but so entranced were they by the music that they killed none. Through the entire night they sat listening to the song, and listening they learned sections of the song. In the morning they returned to the camp and reported what they had heard to their chief. Then said the chief, "That song is for the good of the medicine. You must find the source of the song and discover the medicine that will make us powerful in war and cure all our ills. You must purge yourselves and go again on the morrow." So the young men did as directed and went again to the spring and threw tobacco upon its surface. As night came on they listened and again heard the great song and it was louder and more distinct than before. Then they heard a voice singing from the air and telling them a story of their lives and they marveled greatly. The song grew louder and as they listened they discovered that it emanated from the summit of a mountain. So they returned in the morning and reported to their chief and sang to him parts of the song. Then he said, "You must cleanse yourselves again and this time do not return until you have the medicine, the song and the mystery." So the young men cleansed themselves again and went to the spring and as the thick night came on they heard the singing voices clear and loud ringing from the mountain top. Then said one of the young men, "Let us follow the sound to its source," and they started in the darkness. After a time they stumbled upon a windfall, a place where the trees had been blown down in a tangled mass. It was a difficult place to pass in the darkness for they were often entrapped in the branches but they persevered and it seemed that someone was leading them. Beings seemed to be all about them yet they could not see them for it was dark. After they had extricated themselves from the windfall they went into a morass where their footsteps were guided by the unseen medicine animals. Now the journey was a very tedious one and they could see nothing. They approached a gulf and one said, "Let us go up and down the gulf and try to cross it," and they did and crossed one gulf. Soon they came to another where they heard the roaring of a cataract and the rushing of waters. It was a terrifying place and one of the young men was almost afraid. They descended the slope and came to a swift river and its waters were very cold but they plunged in and would have been lost if someone unseen had not guided them. So they crossed over and on the other side was a steep mountain which they must ascend but could not because it was too steep. Then one of the young men said, "Let us wait here awhile and rest ourselves for we may need our strength for greater dangers." So he said. But the other said, "I am rested; we must go onward somehow." When he had so spoken a light came flying over and sang for them to follow it. So they followed the winged light and ascended the mountain and they were helped. The winged light kept singing, "Follow me, follow me, follow me!" And they were safe when they followed and were not afraid. Now the singing, flying beacon was the whip-poor-will. He led them. After a time the light disappeared but they struggled up the mountainside unaided by its guidance. The way became very stony and it seemed that no one was helping them now and then they wished that their unseen friends would help them, so they made a prayer and threw sacred tobacco on the path. Then the light came again and it was brighter, it glowed like the morning and the way was lighted up. The singing continued all this while and they were nearing its source and they reached the top of the mountain. They looked about for they heard the song near at hand but there was no one there. Then they looked about and saw nothing but a great stalk of corn springing from a flat rock. Its four roots stretched in the four directions, north, east, south and west. The roots lay that way. They listened and discovered that the music emanated from the cornstalk. It was wonderful. The corn was a medicine plant and life was within it. Then the winged light sang for them to cut the root and take a piece for medicine. So they made a tobacco offering and cut the root. As they did red blood flowed out from the cut like human blood and then the cut immediately healed. Then did the unseen speaker say, "This root is a great medicine and now we will reveal the secret of the medicine." So the voices told them the composition of the medicine that had healed the chief and instructed them how to use it. They taught the young men the Ga-no-dah, the medicine song that would make the medicine strong and preserve it. They said that unless the song were sung the medicine would become weak and the animals would become angry because of the neglect of the ceremonies that honored their medicine. Therefore, the holders of the medicine must sing the all-night song for it. And they told them all the laws of the medicine and the singing light guided them back to the spring and it was morning then. The young men returned to their chief and told him the full story of their experiences and he was glad for he said, "The medicine will heal all our wounds."

It was true, the medicine healed the cuts and wounds made by arrows and knives and not one of the Iroquois was killed in their battle with the enemy. When they returned home the chief organized the lodges of the medicine and the medicine people of the Ye-dos and Ni-ga-ni-ga-ah were called the Ho-noh-tci-noh-gah. The medicine was called the Ni-ga-ni-ga-ah (little waters) because its dose was so small.

So started the Ho-noh-tci-noh-gah.[98] The legend here ends.

Neh Ni-ga-ni-ga-ah

The charm medicine is known as the Ni-ga-ni-ga-ah and each member possesses a certain amount of it. The secret of compounding the Ni-ga-ni-ga-ah rested with only one man in a tribe who, according to the teachings of the society, would be apprised of approaching death and given time to transmit the knowledge to a successor whom he should choose. According to the traditions of the Ho-noh-tci-noh-gah the secret holder always foreknew the hour of his death and frequently referred to it in lodge meetings.

It is not my purpose to violate any confidence reposed in me by the Ho-noh-tci-noh-gah who have honored me by a seat in their circle and I will betray nothing when I say that the "little water medicine" is composed of the brains of various mammals, birds, fish, and other animals and the pollen and roots of various plants, trees and vegetables. These ingredients are compounded and pulverized with certain other substances and constitute the base of the Ni-ga-ni-ga-ah.

That this medicine actually possesses chemical properties that react on human tissue was proven by Dr J. H. Salisbury, an eminent physician and a former State chemist, who analyzed and experimented with a small quantity that he had secured from a member of the society.

The medicine itself is of a yellowish hue and when opened in the dark appears luminous, probably from the organic phosphorous that it contains. The utmost caution is employed by the members of the Ho-noh-tci-noh-gah to preserve the medicine from exposure to the air in unsafe places and from contaminating influences. It is contained in a small skin bag and wrapped in many coverings of cloth and skin and finally inclosed in a bark, wood or tin case to keep it free from moisture, disease and dirt.

Among the Senecas of modern times, John Patterson was the last of the holders of the secret and the secret of the precise method of compounding the medicine died with him, he in some way having failed to instruct a successor. The members thus doubly guard their medicine and are loath to use it except in cases of extreme necessity for when it is exhausted not only will they be unable to secure more but by a legend when the medicine is gone the Senecas will forever lose their identity as Indians.

Method of administering the Ni-ga-ni-ga-ah

A person who wishes to have the "little water" medicine given to him for the cure of a wound, broken bone or specific disease must purge himself and for three days abstain from the use of salt or grease. His food must be the flesh of white birds or animals and only the white portions. The system of the patient is then ready to receive the medicine. The medicine man comes to his lodge and an assistant searches the house for anything that might destroy the "life" of the medicine such as household animals, vermin, decayed meat, blood, soiled garments, women in a periodic condition, etc. These things removed from the house, the patient is screened off and the guard patrols the premises warning away all infected or intoxicated persons. An attendant who has previously been dispatched to a clear running stream enters with a bowl of water that has been dipped from the crest of the ripples, as they "sang their way down the water road." Not to antagonize the forces in the water, it was dipped the way the current ran, down stream, and not upward against it.

Everything now being in readiness the medicine man takes a basket of tobacco and as he repeats the ancient formula he casts pinches of the tobacco into the flames that the sacred smoke may lift his words to the Maker of All. The water is then poured out in a cup and the medicine packet opened. With a miniature ladle that holds as much of the powder as can be held on the tip of the blade of a small penknife, the medicine man dips three times from the medicine and drops the powder on the surface of the water in three spots, the points of a triangle. If the medicine floats the omen is good, if it clouds the water the results are considered doubtful and if it sinks speedy death is predicted as a certainty and the remaining medicine is thrown away. In the case of severe cuts or contusions and broken bones the medicated water is sprinkled upon the affected part and an amount is taken internally. A medicine song is then chanted by the "doctor" who accompanies himself with a gourd rattle. After the ceremony of healing, the people of the house partake of a feast of fruit, and the medicine man departs with his fee, a pinch of sacred tobacco. The following description of the house ceremony from the lips of a Seneca will not be out of place. The story is related exactly as it came from the tongue of the interpreter.

Jesse Hill speaking: "Mother scraped off basswood bark, soaked it in water and wrapped it around my leg. Next day we sent for the medicine man. He came at sunset and sent to the creek for fresh water to be dipped where the current was swift, with a pail not against the current. Poured some in a teacup and pulled out the medicine bag. Opened it with a charmed shovel not much larger than a pin. Dipped three times. Cup of water. Floated. Go up or down. Understand it was good medicine. Took some in his mouth and sprayed it on my leg. Told mother to put a curtain around my bed so no one could see me. If any one saw any part of my body, medicine would do no good. Soon came dark. All the animals were put out. Took tin pail and made fire. Put in center of room and all sat around in silence. Medicine man made prayer. Scattered tobacco mother had prepared over fire. Took rattle made of gourd and chanted medicine song loud and louder. Half hour pain had gone. Boiled different fruits together till soft. Put kettle where all could help out with little dipper. Left two doses of medicine. Eat nothing but white things. White of egg of chicken had white feathers and eat chicken if white. Five or six days spoke things. All certain took pain away."

The medicine lodge ritual

The Ho-noh-tci-noh-gah "sits," that is, holds lodge meetings, four times each year; in midwinter, when the deer sheds its hair, when the strawberries are ripe and when corn is ripe for eating. At these ceremonies each member brings his or her medicine to be sung for and if unable to be present sends it.

Only members know the exact place and time of meeting. At the entrance of the medicine lodge, now a private house of a member chosen for the ceremony, a guard is stationed who scrutinizes each person who attempts to pass within. Across the door within is placed a heavy bench "manned" by several stalwart youths who, should a person not entitled to see the interior of the lodge appear, would throw their weight against the bench and force the door shut leaving the

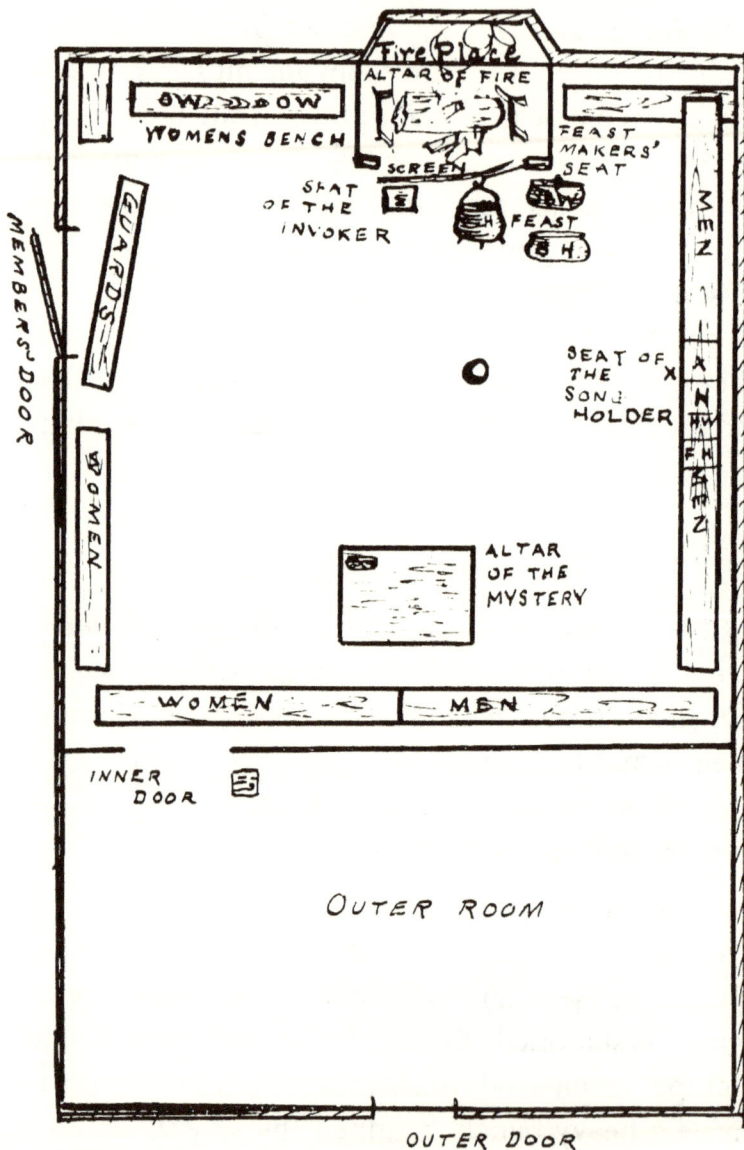

Outline plan of Little Water Lodge

unfortunate intruder to the mercy of the outside guards and incoming members.

Each member entering the lodge has with him his medicine, a quantity of tobacco, a pipe and perhaps a rattle although most of the lodge rattles are in the keeping of a Ho-non-di-ont or officer. As the members enter the room they deposit their contribution of tobacco in a husk basket placed for the purpose on a table at one side and then put their medicine packets beside the basket of the sacred herb.

The ceremony proper commences about 11 p.m. in the summer and in winter an hour earlier and lasts until daybreak. The feast makers enter the lodge several hours previous to the ceremony and cook the food for the feast and prepare the strawberry wine.

The seats in the lodge are arranged around the sides of the room leaving the center of the room open.

When all is in readiness a Ho-non-di-ont takes a basket of sacred tobacco, O-yan-kwa o-weh, and, as he chants the opening ceremony he casts the sacred herb into the smoldering coals. The lights are all burning and the members are in their seats, the only exception being the feast makers whose duties require their attention at the fireplace.

From the manuscript notes of Mrs. Harriet Maxwell Converse, I find the following translation of the "Line around the Fire Ceremony."

The Line around the Fire Ceremony

The Singer, (to the members): "This is the line around the fire ceremony. Now I have asked blessings and made prayer."

The Singer sprinkles sacred tobacco on the fire.

The Singer speaks to the invisible powers:

"Now I give you incense,[100]

You, the Great Darkness!

You, our great grandparents, here tonight.

We offer you incense!

We assemble at certain times in the year

That this may be done.

We trust that all believe in this medicine.

For all are invited to partake of this medicine.

(Now one has resigned. We ask you to let him off in a friendly manner. Give him good luck and take care that his friends remain faithful!)

(To the Thunder Spirit)

Now we offer you this incense!

Some have had ill luck

Endeavoring to give a human being.

We hope you will take hold

And help your grandchildren,

Nor be discouraged in us!

Now we act as we offer you incense!

You love it the most of all offerings.

With it you will hear us better

And not tire of our talking,

But love us with all power

Beyond all treasures

Or spreading your words through the air!

All men traveling under the great heavens

You have invited, your grandchildren and all nations!

Oh you, that make the noise,

You, the great Thunderer!

Your grandchildren wish to thank you!

All your grandchildren have asked me

To offer this incense upon the mountain to you!"

(Speaking to the Great Spirit, Sho-gwa-yah-dih-sah):

"Oh you the Manager of All Things!

We ask you to help us.

To help us make this medicine strong!

You are the Creator,

The Most High,

The Best Friend of men!

We ask you to help us!

We implore your favor!

I have spoken."

After the tobacco throwing ceremony the keeper of the rattles gives each person in the circle a large gourd rattle and then the lights are extinguished leaving the assembly in total darkness. The watcher of the medicine uncovers the bundles exposing it to the air and as he does so a faint glow like a luminous cloud hovers over the table and disappears. The leader or holder of the song gives a signal with his rattle calling the assembly to order and then begins to beat his rattle. The people shake their rattles in regular beats until all are in unison when the holder of the song commences the song, which is taken up by the company. And such a song it is! It is a composition of sounds that thrills the very fiber of those who hear it. It transports one from the lodge back into the dark mysterious stone age forest and in its weird wild cadences it tells of the origin of the society, of the hunter of the far south country and how when he was killed by the enemy the animals to whom he had always been a friend restored him to life. It tells of his pilgrimage over plain and mountain, over river and lake, ever following the call of the night bird and the beckoning of the winged light. It is an opera of nature's people that to Indian ideas is unsurpassed by any opera of civilization.

The first song requires one hour for singing. Lights are then turned up and the feast maker passes the kettle of sweetened strawberry juice and afterward the calumet from which all draw a puff of the sacred incense. Then comes an interval of rest in which the members smoke sacred tobacco and discuss lodge matters. The medicine is covered before the lights are turned up.

With a chug of his resonant gourd rattle the leader calls the people together for the second song which is wilder and more savage in character. The whip-poor-will's call is heard at intervals and again the call of the crows who tell of a feast to come. The whip-poor-will song is one that is most beautiful but it is played on the flute only at rare intervals and then it is so short that it excites an almost painful yearning to hear it again but there is art in this savage opera and its performers never tire of it because it is wonderful even to them. During the singing every person in the circle must sing and shake his rattle, to pause is considered an evil thing. It is no small physical effort to shake a long-necked gourd a hundred and fifty times a minute for sixty minutes without cessation. This I soon discovered when as a novitiate of the society I was placed between a medicine woman and man and given an extra heavy rattle. Every now and then a hand from one or the other side would stretch forth from the inky blackness and touch my arm to see if I were faithful and sometimes a moist ear would press against my face to discover if I were singing and, listening a moment to my attempts, would draw back. The song in parts is pitched very high and it is a marvel that male voices can reach it. At times the chief singers seem to employ ventriloquism for they throw their voices about the room in a manner that is startling to the novice. At the close of the song lights are turned up and the berry water and calumet are passed again and a longer period of rest is allowed. There are two other sections of the song ritual with rest intervals that bring the finale of the song close to daybreak. The feast makers pass the berry water and pipe again and then imitating the cries of the crow the Ho-non-di-ont pass the bear or boar's head on a platter and members tear off a mouthful each with their teeth imitating the caw of a crow as they do so. After the head is eaten each member brings forth his pail and places it before the fireplace for the feast maker to fill with the allotted portion of o-no-kwa or hulled corn soup. When the pails are filled, one by one the company disperses into the gray light of dawn and the medicine ceremony is over. At the close of the last song each one takes his packet of medicine and secretes it about his person.

The medicine song according to the ritual of the society is necessary to preserve the virtue of the medicine, It is an appreciation of the founder of the order and a thanksgiving to the host of living things that have given their life power that the medicine might be. The spirits of these creatures hover about the medicine which they will not desert as long as the holder remains faithful to the conditions that they saw fit to impose when it was given to the founder. The psychic influence of the animals and plants is the important part of the medicine and when the medicine is opened in the dark they are believed to be present in a shadowy form that is said to sometimes become faintly luminous and visible. Members are said frequently to see these spirit forms, not individual members only but the entire company simultaneously. There are marvels and mysteries connected with the ceremonies of the Ho-noh-tci-noh-gah, the Indians say, that white men will never know, nor would believe if told. The Indian believes that he has some sacred mysteries that will die with him, and that even in this age of inquiry, these mysterious things will never become the property of civilization.

Someone has suggested that Indian songs are not stable but vary from time to time, but this idea is at once dispelled when we see a company of fifty young and old chanting the same song without a discord from night till morning. The song is uniformly the same and probably has varied but slightly since it originated. It is still intact with none of its parts missing, although the words are archaic and some not understood.[103]

The medicine men teach that if a packet is not sung for at least once in a year the spirits will become restless and finally angry and bring all manner of ill luck upon its possessor. The spirits of the animals and plants that gave their lives for the medicine will not tolerate neglect, and relentlessly punish the negligent holder and many instances are cited to prove that neglect brings misfortune. The medicine will bring about accidents that will cause sprains, severe bruises and broken bones and finally death. In every Seneca settlement the story is the same and individuals are pointed out who, having neglected their medicine, have become maimed for life. Should some member of a family die leaving his medicine, it is claimed that it will compel the person who should rightly take the dead one's place to respect its desires. The members of the

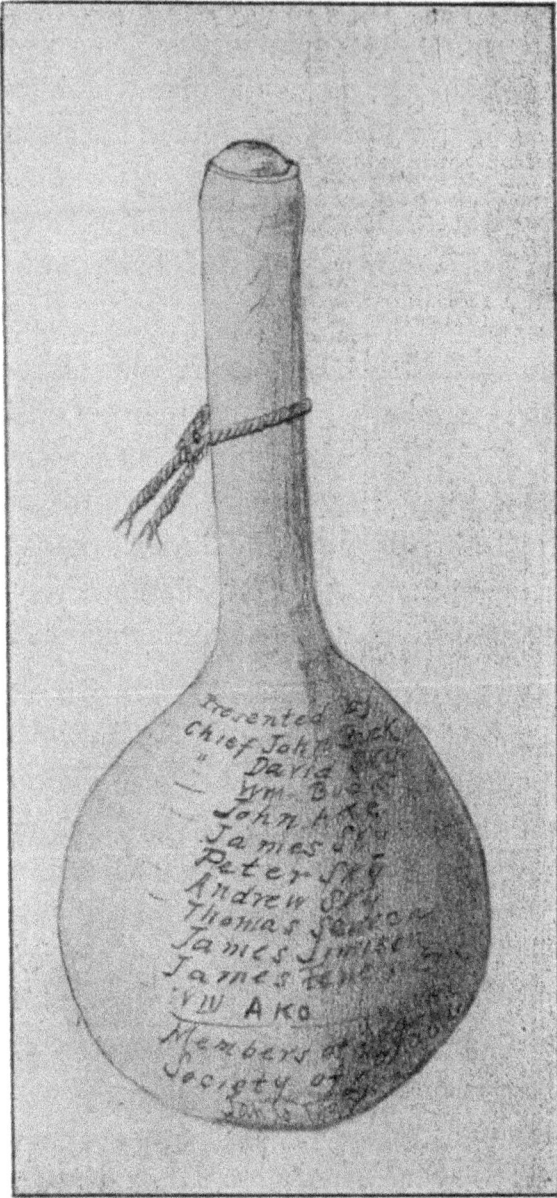

The medicine rattle presented to Mrs. Converse
by the Canadian Medicine Society

society relate that when John Patterson, the last holder of the secret, died, he left his medicine in the loft of his house. His son, a well educated man of wide business experience, one of the shrewdest men of the Senecas and a person seemingly free of superstition, thought that he would allow the medicine of his father to remain idle. He wished to have nothing to do with the old-fashioned heathenish customs of his father. Indeed he did not take interest enough in the medicine to look at it. Several medicine sittings passed by and the man began to suffer strange accidents. One evening as he sat with his family on the veranda of his home, a modern dwelling such as is found in any modern town, the members say that he heard the medicine song floating in the air above him. He was startled and each of the family was frightened. The singing continued until at length it grew faint and ceased. Upon several occasions the family and visitors heard the song issuing from the air. Mr. Patterson sent for the leader of the lower medicine lodge, William Nephew, who asked where the medicine was hidden. No one knew, but after a search it was discovered. Mr. Nephew ordered that a feast should be made and the rites performed. Then was the modern educated Indian forced to join the lodge and take his father's seat. This story, of which I have given but the bare outline, is commonly known among the Senecas, Mr. M. R. Harrington, an archeologist and one time field instructor in archeology of Harvard University, being perfectly familiar with the facts of the case which he took pains to learn while staying at the Patterson home. Howsoever this may be explained, it is nevertheless considered one of the mysteries of the medicine and the instance is not a solitary one.

Few white people have ever been allowed in a medicine lodge and when they have been they have not witnessed the ceremony in full. I know of only two who have ever become members, holding the medicine, Mr. Joseph Keppler and Mrs. Harriet Maxwell Converse. When Mrs. Converse was initiated into the society she took notes of everything said and done. Her account is a most interesting one and its value is not to be underestimated. When she entered the lodge the leader addressed her in the following words, which she has recorded in her notebook:

Address to the candidate

All things are now ready for opening these ceremonies in the proper manner. We are now ready to commence. We are thankful that we are able to say to the Creator that we are in good health.

It was appointed that we should meet in June when the strawberries were ripe, but at that time all of us were busy with our season's labor. Now the ordained period has nearly passed by and we have not sung. Thus it is arranged that we meet at this time and carry the ceremonies through before the berry festival. You (speaking to the candidate), may then know how the Little Water Medicine came to mankind. We older ones, whose experience with it is greater, will tell you.

It shall be done and I, John Jacket, understand the

traditions and offer tobacco to the various beings who are a part of this medicine. I am the holder of this song.

We are thankful to the Creator that we are here. Some of our number are absent. Some are dead. Some have gone to Christ's religion. Some are sick. Nevertheless, we will proceed, we few who are here.

It would require a long time to relate the entire story of the medicine and thus we will tell the principal part only.

(During these preliminary remarks each member lays his sealed box of medicine on the table. An interval of smoking follows the remarks of the holder of the song.)

The medicine lodge epitome of the origin of the medicine[104]

Long time ago in the days of our grandfathers men journeyed great distances in search of good luck and adventure. We are about to relate of one of these ancient journeys.

It so happened at one time that a band of On-gweh-o-weh, (Iroquois) with members of other nations, journeyed far into the south country. They had planned to engage in warfare and bring back a great number of scalps. But it so happened that as they were out the enemy attacked them suddenly and, being unprepared, our party was nearly exterminated. Among those left dead upon the field of battle was a certain Seneca, a chief, who had always been a friend to the birds. It had been his custom to slay some animal and after skinning it to cut it open and shout for the birds saying, "I have killed something for you to eat!"

As he lay dead upon the field the birds hovered over his form strangely attracted by it. They deliberated "We had a friend who looked like this; he used to call us often and it may be he who lies here killed by a blow on the head." While they were yet speaking two wolves came and wailing said, "Here lies our friend. We are orphans now! He always gave us food to eat. Let us try to restore his life! All of us animals he has fed and we must do something for him! It is our duty to bring back his life!"

All the animals and birds came together where he was lying and counseled, saying, "O what can we do? Can we bring him to life?" The presiding chief of the council was a wolf and he asked, "Is there no way to bring him to life?"

Affectionately the animals licked his head and saw where it was crushed and scalped. An owl asked, "How are we to find the scalp?" The hawk replied, "I can get it for I know where it is. I can get it at night on the eaves of the lodge in the settlement," and then he flew away on his errand. Returning successful he placed the scalp on the ground, asking the big crow to vomit on it and stick it on the dead man's head. Then the assembled council rejoiced because the scalp grew fast. The dead chief felt something trickling down his throat and seemed to hear a far away singing. He began to move and there was life in him and he began to talk the same language they talked and they understood him. And when he became fully conscious the birds and animals had gone.

Leaping to his feet he returned to his people and told them what had happened as he lay dead, how he had heard singing and had learned the song. The people marveled and were convinced.

After a time men, those who were warriors, volunteered to go and fight another battle with the south country enemies. Thus an expedition was fitted out and the same chief who had been dead said, "That's the right thing" and he went with them. Now they had certain plans when they stopped for provisions.

Their camping place was on a grassy place near certain deer licks where bears and other animals came to eat. At this place there was a kind of brook and spring. Being a distance from this place two young men who were perfectly virtuous were sent by the party to get game. Now they started and went. Arriving at the lick they sat down and listening thought that they detected the sounds of music, so they harkened. The sounds seemed to issue from a mountain and ring all about them. It told them of all their doings, and so entranced were they that they could do nothing but listen all night, though they should have returned to the camp. The next morning they returned and made report, that they had gone to the lick for game but there was something else there, and told the full story of the happenings. Then the once dead chief said, "It seems that we have met great luck, so return to the lick again. For this we will cleanse you and you may learn the import of the singing." So that night they gave them medicine and cleansed them and started them back again. And as before they heard the singing, this time very loud and distinct It came from away up the hill mountain and they went toward it hoping to learn the words and music. Again returning to camp they sang parts of the song they had learned and the chief who had been killed recognized it and said "It is for the good of the people!"

Again the young men were purged and again they went by night, this time under the orders to follow the sound of music to its source. Reaching the lick the voices came as before and the young men said, "Now is the time to go!" They started and came to a windfall where the path was filled with fallen logs and it was very dark there. After a time they came to a place where they heard the roar of waters and there were two gulfs. Then a big light came singing to follow it. Then the young men said, "Let us go up and down the gulf," and when they went down they found that they could ford the river. And the light began to glow like morning. One warrior was timid and said, "Let us rest for we may encounter great danger here," but the other replied "I am rested," and they went up the mountain.

The voices seemed very near yet they could not find the singers. At length they reached the top of the mountain and found a large cornstalk, from four to six inches around. Its long leaves swept the ground and kept it smooth and clean. It grew from a large stone and its four roots spread out, one to the east, one to the west, one to the north and one to the south. One warrior said, "It must be this corn that sings."

For a time they deliberated and said "The root must be cut. We must have a piece of the root. This must be medicine." They built a fire and offered tobacco incense; then taking an axe they chopped portions of the roots off and the juice was red like blood and immediately the cut ends came together and healed.

The singing continued and seemed accompanied by a rattle made of a squash.

The young men with the words of the song ringing in their ears, bearing the sacred root started down the incline and all the animals and birds being invisible followed the two virgin men and told them all that was in the medicine. They returned to the camp and the song was called a great blessing. They scraped the root and put it in water and made incense of it. Drinking the mixture they became so strong that they could not be shot though shot at seven times.

(The holder of the song pauses after the story and then turning to the candidate says)

"We have this medicine good and strong. We have faith. It is many extracts. For its preservation we sing four times a year. It is the same music. We sing all night and the spirit of the medicine sings with us as it did upon the mountain.

Now you have heard the report that the old people made to me and I surely believe for I have seen and had experience. I have seen men who had been shot by accident or hurt in other ways who after using the medicine recovered. When I was young once, forty years of age, I was appointed to practise this medicine and ever since I have done so. After a while some church members objected to it, but I have always had faith in it and thought it aright to come true through music. When the Christians hold their service they always have music and praise God in music. God gave this music and all good gifts and he never thought it wrong. (The medicine and the medicine song) Now I am getting old and I have spoken from experience believing all I have said faithfully."[105] [It took an hour to relate and interpret this. H. M. C]

Instructions to the candidate[106]

The medicine birds

In order to get the bird most important in the medicine, a young man must cleanse himself, a virgin, never known woman, Ho-yeh-de-wa-doh, pure man. He goes up to get the charmed medicine. Lives on meat only for two or three months. Sent by company of medicine men, birds, he goes up a mountain and hides it, medicine. Then he calls all the birds of the air. All the birds come and the first bird comes. He shoots him. Crows, turkey buzzards come first and make an awful noise. Second bird white bird. Forbidden to kill him because he brings the third bird. This last bird is red, supposed to be red eagle, extinct, and he kills him and he vomits blood. Takes the heart and brain for medicine.

Employment of the songs

Four times a year we sing all night to the birds and animals. Sit in a circle and burn the sacred tobacco. One draws out a coal and burns it. All the birds and animals invited to take tobacco (all that are connected with the medicine).

Tell the darkness to take some medicine. Sing to He-no, the Thunderer, last for he said, "The Medicine People are my people. I want to help them all I can." Sing to animals to keep them on friendly terms. If any one has medicine and has bad luck, sing and the medicine will make them feel better. Strong in their work, sometimes they dream someone gets hurt and if they don't sing to the medicine someone of the family will get hurt.

Some members of the band keep it. Several bands keep it. Three or four keep it.

Animal and bird members of the medicine

The animal and bird members of the medicine are the deer, snipe, white heron, hawk, big crow, big deer (moose or elk), bear, mud turtle, beaver, wolf, eagle, whip-poor-will, owl, crow and otter. These accompanied the young men on their night journey.

The fruit members

The fruit members are strawberries, blackberries, apples, huckleberries.[107] The tree is the maple because it yields the sweet water for the drink. The plant is the

255

tobacco only, its root is a deadly poison.

The ingredients of the medicine

The ingredients of the medicine are supposed to be unknown but tradition relates that it is composed of portions of all the birds, animals, plants, trees, and fruits that are members of the Ni-gah-ni-gah-ah, their brains and hearts, etc., etc.

Duties of members

Every member must be kind and forgiving. He must forgive his enemy before he can sing. Must be pure. Must not ask for money to take it for service.

No one must sing the songs to learn them or even repeat them to any one only in the lodge.

Any one of good reputation can come in and sing in the outside room if he believes in the medicine and those to whom it has been administered, but only members of a band can hold it.

———————

After her initiation to the Medicine Society Mrs. Converse published in the *St Louis Republic* two accounts of her experience. These are too valuable to become lost within the files of a newspaper and should be placed on record. For this reason I have seen fit to copy them entire.

THE SOCIETY OF THE MEN
WHO MOVE SPIRITS[108]

"Little Water Medicine" which is called the Indian's elixir of life. Some of the strange habits and superstitions of the doctors.

(Mrs. Converse, the author of this strictly true narrative was in 1884 formally adopted into the family of the Seneca chief, Tho-no-so-wa, a descendant of Red Jacket, that she might thus become a great-great-granddaughter of the chieftain whom her father had powerfully befriended. Later she was made a member of the Onondaga, Oneida, Cayuga, Tuscarora and Mohawk nations. Since writing this story she has been made a chief of the Iroquois League in recognition of her public services for the welfare of the eastern tribes of Indians.)

The Ne-gar-na-gar-ah[109] Society is known to all the North American Indians.

Its rites are the same everywhere although the location of tribes and the animal and bird inhabitants of the localities govern somewhat the character of the sacred song which is recited at the four yearly conventions.

It is with the consent of the Iroquois members that I relate some of the ceremonies at my own initiation into this great secret medicine society, to correct false ideas among the "palefaces." Certain vows of silence prevent a complete account.

The Indians have been accused of conducting the rites of the Ne-gar-na-gar-ah with pagan profanities.

This is not true. A moral and deeply religious spirit prevails. If there be superstition in the legend of the origin of the society, there is none the less undeniable remedial and curative virtue in the "Little Water Medicine" prepared by the mystery man especially in the case of gunshot and arrow wounds.

I had been told the traditionary perils attending the initiation into the society. I had been warned that an evil spirit might take possession of me whereupon I would be transformed into a witch and could assume the form of bird, beast or reptile, just whichever would best serve my plan in carrying out any horrible purpose. Moreover if I were discovered in my practices or if I were even complained of by any outside person I would be secretly poisoned or shot. I might be compelled to join a band of invisible demons who hold secret meetings in the darkness for which the initiation fee is a human life, they to select the victim. I might be condemned to murder my dearest friend. Indeed it was the privilege of the demon band that the most precious should be sacrificed in its cause. Or, I would be given a "charmed life" and held at the mercy of these demons which they would bestow upon some other human member of their band to be used in case of my disobedience.

Nevertheless, I accept with pleasure the invitation of my gentle friends, the Iroquois members of the Ne-gar-na-gar-ah society, to "sit" in the Moon-of-the Berries convention in June 1888. As the legend of the origin of the Ne-gar-na-gar-ah is of importance in understanding the rites at my initiation, I will introduce it just here.

Origin of the Ne-gar-na-gar-ah

A member of the Canadian Medicine (Little Water) Company

In the "old times" Indians understood the language of animals and birds.

Among the special friends of the fur and feathered tribes was a certain giant chief, known far and wide for his goodness and valor.

The chief through whom came the Ne-gar-na-gar-ah, is not claimed as the ancestor of any special nation, but is acknowledged by all tribes to be the "governor" of the medicine. His influence among the Indians yet endures as the "Doer of the Good."

Notwithstanding his vigilance, this chief one day during a hunt, was suddenly overcome with exhaustion and fell in a dead stupor. At this moment the chief of a hostile nation chanced to pass by, and lifting his stone axe, dealt him a death blow, took his scalp and fled with the trophy to his own people.

"By the good that comes," as the red men say, a wolf found the dead chief, and recognizing him as the friend of his tribe, gave a piteous death cry that summoned other animals and birds to his aid.

A bear, hurrying to the chief, discovered warmth in the body and clasped it close in his hairy arms and commanded life to return.

An eagle fanned his great wings above the chief's head and summoned the noon air to bring back his breath.

A swift hawk flew to the camp of the enemy where the chief's scalp, painted with red blood and stretched on a hoop, was fluttering from a pole around which the warriors were celebrating a victory dance. The quick wings and keen eyes of the hawk were too cunning for the flying arrows of the warriors. With one swoop he seized the scalp in his beak, softening it with his feathers dipped in a gentle stream, he carried it to the forest doctors, who quickly restored it to the gaping wound on the chief's head.

In the council held by these forest folk it was

determined to compound a medicine to which each bird and beast should contribute some vital portion of its own body. To this was added curative herbs, and then the mixture was administered to the chief in the cup of an acorn, and it quickly restored him to life.

The legend states that the chief persuaded these forest doctors to reveal to him the secret of this wonderful "life creator." The story of his night journey to obtain this secret is the foundation of the initiation ceremony of the Ne-gar-na-gar-ah society.

The date of the organization of the order, Indian history does not tell. But it has existed for centuries and there is reason to believe that as far as is possible with the encroachments of the "paleface" into the territories of the red man, the exercises at the conventions today are conducted according to the primitive rules of its origin, and the seasons at which these gatherings are held are the same among all the North American Indian nations and the watchwords and signs are recognized everywhere.[110]

Legend of the chief's initiation

It is night, a night of darkness impenetrable. There is no sound save the waterfall and the river. In the forest the chief, patient and listening, is waiting for the sign promised him.

Will it be given?

Yes. Birds and beasts do not lie.

The chief trusts and waits until a strong voice that

has come out from the stillness and the darkness is saying: "Hast thou cleansed thyself from mortal guilt and impurity?"

The chief replies, "I have."

"Hast thou ill will toward any of thy fellow creatures?"

"I have not."

"Wilt thou trust and obey us, keeping thyself always chaste and valorous?"

"I will."

"Wilt thou hold this power with which we endow thee for thine own people only?"

"I will."

"Wilt thou endure death and torture in its cause?"

"I will."

"Wilt thou vow this secret never to be revealed save at thy death hour?"

"I will."

"Thy death hour will be made known to thee, thou wilt be let to choose thy successor, and at the end of thy journey thou wilt be rewarded for thy faith and obedience!"

There is a rustling as if a hurrying wind were flying through the forest, and again the silence!

Yet in the darkness something glows, flickers, disappears, returns, fans sideways, wings to and fro near the chief, and at last fitfully hovers over him, as a whip-poor-will with its night voice softly sings, "Follow me! Follow me!"

It is the promised sign. The winged light vanishes and the believing chief follows.

On and on through stretches of tangles that test his endurance, through the shadowy horrors of endless swamps, the chief is guided by the voice of the whip-poor-will, "Follow me! Follow me!"

In the forest depths he is attended by all the night folk each of whom reveals to him the secret of the portion it added to the medicine, until he knows each of its elements. His trail widens as he speeds on and there are "stations" where he is permitted to rest. At these moments the forest folk vanish but the winged light returns to cheer him.

He thirsts: an invisible bird, bearing the night dew in the hollow between its wings, brings him a drink.

He hungers: an invisible animal brings him food that nourishes him.

Thus refreshed he wanders on, at intervals, until he reaches a frowning mountain of rocky steeps that are insurmountable by human will or skill.

As this monster mountain threatens the chief the east sky seems nearer to him, the voice of the whip-poor-will grows faint and at last silent, the forest folk have fled, the winged light does not return, yet the deserted chief believes and waits.

At last in the distance of the fair skies he hears the

screaming of an eagle. He is suddenly possessed with a power that leads him up the mountain, where he finds at its summit nothing but rocks and barrenness, except one majestic plant that stretches its leaves far out toward the east, west, south and north skies.

A voice directs him to divide the plant into two portions. As he cuts it, a stream of blood flows from the wound down the rock side. A substance is laid in his hand which the voice bids him hold close to the bleeding plant stalk, whereupon, the prostrate plant lifts itself and its wound closes, leaving no sign to tell of its bruise save a seed sheathed, tasseled and golden. This is the maize or wild corn plant. In this manner was the chief endowed with life's great restorer, the medicine, the Ne-gar-na-gar-ah.

How the medicine is dispensed today

The conventions of this society are held four times a year; when the deer sheds its coat, at the berry moon, when the corn is ripe and in midwinter.

The curative handed down from the chief is held by one medicine man or "mystery man" of a nation or league of nations, and at these conventions is distributed by him to certain bands of the order who are entitled to use it for the people. This head man holds the secret of compounding the restorer until his death warning when he reveals it to his successor whom he has a right to choose. It is told that "he who holds the medicine" never dies suddenly, for, as the red men say, "he has time to die."

Tradition says that when the medicine is exhausted the red man will disappear from the earth. It is a fact that the medicine is very scarce among the eastern Indians and that, by reason of the extermination of certain animals important to its ingredients, it will be nearly impossible to replenish the stock. The passing away and total annihilation of many of the eastern tribes is noted by the red man as a fulfilment of the prophecy.

The first chief was given permission to kill any beast or bird from whom it was necessary to extract the life principle for the medicine. He was also given the right to kill in the hunt for food or furs to cloth his body any of the medicine beasts or birds if he would first ask its consent and pardon. If refused he could not inflict upon it a death wound by his arrows or otherwise. The true medicine man still abides by this law. Entire secrecy is imperative in this organization. If revelation is made of its primal important secrets the penalty is swift and certain.

Precautionary measures in relation to cleansing and purifying the body are rigidly observed before participating in its conventions or singing for the benefit of the sick. The indulgence in any sensual appetite destroys the "charm" or efficacy of the medicine. The sacred song is usually recited by one chanter who visits the different tribal medicine bands of the nation. The gentle old chief who officiated at my initiation has been the national chanter of the Iroquois League for 47 years. If the song is repeated by any one without the knowledge of the chanter, it is expected that evil results will follow.

When "called" to administer to a wounded or ill person, it may happen that the patient fails to receive full recovery by one visit of the society. In this case, as the "medicine" does not solicit patients, it must be called again a second time and given a feast, when the patient will be restored to health, if it is the will of the Great Spirit, who is always asked to guide the red man and choose for his best always.

THE SENECA MEDICINE LODGE

MRS. CONVERSE'S STORY OF HER INITIATION[111]

"Twenty-four hours before the berry moon first hangs her horn in the night sky." This, the traditional call I understood when I received it from the New York State Iroquois Ne-gar-na-gar-ah.

A day's journey by rail, 48 hours before the first quarter of the June moon, brought me to the appointed place, the comfortable farmhouse of an Iroquois chief.

No person except a member of the society can touch any article that is to serve in its ceremonies. After the room, in which the society is to meet is prepared, no person except a member is permitted to enter and a watcher is stationed at each window and door. At least one representative of each of the clans must be present to form a quorum. These clans, the Wolf, Bear, Beaver, Turtle, Deer, Snipe, Heron and Hawk and others which include all the animal and bird inhabitants common at one time to all latitudes between southern Canada and Louisiana, represented the procession that accompanied the chief in his night journey to discover the secret of the Ne-gar-na-gar-ah.

At certain "stages" in the ceremony the representatives are required to give the voice sign of their clan bird or animal, thus signifying that it has entered the room.

Although the Bear, Wolf, Hawk, and Eagle were prominent in restoring the chief to life, as he proceeded on his journey all the nightfolk of the forest joined him. So, in the celebration of the mysteries of the Ne-gar-na-gar-ah, all these clans join the procession. The song chanted relates the story of the night travel, each stanza announcing the arrival of some bird or beast.

The ceremony, which begins at 9 p. m. in winter and 10 p. m. in summer, continues all night. The feast is served before dawn, and the members depart before the sun rises. The song is chanted three times during the year, June, September and January. On these occasions a feast is given. The spring and fall conventions are held for the benefit of the sick. If at any time a member should, by dreams or otherwise, have a premonition of danger coming to him he can order a "special" meeting.

Preparations

Before dawn of the appointed day my host, the Iroquois chief, had brought from the forest a few hemlock logs, which he deposits in an unoccupied outshed and bars the door. He also spreads leaves of Indian tobacco yet wet with dew under the stove in the summer-cooking room.

The provisions for the feast consist of a few quarts of freshly gathered wild strawberries, sugar to sweeten the "strawberry water," a hog's head and a few dozen ears of flint corn.

When these are put in place, the night has come with its starless darkness, the members are assembling, the hemlock logs are kindled to a blazing fire under a great iron kettle and the hog's head and hulled corn begin boiling. This, the feast, is superintended by an aged matron, wife of the chanter. I offer to assist and am stirring the soup with a large ladle when a chief summons me to the ceremony and I follow him. In the room, the common winter living apartment of the chief's household, about 20 feet square, the members are seated close to the wall on benches arranged in a hollow square; in the center are a large stove and a table; on the latter are a large pail and a dipper for the strawberry water, a lot of small parcels, some carefully wrapped in cloth, others in strips of birch and elm bark, a dozen gourd rattles, two quaint looking flutes and a small oil lamp that renders the corner shadows darker and more weird by its flickering.

I stand at the door unnoticed. Were it not for my knowledge of the customs of the red men I would retreat.

I know by their mute language that they are discussing me.

I know that they will give me a sign by which I do finally enter the room and take the seat appointed me in the northeast corner.

The initiation

The venerable chief walks to the table, takes a box and passes it to all. It is the sacred or incense tobacco of which each member receives a small pipe portion. He offers me a new clay pipe and lights the sacred tobacco with the punk kindled by the flint fire and whispers to me, "Smoke, sister, smoke!"

As I receive the pipe he awaits for my assent. I make a sign motion with the pipe, and, raising it to my lips, with one inhalation promise and declare loyalty forever to the silences of the Ne-gar-na-gar-ah.

After my vow the pipe of each in the room, including those of four elderly women, is lighted by the chief, who carries the burning punk in his hand; thus performing the rite of "community of friendship."

During the smoking the legend of the Ne-gar-na-gar-ah is related to me by a chief of the Wolf Clan and interpreted by my host who sits by my side.

After a wait of a few minutes the lamp is blown out and all is darkness. I sit near the window, but I can not see the lowest branch of the apple tree, which, blown by the wind, is scratching the panes with a ghostly touch. The hush is heavy and stifling. Can there be around me twenty-five people in this dark stillness? I clasp my hands together with a pinching clutch, and recall the injunction of my host to "continually remember the legend of the chief's journey."

I remember then that this darkness must symbolize the awful night that came upon him.

Sure that the "winged" light will float into the room from some place, I wink my eyes wider open, and at last see a faint light where the table stands. Yes, the light that comes and goes is clearly defined. I know that there is nothing supernatural in the ceremonies of the Ne-gar-na-gar-ah but I still sit and wonder.

My host whispers: "Watch, they have uncovered the medicine."

I comprehend. I had been told that the Ne-gar-na-gar-ah, possessed of certain phosphorescent elements, would emit a luminous glow when first exposed to the air and darkness. At the same instant a small blaze glows from the top of the stove. By this brighter and stronger light the medicine light fades away. Outlined in the darkness I see the venerable chanter standing by the stove. He is throwing the sacred tobacco on the blaze and in a low voice is saying: "Oh thou, the Great Spirit, the giver of the darkness and repose, we thank thee for all the silences of the night." This invocation is followed by an offering of gratitude, also numerous petitions for the preservation of the medicine, the quick recovery of any to whom it may be administered, and the spiritual and temporal welfare of each member of the society. He also asks of each life that may be preparing to fly unasked from some human body to

A Mohawk Medicine Woman

remain a while longer and not go until the Great Spirit is ready and invites it. At the end of each sentence he rests and throws tobacco on the flame until the little blaze has expired and the darkness is again in the room. Then the chief in the invitation rite requests all the night folk of the forest, including those who run under the ground, to protect us on our journey to the morning. The chanter then recites a weird melody;

The darkness song

Ha go wa nah u na
Ha go way nah u na ha ha ha go way
Ha una ha na ha ah,
Ha go way,
Na sa ha nee ga ha do wayhe ah
Ha u na ha ah ha go way!
We wait in the darkness!
Come, all ye who listen,
Help in our night journey:
Now no sun is shining;
Now no star is glowing;
Come show us the pathway:
The night is not friendly;
She closes her eyelids;
The moon has forgot us,
We wait in the darkness!

There is a short pause, the chiefs take their rattles, and the invitation song begins, the chanter singing alone, the chiefs softly shaking their rattles in rhythm with his voice, and the members of the clans in turn responding to the "invitations" by imitating the call or cry of their animal totem.

Preceding this song the cry of the whip-poor-will, the bird protector that guided the chief on his journey, is wondrously imitated by the flute player.

As literally as possible I translate:

The invitation song

Ha wa ga na hoe
Ha wa gah nae
Na ho oh ha na
Ga na ho hi-e-e-e-e-eh!

So says the whip-poor-will
Follow me, follow me!
So says the chief to him,
Yes I will follow thee!

See the night darkening;
The shadows are hiding,
No light to follow for.
So says the waterfall,
So sings the river voice!

Someone is nearing me.
Soft he comes creeping here,
Two eyes glare close to me.
Lighting the forest path—
Hear how his breath blows by!

Fol-low me, fol-low me,—
So sings the whip-poor-will!
Yes I am following,—
So the chief answers him.

Cries announce that the Wolf and his mate have entered the room.

Here there is a rest interval; the lamp is lighted, the

sweet strawberry water is passed, pipes are smoked and the conversation is carried on in whispers for about 20 minutes; afterward again the darkness and the song continue:

> Hark, the trees bending low,
> Something is breaking them,
> Not the strong north wind's hand,
> Something stalks broad and swift,
> Snuffing and panting loud!
>
> Hark! How the tangles break!
> Fearless the footfalls pass,
> Strong trees stretch far apart.
> Great horns dividing them.
> (Whip-poor-will chorus)

The Buck and Doe, with cries enter the room; another rest interval, with smoking and drinking.

The song continues:

> How the cold shivers me!
> No snow is falling now,
> Where does the sun's fire hide?
> Something comes roaring loud
> Swift footed warning me!
>
> Its breath blinds the night eyes.
> Like rainy vapor falls!
> Now it walks close to me,
> Warming and coaxing me.
> Where the black forest frowns.
> (Whip-poor-will chorus)

The Bear and his mate have come and after a rest interval the song goes on:

How the wind travels now,
No one dares run with it.
Great trees bend low to it.
Rivers fight back to it,
Roaring and splashing it!

Hear its wings flapping strong
Far in the hidden skies!
Swift it flies northward high,
Whistling and calling loud.
Hunting its running prey!

The Hawk and its mate are announced. Although these four attendants mentioned in the journey legend are the royal guests of the society, yet the song continues with its intervals of rest until all the forest folk announce their arrival.

There are also rites that symbolize the dangers of the forest tangles and swampy horrors. Through these I am taken, yet guided by the whip-poor-will return safely to my seat. By the legend the Eagle must dismiss the meeting. His coming which is imitated on the small flute announces the day. The cold gray light of dawn steals into the room as this, the final stanza, in the chorus which we all join, is chanted:

The Eagle Song

Deep the dew water falls
No one comes close to me!
Where are you whip-poor-will?
Why am I waiting now
Calling your voice again?

Screaming the night away.
With his great wing feathers
Swooping the darkness up;
I hear the Eagle bird
Pulling the blanket back
Off from the eastern sky!

How swift he flies bearing the sun to the morning.
See how he sits down in the trails of the east sky!
Whip-poor-will, Whip-poor-will, no more I follow thee!
When the night comes again, wilt thou say "Follow me"?

The singing ends and the matrons bring in the kettles of soup and distribute it to all.

A few words in which I thank my Indian friends for consenting that I may hereafter "sit" with them and their friendly replies fill the moments that are swiftly bringing the day. It is the law that the sun shall not see us separate.

As I stand in the farmhouse door and hear the rumble of wheels grow faint and fainter, the sun casts a foreglow of its coming in the east sky, and the night seems a dream and it is difficult to realize that it has made me a member of the most ancient order of North American Indians.

APPENDIX A

ESQUIRE JOHNSON'S ACCOUNT OF THE ORIGIN OF GOOD AND EVIL AS IT WAS TOLD HIM BY THE OLD MEN[112]

The old times among the Non-do-wat-gaah

Dated, Oct. 25, 1875

When there was yet no land, but all was one extensive lake there were multitudes of ducks and geese, one, Gwi-yuh-gee, looked up and saw something dark in the sky above them, and called out to the rest that something was coming down to the earth. He immediately called a council of the waterfowls as to what they should do for a place for the being, whoever she might be, to rest upon. One duck offered to dive to see if there might be some bottom to their lake which might be brought up for that purpose. After some time she came up but was dead, the struggle having been too great for her strength. She shot up into the air and dropped back lifeless to the surface of the water.[113] Several others made the attempt with like results until at last a muskrat made the attempt in a like manner and came up dead but with a little earth in his claw which when the others saw they commenced their efforts anew and many were successful in bringing up a small quantity which they placed, at the suggestion of their chief, on the back of an immense turtle who was willing to become the foundation of an island for them.

At length the dark object which was all this time becoming plainer to their vision, reached their view, reached the island and was found to be a woman with child. The waterfowls received her and provided for her wants, feeding her with crabs and other small fish to keep her alive. When the woman was taken in labor, they discovered that there were twins and that they were already endowed with the gift of speech, and were heard to converse together. One declared that he thought he saw a light under his mother's arm, which he thought must be the way of egress into the world. The other said no, that he felt attracted in the opposite direction. But one at last burst through his mother's side which caused her death immediately, while the other was born the natural way. The last born was God, the first was the Devil.

God immediately said, "I will take my mother's face and make the sun, and her bright and beautiful eyes shall give light to the whole world. Of her body and limbs I will make the moon to give light by night on the earth" and the light of day was there established and also the light of the moon at night. Then began to grow upon the earth grass and flowers and trees and grains and vegetables for food for men and animals.

After some time God met his brother the Devil on the shore of the island and having discovered that he was intent on spoiling everything he made, he rebuked him sharply and told him he must stop doing mischief and not spoil his work any more. The Devil answered that he had a right to control things as well as he, that he could make wise things too. God said, "Well, try

278

then now, and let me see if you can make a dish which will be useful." The Devil went to work and did it very well but when he put water in it it fell to pieces and was useless. God then took the sand on the shore and formed a dish and took it and dipped water and set it down and it was whole and useful.

APPENDIX B

THE STONE GIANTS[114]

As God was walking about on earth and taking care of the things he had made, he met a company of people whom he accosted in a friendly way and asked them who was their master and where they were going and what was their business. They said that they were independent and that they were going to find some people who lived over that way and were going to kill them and eat them. God told them that they had better not go, that they might get killed themselves, but they persisted in going on. As soon as they were out of sight he took some coal and blackened his face and took a long circuit and ran with great speed to a place where he thought he could intercept them. He broke down an oh-so-ah tree and carried it for a club. When he met them he gave them battle and killed all but two, who ran away. God took the same path back to where he met them and having washed off the crock from his face he stood waiting their approach. He said, "Well, what luck did you have?" They said, "We are all dead but us two." "That's what I told you," he said. The people were clothed in garments of stone and were called Ga-nos-gwah.

APPENDIX C

THE DE-O-HA-KO[115]

Spirits of the Corn, Beans and Squash

These plants are considered special gifts from the Great Spirit to the red man, and the welfare of each is intrusted to an individual guardian, one of the three spirit sisters, daughters of the Earth, the "Great Mother" of the Iroquois. The beans, corn and squash were, in the "old time," planted together in one hill and it was therefore consistent that their protectors should dwell in peaceful community. These chaste maidens are possessed of great beauty and unswerving fidelity. Ever watchful in their guardianship, clothed in the leaves of their respective plants and friendly with the dews, at nightfall in the growing time they solicit their moisture to refresh and invigorate the fields over which they preside, protecting them from blight and the infection of creatures that might corrupt the ripening. These gentle defenders have no individual names and are known only as the De-o-ha-ko.

There is a legend that the corn once grew spontaneously and abundant and that its grain was heavy with rich oil, but the "Evil Minded," envious of the goodness of the Great Spirit in this gift to his people and having a limited power to destroy, one night detained the Spirit of the Corn while he sent forth one of his emissaries who cast a blight over the corn. From that time the result has been apparent, the corn yielding less abundant and being more difficult to cultivate. Since this fatal blight and captivity, the Spirit of the Corn has been compelled to hold her vigils alone in the fields where the corn now grows, separated from its sister plants. In her loneliness she dare not leave her charge to seek the dews, hence the droughts; but the pitying dews frequently visit her, refreshing the fields and comforting her in her solitude.

In the winds that moan through the rustling corn leaves, the red man hears the voice of the Spirit of the Corn who, in her love for him, bewails her blighted fruitfulness.

The conception of He-no, Ga-oh, and the De-o-ha-ko is, to a degree, similar to that of Jupiter, Aeolis, and Ceres of the Greeks; yet the red man, believing these myth guardians of nature to be subject to the one Supreme Ruler, the creator of man and the source of all good, reached a more definite conclusion respecting the existence of a Deity and entitled him to a supreme religion of purity and dignity.

APPENDIX D

THE LEGENDARY ORIGIN OF WAMPUM[116]

Among Mrs. Converse's correspondence I find the following letter from General Parker. It is evidently a reply to one of her inquiries. EDITOR

New York, July 9, 1885

Yours of the 8th received. There are several legendary tales concerning wampum floating confusedly through my brain, and belonging to various Indian tribes, but you desire the Iroquois general legend. I use the word *general* because each tribe has tales of its own varying from the general one, related in rehearsing the origin of the great league. It is very simple and is told as follows.

Hy-ent-wat-ha, an Onondaga, failing to enlist To-do-do-ha, also Onondaga, as an associate to perfect the league left the council fire, which had been evoked by his persuasions, and journeyed toward the rising sun and thus journeying he came to a beautiful lake (supposed to be the Oneida) which he was compelled to cross in a canoe. In passing over the lake he noticed that the blades of his paddles brought up from the bottom quantities of white and purple shells. Upon landing, he further observed that the shores were lined with a great abundance of them. I am not conchologist enough to designate what species of mollusks these shells belonged to but they were gasteropodous.

Hy-ent-wat-ha, being a wise man, at once bethought him how to use these shells to advantage. So he gathered

282

a large quantity, filling his traveling pouches, and in the occasional rests of his journeyings he made a belt out of the shells representing a pictorial history of the league. The foundation of the belt was white and the pictorials purple. There stood the five cantons and the five brothers in front with joined hands in token of brotherly union. He also made a large number of strings, each string representing some law or fundamental principle of the league. Before reaching the country of the Mohawks, the keepers of the western door at Albany, he had every idea and principle of the league perfectly formulated in these belts and strings. Thus he reached the Mohawk country armed, we may say, cap-a-pie with every idea, principle and ceremony required for a perfect league of wild, untutored Indian tribes. Reaching a Mohawk village, or cantonment, he camped on the outskirts thereof. He was discovered and noted as a stranger, and though informally invited by individual Indians to partake of their hospitality, he silently and invariably declined. His strange conduct was observed. It was surmised that he was queer though harmless.[117] He was noticed to be always talking about something, and constantly handling belts and strings made of curious white and purple shells. The head men of the village ordered strict watch to be kept over his every movement, and every word he uttered to be carefully and strictly noted, so that it might be determined what kind of a man he was. It was ascertained that these belts and strings of shells related to some sort of a league, its principles, its laws and ceremonial observances, also that with certain belts and strings he had formulated a tribal, or international code of etiquette, a conventional decorum to be observed towards each other or their representatives.

All this being duly and fully reported to the head man or patriarch of the village, he properly apprehended that the stranger was no ordinary person, and determined to invite and receive him as his guest, and being already informed as to the observance required to invite and receive distinguished guests, he sent a special messenger to the stranger asking him for the loan of certain of his shell belts and strings. Having obtained them, with all the exacted observances, he formally invited and received the stranger into his lodge. He gave him the place of honor, seating him upon a throne of skins, similar to his own. He informed the stranger that he was to be his brother, that they were to have equal rights to everything in the lodge and that equal respect should be paid by the people to both, and that they should jointly govern the people.

This much pleased Hy-ent-wat-ha and he accepted the proffered contract in the same spirit, which to him seemed to govern the tender. But to the extreme mortification of Hy-ent-wat-ha no inquiry was made of him as to whom he might be, who his people were and where and on what mission he was bent. He complained to his brother of this neglect and told him it was his (the brother's) duty to send out runners to look for the smoke arising from the camp fires of his people and finding them to go in and ascertain the news. The brother (he is called brother, for he is yet not named) apologized for his stupid neglect and at once sent a deputation westward in search of the home of Hy-ent-wat-ha and his people.

For a while things went smoothly with Hy-ent-wat-ha. The compact announced by the brother was strictly and faithfully kept, but after a time and while the delegation was yet absent, a party of some special friends came to visit the brother. Sitting room to accommodate all the party was scarce, but some room could be made if Hy-ent-wat-ha would give up his place. Accordingly the brother asked him to vacate his place in front and take a place behind him. This of course was a breach of the compact though unwittingly committed. Hence, as soon as Hy-ent-wat-ha could gather his personal effects, he left the lodge and reoccupied his abandoned camp, on the outskirts of the village. The brother sent to know the cause of this abandonment and on being told, made the most ample apologies and Hy-ent-wat-ha returned to the lodge. The compact was never again broken and they remained brothers indeed.

The prospecting deputation now returned and reported that on journeying westward they had perceived a column of smoke rising from the earth till its head seemed to pierce the heavens. They had proceeded to its base and there found a large concourse of people, who announced that they had been called together by a great and wise man who had mysteriously disappeared and they were waiting for his return to tell them what they should do. That they were ruled by a wicked monster in the form of a man, whose name was To-do-do-ha, whose hair was a tangled mass of hissing serpents. Whenever this human monster turned his gaze upon others, they were invariably turned into stone. All of the people, including the snaky monster, were anxious for the return of the man who was last seen making his way eastward.

Hy-ent-wat-ha then explained that it was he who had called the people together for the purpose of organizing the Indians into one great family and establishing a perpetual peace among them; that the snaky headed chief had objected because he would be shorn of his great influence and demoniac powers. But that as the council fire which he had kindled, from the red willow was still burning, it was plainly his duty to return and complete his task. But he could not do it alone. He must have help and his brother must be the helper. He therefore named him Da-ga-ee-oga meaning *the word between,* implying a speaker. That is, Hy-ent-wat-ha was to do the work and his brother the necessary speaking and talking. At the same time Hy-ent-wat-ha instructed his brother in all the ceremonials and language of the belts and the strings.

The shells have since been called wampums. Hy-ent-wat-ha made the white shells emblematic of peace and the purple of mourning and war. The two colors combined were used in recording their laws and councils. It may be said that Hy-ent-wat-ha consecrated the little shells to certain specific uses which the Indians generally have observed ever since.

[Signed] Do-ne-ha-ga-wa

The Wolf

286

ENDNOTES

[1]Although Ely S, Parker possessed a great store of information relating to his people, the Iroquois, his busy life as an army officer and engineer gave him little time to record in Srint much of his knowledge. He seemed better able to inspire others to study and write, Morgan's League of the Iroquois contains some of his essays and indeed Morgan acknowledges Parker as his collaborator. If Morgan is the "father of American anthropology" Parker gave him the inspiration. It is not strange, therefore, that he imparted to Mrs. Converse the impetus for her researches.

[2]The manuscript as found among Mrs. Converse's papers embraced but 22 legends. From her rough notes the editor has added 14 other myths and folk tales besides a number of miscellaneous papers.

[3]See Appendix A, p. 277.

[4]Ata'-en'-sic. This is the Huron name for the first mother, and not that of the (confederated) Iroquois. The Senecas usually give this character no name other than Ea-gen'-tci, literally *old woman* or *ancient bodied*. This name is not a personal one, however. Mrs. Converse has therefore substituted the Huronian personal name for the Iroquoian common name.

[5]Hah-nu-nah. The mystic name of the turtle. This name is used in the lodge ceremonies of the Little Water Company. The ordinary name for the turtle is Ha'-no'-wa.

⁶The term Great Spirit is not Iroquoian but Algonquian and a literal interpretation of their word, *Tchi Manitou*. The Iroquois equivalent would be Notwais'ha-gowane, (Spirit Great), a term never associated with the idea of the Supreme Deity. Morgan used the term Great Spirit in the League of the Iroquois but probably because it was the popular name with white men. The idea of a Supreme Being was not a well developed one until the advent of white missionaries.

The present religious system of the Iroquois requires that The Maker be addressed as Ho-dia-nok'-da Hed'-io-he, Our Creator. This custom was inaugurated by Ga-nio'-dai'-io', the Seneca prophet, and is found in section 49 of the Gai'-wi-io' code. The Blue Sky translation which the writer has at hand reads as follows:

So now another one I will tell you.

There is a controversy in the upper world. Two beings are disputing over you-the children of earth. Two beings are disputing. One is the Great Ruler and the other is the Cave Dweller. And you who know only of the earth know nothing of the discussion.

So now the Evil One said, "I am the ruler of the earth because when I command I speak but once and men obey."

Now Haweni'io said this to the Evil One, "The earth is mine for I have created it and men and you did no part of it."

The Evil One answered, "I do acknowledge that you have created all but I say men beings obey me and do not obey you."

Now Haweni'io said to the Evil One, " The children (at least) are mine for they have done no wrong."

So answered the Evil One, "Now I tell you the children are mine for when I say 'Pick up a stick and smite your playfellow.' they do. Aye, the children are mine."

Then Haweni'io said, "I will send my messengers once more to tell how I feel. In that way I will claim my own."

288

The Evil One replied, "Even so it will not be long before they forget and transgress the law of the prophecy. And this I will say, one word, and they will do what I say. It is true that I delight in the name, Ha-nis′se-o-no. It is true that who speaks of me, though on the other side of the earth, will find me at his back."

Then spoke Haweni′io and said to men beings. "Now you must not say Haweni′io, Ruler, because the Evil One calls himself Ruler. And whoever is mine must say, Ho-dia-nok′-da Hed′-io-he, Our Creator, and when you speak of the Evil One, say Se-go-ie-wat′-ha, Tor-mentor, for then he knows that you are aware that he is the punisher of evil souls that leave the earth."

So now they (the messengers) said it and he (Ga-nio′-dai′-io′) said it. Nia′-ie-huk (So it was).

⁷The central tree in the heaven world was the apple. This tree figures in all the various Iroquois cosmogonic myths. Later in the center of the lower world the Good Mind created another tree, the tree of light.

⁸The light was made by the Fire Beast, Ga-ha-shein-dye-tha.

⁹The belief that the earth is supported by a gigantic turtle is one that is shared by many races. In the ancient myths of the Hindoos, for example, the earth is described as resting on the back of four elephants which stand upon the back of an enormous turtle. In Iroquoian ceremonies the turtle symbol plays an important part.

¹⁰In this version the twin boys are made the firstborn. The full versions always relate the birth of a daughter who becomes impregnated by the wind and gives birth to the twins, dies upon their birth and leaves them to the care of the Sky Woman, the heaven mother.

¹¹The idea of moral dualism is found more or less developed in the beliefs of most primitive races. Probably in its most primitive form the idea is not

of a moral dualism but the idea of the conflict of constructive and destructive forces. Evolving either naturally or changed by contact with civilized peoples, the dualism of warring powers took upon itself the dualism of the moral forces. The modern cosmologic myth names the two spirits, the Good and the Evil, but when Father Broebeuf visited the Hurons in 1636 he found them named Iosk-eha, the *White One* and Tawiscara, the *Dark One.*

The Wyandot names are, Tseh-seh-howh-hooh-nyk, Man Made of Fire, and Ta-weh-skah-sooh-nyk, Made of Flint.

The idea of the Light God and the Dark God is a mgst significant one and leads to fields of fruitful research. The idea is fundamentally that of light and day, and darkness and night: day with its sun light and activity and night with its blackness and unseen terrors. This underlying idea has influenced the dualistic theology of all nations. The Egyptian god Osiris is the Sun God, and Seti his brother the God of Darkness. In the Zend-Avesta, in the conflict of Light and Darkness, Ahura-Mazda and Anra-Mainyn, are the good and evil spirits, Ormuzd and Ahriman, and in modern Christianity where the Spirit of Light is in conflict with the Prince of Darkness.

12The Senecas still honor the Sun, En-de-kă Dä'-kwă, in a sun dance and call the ceremony En-de-kă Dä'-kwă Da-non-di-non-io (sun thanksgiving). The ceremony has no certain time but is called by any one who dreams that it is necessary for the welfare of the settlement. The dance begins at noon, when arrows are shot up at the sun while the people give their war cries, for the sun loves the sound and symbols of battle. The rite takes place in open air and begins with the chant of the sun song holder who casts tobacco into a fire. Twice again showers of arrows are shot as offerings to the sun when the great feather dance is performed in honor of Endeka Dakwa.

The moon is likewise honored by the Senecas in the ceremony of the Soi-ka-dä-kwa Don-di-nion-nio, *moon thanksgiving*. The ceremony is called by any one who may be commanded by a dream to do so, or may be ordered through the advice of a *diviner*, teller of the future and of necessities. In the moon ceremony the holder of the moon song recites his thanksgiving ritual and casts the sacred tobacco upon the flames of the ceremonial fire. The moon is "amused" by the game of peach stones, though' anciently deer bone buttons were used. The ceremony takes place after sunset and lasts until midnight when a feast is distributed to terminate the rite.

[13]Darkness, called either So-son'-do-wa, *great darkness*, or De-io-da-son-dai-kon, *thick night*.

[14]In the writer's version the Good Mind (Light One) was bidden by his father "to the East" and when he found him, to ask for power. The father was found in the top of a high mountain in the east ocean and appeared in a blinding glare of light. The Light One was ordered to prove himself a son, commanded to cast skyward great rocks, withstand winds, floods and

flames. He triumphed in the ordeal and his father gave him power over the four elements. This is nothing less than a sun myth, the sun being the father of light.

[15]The pit is the underworld and is called the "cave."

[16]The first beings of earth were a race of gods who returned to the sky world when the Good Mind created men-beings. This creation was accomplished as follows; After the Good Mind had pulled up the tree of light he beheld his face in the pool of water in which it had grown. This gave him the idea of molding images in red clay which he afterward transformed into living beings. Thus did the human race take origin. The idea of creation "in his own image" is not necessarily of biblical origin. It is a primitive idea and one that might be developed independently by widely separated peoples.

[17]Ga-oh is the name of the wind spirit according to Morgan. The name for wind, however, is Ga-hä (Seneca). The whirlwind is called Sha-go-dio-weñ'-go-wa, *he defends them*. This is also the name of one of the False Faces.

[18]Ga-oh dwells in the west sky according to the researches of the writer, agreeing with Morgan who names the western sky as the abode of the wind spirit and calls his dwelling Da-yo-da-do-go-wa. Ga-oh is not an evil being, howsoever his four winds may rage, but on the contrary, solicitous for the welfare of men and ever obedient to the commands of the Creator.

[19]The American Indians of both continents personified the four winds and the allusions to the wind spirits in their mythology are strong and beautiful. The

four winds are usually regarded as the spirits of the four cardinal points, or the four corners of the earth. The subsequent development of a simple myth has often obscured the original meaning but in the wind myths the inferences are so strong that the winds as the four characters are not long hidden to the careful student.

The Algonquins and Sioux trace their origin to four ancestors which inquiry reveals to be the four winds. In Iroquois mythology the daughter of the sky woman in some versions is said to have been "wrapped around" with a wind by whom she became the mother of twin boys. The Creeks are more specific and say that they sprang from four beings who came from the four comers of the world and built a sacred fire where they met. In many of the American languages the names for the four directions are the names for the winds of these directions also. The Sioux call the four quarters of the globe, ta-te-onye-toba, which literally means, *whence four winds come*. Among the Mayas the names for the cardinal points are the names for the winds. Invocation to the winds has been a common practice among all nations. The Aztecs prayed to Tlalocs, the god of showers: "Ye who dwell at the four corners of the earth, at the north, at the south, at the east, at the west [Sahagun. Hist. de la Neuva Espanas, p. 375] The Eskimos invoked Sillam Innua, the owner of the winds, and believed that his abode was the haven of departed souls. Thus in sickness they prayed to the four winds to summon a new soul for the afflicted person, and called each wind by name, Pauna (east), Sauna (west), Auna (north), Kauna (south) [Egends. Nachrichten von Grönland]. One of the most beautiful invocations of the Iroquois is the wind song sung by the priest of the Gai'wiio' as he stands at the northeast corner of the Long House and sings the wind song to greet the rising sun.

Some of these references will be found in Brinton's *Myths of the New World.* Kirkland relates that the Tuscaroras told him that in their religion were four "little gods." In the east was Tyogetaet, *rising up* or *making his appearance,* (sunrise or dawn): in the west was Yucataghphki, *twilight;* in the north was Jothoel, *somewhat cold;* in the south, Unte.

Invocation of the winds by Aryan and Semitic races was a common thing, nor are instances lacking in the sacred scriptures, see Ezekiel 37:9 and Revelations 7:1.

[20] Naturally one of the most universal myths is that relating to the spirit of thunder. Many regarded the Thunderer as the great heaven deity and although subsequently the thunder or rain god became the servant or subordinate of the greater god, he was yet feared and propitiated. Thus, the rain or water god of the Aztecs, Tlaloc, who holds the thunder and lightning, to the primitive mind emblems of power, was once the great heaven god of the Nahuatl people.

[21] Hi' '-no, Spirit of the Thunder, hates all mysteries, he despises monsters, unclean beasts and witches. He pursues with relentless fury the myth monsters and strikes them dead with his thunder fire whenever they appear. He hates the creations of witches, such as images made living and witch transformations. The

great horned serpents, the saistah-gowa jodi''hgwadoh, and the underwater people fear him and often when they attempt to visit the earth world they are discovered by the vigilant storm clouds who immediately report their movements to Hi''-no. He hates the False Faces and all manner of sorcery. He must not be spoken lightly of or trified with but frequently soothed by offerings of tobacco incense, for he loves oyankwa-oweh, the sacred incense.

Hi''-no called the Iroquois his grandchildren and they, in the thunder dance, in his honor, affectionately call him, Tisote, *grandfather*. Likewise he said the "medicine people are my people" and the Little Water Company always offer him tobacco and implore his favor.

The Senecas hold a special ceremony called We-să'-ze every spring in honor of the Thunderer. The sound of the first thunder rumble is the sign of his first awakening and the call for the dance. A thanksgiving speech, Don-di-nion'-nioh, is recited and at its close the warriors start the war dance and dance into the Long House where the ceremony is concluded.

[22]The thunder spirit has also a large family of noisy thunder boys. Every storm cloud is moreover a scout whose duty is to spy out the otgont (magically malicious) forces, such as the creations of the evil mind, witches, the underground buffalo and the like.

[23]Among the Iroquois there are several beliefs connected with lightning. Two notes from the editor's collection may be found of interest.

The thunder medicine. One of the most potent charms of the medicine men is alleged to have been the foam that is said to ooze from the roots of a tree immediately after it has been struck by lightning. This foam is scooped up by the medicine man who quickly transfers it to his mystery pouch. This mystic medicine is the magical gift of Hi''-no and is reputed a wonderful cure for extreme cases or as a final resort.

Lightning struck trees. When his gleaming missile has crashed into a tree, no man must with his naked skin touch the punished wood, for some of the ragged fire that has splintered it may yet linger to blister the offender and cause an irritating rash to break out over his body. Nor must the wood be burned for the smoke will anger Hi''-no who in his fury will burst a black cloud over the offensive flames to destroy the unsavory incense. Even then his anger may not subside but he may send great rains over the land to remind men that his wishes must not be lightly held.

24The following account of Hi''-no, as told by Esquire Johnson, an old Seneca chief, will be found of interest: Sometime afterward God met a man walking about by himself and addressing him in a pleasant way, asked him what he was looking for. He said he was amusing himself looking around the world, that he had a great many grandchildren not far off, that he was in fact the Thunderer and had many grandchildren near and loved them much. Moreover, that he wished to be set about some great work and asked God to give him something to do. God said to him, "What can you do?" He said, "I can wash the world if you want me to." "Very well," said God, "that would be a good work for you to do and I will employ you to do that work for me. You can make it rain and wash the earth often." (Taken verbatim from the manuscript notes of Mrs. Asher Wright, a misionary who interviewed Johnson in 1876.)

25 Orphans and neglected children in Iroquoian folklore were commonly adopted by the nature spirits who taught them mysteries and ceremonies. In Iroquois mythology there are several stories of the adoptions by Hi''-no.

26 The black clouds are thunder spies.

27 The serpent is one of the-sais'-to-wä-ne of the Senecas or O'-nia'-hri-ko'-wa of the Mohawks. These creatures are divided into two tribes, the Oñ-gwi'-ias and the Jo-di''-kwa-do'. Both are "underwater" people but the Oñ-gwi'-ias are evil men-devouring creatures while the Jo-di''-kwa-do' are not necessarily malicious for they sometimes help the distressed who may be lost on lone islands or those cast by treachery into the water to drown. Both tribes however are great sorcerers and therefore hated by Hi''-no who pursues them whenever they appear in daylight above the water. There are several tales telling how the underwater people coaxed boys and girls away from the land and cast upon them the spell by which they were adopted. They are human in form but assume the form of homed serpents by dressing in snake skin garments. They have houses beneath the waters and there appear as ordinary men. Their daughters are especially beautiful and captured

landmen at once become enamored with them and are quite willing to don the shining suits (snake skins) and big feathers (horns) which make them forever Jo-di''-kwa-do'.

[28]Should be Os-hă-dă-ge-a'.

[29]The Sun, according to a myth in the writer's collection, is the chief messenger of the Creator. It is his duty to observe all the activities of men and nature and report them to his superior. "He is the eye of the Creator," said Soson'dowa who related the tale. The sun is especially the patron spirit of war and lingers as he watches the conflict. Thus days of battle are longer. Each morning he emerges from under the sky dome (horizon) where its rim touches the far east sea. The east wind blows as he mounts the sky path, though "maybe it is the wind of the bowl when it is lifted." When Endē'ka Da'kwa descends on the west water, the bowl lifts again for the fraction of a moment and he shoots under and leaves the world to Night. The raising of the sky dome twice each day makes the tides of the ocean "but they don't come even now days" remarks the myth teller.

[30]In some respects the Dew Eagle has its counterpart in the Thunder Bird of the Dakotas and Algonquins. In the instances of the Dew Eagle and the Thunderer we have examples of the complex character of the Iroquoian mythology. The Eagle (Thunder Bird) has been stripped of the thunder power with which the other races endowed him. Hi''no has taken the thunder and rain-making office but the Eagle is made the dew maker and labors faithfully when Hi''no fails to come.

There is a legend that an enormous white eagle will come from the east ocean and battle with the Dew Eagle until he dies. Then will the Oñgweh′owe no longer have woods and fields, but dry desert places where they will starve. The Indians' Dew Eaprle has probably been dead for some time.

31This is a variation from the writer's version of the myth which makes Ga-sho-deē′to, not De′-on-iot, the Soul Gatherer. Rather is he the herald of disaster. An extract from my manuscript notes may be of service in giving an idea of the myth. "And did no warning sign appear?" asked Ohoosta. "Yes, but we did not know it was an omen until too late. Then we remembered a blue (sky colored) panther floating high over the trees. He had no face but from his tail shot flames of fire." (A comet). "So now then you will remember to offer (throw) tobacco upon a fire," said Ohoosta. "Tobacco incense is a sign that death and trouble are not wanted and when he has breathed it Ga-sho-deē′to will go away and turn aside the danger."

32The milk way.

33Son-do-wĕk′-o-wă is the angel of death.

34Another version states that the dancing party consisted of eleven young men and boys, the oldest of which was chosen the chief. They were training for battles which the future should bring and requested the parents to furnish them food to eat during their period of training. The request was refused several times. The chief kept up their spirits by singing and beating the water drum whose ringing rhythm charmed their feet to the war dance. Their spirits were high when they finished their dance and they again implored their several parents for food. The chief was angry when it was refused, and grasping the wet drum again said: "We will dance ourselves away from earth and leave it forever." He sang the Ji'-ha-ya (the witch) song and roused the dancers to high enthusiasm, bade them dance and look upward and listen to no plea that might be wailed up through the trees. Thus they danced up to the sky, all unheeding of the cries of terror and distress from below, save one who looked down and fell.

35Only seven of the brothers are now commonly visible because some are very small and dance behind the rest. On very clear nights those with good eyes can see the others.

36The myth setting forth the origin of the pine is a part of the Pleiades (Dancing Stars) myth, though of a version a little different in some parts from the one recorded by Mrs. Converse. The legend relates that the chief of the skyward dancing party hearing the cries of his mother looked down. His act was a fatal one for he immediately fell like a stone into soft clay, for when he struck the earth he entered it and disappeared. The mother mourned and watched over his grave spot for a year and when springtime came again she saw a tiny green shoot springing above the sod. When the years passed by, it became a lofty evergreen tree and the people called it O'-so'-ä (gē-i). It was the first of its kind and the soul and blood and body of the chief were in it. This the people knew for they heard it sighing and moaning to its mates in the heavens at night. A thoughtless warrior slashed its bark with his knife and red blood poured out, and it was human blood. "After many years," says the story-teller, "the feathers that dropped from the wide branches sprang up into the pine trees and these have thick sticky blood, but it is good for many things, canoes, ropes and medicines. So it's a good thing he looked down."

37The religious philosophy of the Iroquois teaches that each soul has its individual path leading from the soul house, the body, to the great sky road, the Milky Way. The good sky path is called Ga-o-ya''-dē he-io-o'-dio' and the evil soul's road, o-a'-gwĕnt.

38The term Happy Hunting Ground is not strictly Iroquoian. The modern believers in the Gaiwiu term their heaven, "the Land of the Creator." It is described, however, as a place where Indians will enjoy again the things which a red man most loves. Should be "Place of the Maker." Sometimes the world of spirits is called gä-o-ya''-gē, Sky Place.

39Handsome Lake described very vividly in the Gaiwiu his experience on the road of souls, the Milky Way, and said that most of the tracks that he saw in the road were those of children. Going further and looking at the downward fork he saw the footprints of adults only. The Milky Way is called dja-swĕn'-do.'

40The three brothers were named as follows: the oldest Tŭg-a-wa-ne'; the next younger, Ha-da-wa'-sa-no or Ho-wē-ta-ho' and the youngest, Hos'-to'. The youngest was a quiet, bashful fellow, the next older given to much speaking while the oldest was a great braggart.

[41]Hos'-to', the youngest, bore the fagots and Ho-wē-ta-ho', the next older, carried the kettle in which to cook the bear.

[42]O-nä'-o' means corn. The parched com cake is called onă'-so'-kwa by the Senecas and o-nă-gwĭtz-orä by the Mohawks. It was made by roasting dry shelled corn on a flat stone and afterward beating it to a meal in a mortar. The flour was mixed with maple sugar, wet, pressed into cakes and dried. Dried chokecherries were sometimes pulverized and added. This food must be eaten sparingly and with plenty of water to prevent cramps.

[43]The net in my version is a cave and is the constellation of Corona borealis.

[44]The older brother is the actual hunter, his next younger brother carries the kettle in which to cook the bear while the youngest bears the fagots for the fire. The boastful older brother fell behind in the chase And the youngest passing by his next older brother hurried on and killed the bear with his chunks of fire wood. The blood dripped down and turned the maple leaves red while the fat, melted to oil in the heat of the chase, dripped down and turned others yellow. The bear; miraculously revives before the fire is kindled and the pursuit goes on again.

[45]The stars outlining the bowl of the "dipper" represent the bear and the handle stars are the hunters.

[46]The myth of the celestial bear chase is one of the most widely distributed in America. That the Ursa Major of the white man's astronomical lore should be

the same thing in the Indian's seems remarkable at first, and yet, when the elements which suggested the component ideas of the myth are examined it will be found that to human minds in the same cultural stage, though separated by space and time, the same factors suggest the same ideas or combination of ideas. That the idea of things should be similar, therefore, does not seem so strange.

The story of the bear constellation as related by the Indians is Precolumbian without a shadow of doubt. The earliest explorers and missionaries heard the myth from the Point Barrow Eskimos and from the Zuni Pueblo dwellers of Arizona, from the Sioux of the Dakotas, from the Micmacs of Nova Scotia, and from the Siwash tribes of California. Still it may be objected that the myth was of recent introduction, but if it were, its details would not have presented so much of a variation but rather have conformed to the myth supposed to have been derived from European sources.

The suggesting factors which gave origin to the idea of the *bear* as associated with the constellation deserve some consideration here. The North American Indians, in common with other primitive people, were deeply impressed with all the phenomena of nature and curious regarding their cause. Any similarity between the known and the unknown was noted and where several real or symbolical similarities were observed, the unknown was compared to, symbolized by and named from the known. Real or pretended similarities were adduced both from actual knowledge and experience and from preexisting myths. The primitive mind drew no dividing line between the real and unreal, between ideas derived from objective and subjective sources. One supplemented the other in his store of data. Each element formed material for his premises and he regarded his conclusions sound. A myth once evolved was the precedent upon which other and more elaborate myths of other things might be built. If we knew what the primordial myth of any people was we might be able to trace step by step the history and evolution of myths. But then we should also be compelled to ask what ideas suggested that myth and at length we should be reduced to an analytical study of the evolution of ideas. We can not do this in a footnote and, therefore, we can not clear every question which may arise regarding a myth.

The bear constellation is one of the most prominent in the heavens and must have early attracted the attention of leaders who probably thought somewhat as follows:

The four stars (which compose the "dipper" bowl) suggest the four tracks or feet of an animal. What animal ? . . . The den *(Corona borealis)* suggests a cave in the rocks. What mysterious animal is it that never dies (disappaars), and though it may turn on its back (become inverted like the constellation in late autumn and winter) to sleep, yet returns living again? And who are the stars, the seven stars that follow the beast, four to become lost and three ever in sight? Surely some magical animal this is, it must be a bear (regarded by the Indians as a most wise and mysteriously magical animal). Its den is like a bear's den. It never dies, no, a bear never does (from natural causes, the Indian thinks). Yes, it is a bear. The seven stars are the pursuers, the three always visible are the hunters. Do they slay him? Yes, for he turns over. Now, why do leaves turn red and yellow when he turns over? Because his blood and oil spill down. Then how does he come to life again? Ah, his spirit hides in the cave, enters a new body and starts out again in the spring. So this is the reason for that group of lights. I have discovered what they are.

A very slight suggestion may start and give direction to a train of thought that results the same in independent minds. Thus undoubtedly the bear constellation myth had its origin. The reader who is interested in the bear myth is directed to Salisbury Hagar's masterful essay in the *Journal of American Folk Lore*, volume 13, page 92.

[47]So-son'-do-wăh means Great Night.

[48]The name is usually written Jo-naën-dă'.

[49]The Iroquois call the morning star, Gĕñ-deñ'-wit-hă, It Brings the Day.

[50]The crow and raven are among the most magical of all the "medicine" creatures. The Iroquois believed that the crows possessed great intelligence and sagacity since they "hold councils and have chiefs." The spirits of the crow and the raven figure prominently in the rituals of the Little Waters Society and the Ih'-dos Company.

[51]The three vegetables, the corn, beans and squash were known to the Onondagas as tu-ne-ha-kwe meaning "these we live on," and to the Senecas as Dio-hē'-ko, meaning "our true sustenance." It is interesting

to note that among the ancient Aztecs the spirit of the maize was called Tonacayohua, She Feeds Us.

In the rites of the green corn thanksgiving the Dio-hē'-ko are saluted in the words daiet-i-non-nioh dio-hē'-ko, *we salute our true living.*

The Seneca women have, (and probably all the other Iroquois had), a society called the To-wiis'-săs, a society composed solely of women. The Towi'sas people call themselves the friends of the Dio-hē'-ko. Their object is to attend to the wishes of Naidiohe'ko, spirits of the three sisters, and preserve the rite by which they may be supplicated.

Owing to the capture of an entire lodge on its march from one village to another, two warriors are now admitted as guards and to keep them interested the women have them sing one part of their ritual while the women, for a ceremonial purpose (not because of appreciation), clap their hands.

[52]Meaning "standing rock."

[53]The Bird dance seen in the Long House ceremonies at the Indian New Year's ceremony is the public exhibition of the Eagle Society, one of the (once) secret fraternities of the Senecas. The dance is called the ga-ne-gwa-ē. This society is one of the most influential, next to the Ga-no-da, Ho-noh-tci-noh-gah (Little Water Society). The sign of membership in the Eagle Society is a round spot of red paint on either cheek.

[54]Jo-wiis means "chipping sparrow," and as a name was regarded as one of the preferred.

[55]Jo-wiis is regarded as the founder of the Eagle Society.

[56]All magic beings who possessed *otgont,* or wizardly power seem to have been vulnerable only on this portion of their anatomy. The Niahgwahe, another myth monster, is another example of an otgont creature who could not be killed otherwise.

[57]The mask to become the habitation of the Gagonsah spirit which lives in the tree must first be carved on the living tree. A ceremonial fire is kindled and an invocation made asking the life of the tree to enter the mask and thereby furnish it with life that the Gagonsah spirit might enter. The tree was then propitiated by offerings of tobacco and the mask cut off.

[58]According to the teachings of the Jadigohsashooh, the False Face Company, each tree has its own voice which the initiated can recognize. When the hurricane twists down a tree the Indian who hears the death groan as it falls, says "that is a hemlock," or an oak according as he interprets the "voice." Generally he is right in his statement, it is said.

[59]The proper wood for "medicine masks" is the basswood. A mythical reason is given for its empioyment but the practical reason is probably that it is easy to carve. The Indians also ascribed medicinal virtues to its bark and used the sap as a lotion for wounds. The bark furnished fiber for twine and fabrics and also when peeled off in troughs furnished conduits that conveyed water from springs.

[60] The lost hunter became the founder of the False Face Company and instructed the first band in its ceremonies and ritual. The editor found one of the Stone Giant's masks in the possession of a member of the Cattaraugus Company and purchased it for the State Museum. It never was used in public ceremonies in the Long House but always within the company's lodge.

[61] This is one of the legends which David Cusick included in his *History of the Six Nations*.

[62] In some myths the flying heads are false faces. The Mohawks instead of making the Stone Giant the founder credit the Flying Heads with being the original False Faces.

[63] The Oh-gi-we is a society with regular leaders and fixed rites. It is sometimes called the "Talkers with the Dead." When the unhappy soul of the dead member appears to one of the living either in a dream or in a waking vision, the ceremony is ordered in all haste. The formula by which souls are released from influences which bind them unhappy to earth forms the bulk of the Oh-gi-we ritual.

[64] Another version of this story relates that the evil spirit was transformed into the screech owl. The burning of otgont beings is common in myth tales and the bursting of their heads, from whence a beast or bird typifying their evil disposition flies, is another common feature.

[65] The mystery of dreams was one that profoundly impressed the Iroquois but in this they did not differ from most primitive people. With them every dream

had a meaning which the dream interpreter could reveal. One of the ceremonies at the midwinter festival was the guessing of dreams. The Jesuit missionaries have left some interesting accounts of this custom. Dreams determined the assembling of several of the secret societies and some are said to have originated thus.

The influence of dreams upon primitive minds can hardly be realized by any one but the close student of savage races. Some seem to be in a perpetual daze and almost unable to distingmsh between the imaginative happenings of their sleep and the actual happenings of the waking state.

[66]According to Iroquois lore the soul in crossing water must have some material boat or bridge, howsoever small.

[67]Another version, from the Senecas, makes Ha'-to' the Spirit of the Winter and O-swi-nĕ'-don', the Spirit of Warmth. The former is described as an old man who skulks about in the woods and raps the trees with his war club, (ga-ji-wa). When the weather is the coldest he is the most active and any one can hear him rapping the trees. It is a very evil thing to imitate the acts of any nature spirit. The penalty is to be captured by the spirit and pressed into its service. Ha'-to' is deathly afraid of blackberries and never visits the earth when they are in blossom. A boy who had mocked Ha'-to' once vanquished him by throwing a pot of blackberry sauce in his face. Thus the Senecas use blackberries in winter as a medicine against frost bites.

68 The Stone Throwers are a band of elves who are fond of playing harmless pranks. Should one offend them, however, the prank may cease to be harmless. An Indian who discovers that he has been punished by them at once holds a proper ceremony for their propitiation. Mr. M. R. Harrington who questioned the Oneidas regarding their belief in the Jo-ga-oh was told that when a good round stone was needed for a hammer or corn crusher that an Indian would go down to a creek and place an offering of tobacco beneath a flat stone and returning the next day find within the radius of a man's length a stone just suitable for his purposes.

69 It is interesting to note the important part which orphans play in Iroquois mythology. Most of the mystic societies were founded by orphans who had been driven from home to perish and other legends set forth the great heroism and eventual success of orphans who are cared for (or ill cared for) by their uncles and grandparents. The "neglected nephew" stories form a large portion of Iroquoian legendary lore.

70 The youth who founded the Pygmy Society, sometimes called the Dark Dancers, bore the name of Covered-with-excrement, in allusion to the filthy condition in which his uncle kept him.

71 The ceremonies of the Pygmy Society are called at certain times to propitiate the elves and sprites who often wish to be assured of man's gratitude for their favors. The writer has translated the entire ritual and recorded the songs and chants on the phonograph. The Seneca name for the society is Yot-don-dak-goh.

[72]The editor has questioned a number of Iroquois children regarding the Jo-ga-oh and has been told that these little folk have sometimes been seen running through the woods. They generally are dressed in all the traditional paraphernalia of the Indian but sometimes are entirely naked. Two Seneca children who described them said that they were about a foot high and ran very fast. With adults they are more heard than seen and are known by their drumming on the wet drum. The listening initiate who hears the tap of the ringing water tom-tom knows instantly that the elves are calling a council and summons his society to meet and make the proper offerings to these "elves who run in the darkness and who wander upon the mountains."

[73]The elves are naturally unsuccessful hunters. This is not because they lack skill but because the animals have learned to detect their peculiar scent. Because of this the members of the Pygmy Society save the parings and scrapings from their finger nails and tie them in little bags to throw among the rocks for the elves. They are believed to saturate them in water and bathe in it. The animals then think that human hunters seek them and are not afraid.

[74]Ho-non-di-ont, The Company of Faith Keepers.

[75]This is a legend of the puberty ceremony, common in different forms among many tribes.

[76]It is possible for a youth to become a chief but unless he inherited the right to candidacy from his maternal side to become one of the several considered for nomination and then received the nomination

by the women and the confirmation and election by the warriors, he could not hope to become one of the council of fifty sachems who formed the governing body of the league, The difference between chiefs and sachems is the same difference which now obtains between army officers and federal senators.

[77]The name Jis-go-ga is one which has been borne by several noted war chiefs and is considered one of the strong names.

[78]The snake people. Some of the older Senecas say that this legend alludes to the Cherokees. The Seneca name for the Cherokee tribe is *Cave* or *Hole Dwellers*.

[79]Devil song.

[80]This is a variation of the generally known legend of Nun-da-wa-o.

[81]Bare hill on Canandaigua lake.

[82]Canandaigua lake.

[83]This myth strongly resembles the Abenaki legend of *The Woman and the Serpent*, one of the A'tosis stories. It probably came to Mrs. Converse through Mohawk sources. The Algonquin original has the lover a serpent instead of a fish.

[84]In Seneca this name is To-do-da-ho. See Origin of the Wampum Belt, page 202.

[85]Ot-to-tar-ho or To-ta-da-ho became the first presiding sachem of the confederacy. The wampum belt commemorating him is second only in size to the

Wing or Carpet belt of the league. Both belts are in the State Museum.

[86]This legend is probably from European sources.

[87]The adoption of the St. Regis Indians was brought about largely through the influence of Mrs Converse.

[88]Although the active government of the Seneca Nation is the modern republican form, underlying this is the ancient tribal form. This survival is fostered by the pagan party and is the link that holds together the old form of the ancient league. The sachem names are still carefully transmitted and the tribal customs form the basis of the common law held at present.

[89]The eight clans here named were those of the Senecas. The three common clans were the clans of the Bear, Wolf and Turtle. These were the elder clans and the sachems belonging to them were the most influential in the league councils. Among the Senecas, Cayugas and Onondagas the clans were divided into two phratries, the Animal and the Bird. The Animals were called the elder brothers. Strangely the Deers were the head of the Bird phratry, whose other members were the Snipe, Heron and Hawk. Each phratry when in council sits opposite the other.

[90]It is recorded that the Iroquois soldiers in the Civil War were the finest body of men in the army, considered from a physical standard. The Iroquois are still a splendid people physically as is attested by the number of athletes among them who have made world records. The record of Deerfoot in 1864 in which he

ran 12 miles in 62 minutes, 2½ seconds is well known and in modern times the skill of the Pierce brothers on the track and of Thomas Longboat, the Canadian Onondaga, has attracted much attention. A number are expert ball players and a Seneca is a professional athletic trainer.

91Iroquois Indians at present are engaged in many different trades and professions. Some are masons, molders, carpenters, bakers, painters, engineers, railroad trainmen, conductors, clerks in business and banking houses, cooks, shopkeepers, blacksmiths etc.; in professional lines they will be found engaged in the practice of law and medicine, in music, in teaching, both in primary and higher branches, and some are engaged professionally in scientific pursuits. Others will be found as laborers drifting about among the whites, as teamsters and farm hands and the like.

92The census of 1890 was used by Mrs. Converse as a source of information.

93The devout Indian after he has finished his meal always says "Niaweh," meaning, *I am thankful.* Although he apparently addressed the others at the table according to his religion in reality he is speaking to the Creator. The response of the people is "Niuh!" meaning, *it is well.*

94The national belts of the Iroquois were passed into the keeping of the State Museum by the chiefs and sachems of the Onondagas in June 1898. In January 1908 the chief of the Onondagas, Sa-ha-whe (Baptist Thomas), signed an indenture making the Director of the State Museum the wampum keeper of the Five Nations and conferring upon him and his successors in office forever the title Ho-sa-na-ga-da (Ho-seh-na-geh-teh), Name Bearer, the official name for the wampum keeper [See N. Y. State Mus. 4th An. Rep't Director].

[95]This belt is now the property of Hon. John Boyd Thacher of Albany.

[96]This article has been written, so far as possible, from the standpoint of the Indian.

[97]The active membership in the order is limited to actual holders of the mystery packet. In order that the writer might become a full member, Cornplanter resigned and surrendered his packet to him.

[98]Beauchamp in *American Folk Lore Journal*, volume 14, page 158 says the Onondagas call the society, *The Ka-noo'-tah*. This refers to the name of the song which is Ga-no'-da in Seneca, and not to the society.

[99]The Jesuits described a similar ceremony among the Hurons in 1640. In the *Relation of 1670* is an account of the medicine water as used by the Onondagas.

[100]In all cases the word here translated "incense" should read tobacco.

[101]This does not occur when the medicine has been adulterated with powdered roots.

[102]In recent ceremonies each member smoked his own pipe of Indian tobacco..

[103]The writer has recently examined an old book in which a Seneca had recorded the words of the ritual.

There is no variation between the version found in the book and that now used with the exception of an "r" sound in some syllables now pronounced "ah." The writer's conclusion above stated is therefore justified.

104According to the translation by William Jones, a Seneca sachem of the Snipe clan, now deceased. Reproduced almost word for word and sentence for sentence, the only changes being those necessary to correct the more pronounced imperfections of grammar.

105Jacket was an elder in the Presbyterian Mission Church for 30 or 40 years and was considered by the Indians and the missionaries an exceedingly devout man.

106From the speech of John Jacket, Holder of the Song, and here recorded literally, as translated by William Jones.

107Jacket has forgotten to name the corn, beans and squashes as members of the medicine.

108From *The Republic*, St. Louis, Mo., October 16, 1892.

109Mrs Converse has spelled the name of the medicine *ne-gar-na-gar-ah*, conforming to the old form of pronunciation used by the members.

110Medicine societies existed among most Indian tribes but they were not uniform in character nor did they usually recognize each other.

111From *The Republic*, St. Louis, Mo,, Oct. 23, 1892.

[112]Verbatim from a manuscript by Mrs. Asher Wright.

[113]The duck's name Gwi-yuh-gee, means "shot up out of the water."

[114]Verbatim from manuscript of Mrs. A. Wright's interview with Chief Esquire Johnson.

[115]From Mrs. Converse's manuscript notes.

[116]This legend was published in a small handbook issued by the Regents at the ceremony of the passing of the wampum belts to the State in 1898.

[117]His strange conduct may have given rise to one of the translations of his name, *He who seeks his mind knowing where to find it.*

www.ingramcontent.com/pod-product-compliance
Lightning Source LLC
Chambersburg PA
CBHW031234090426
42742CB00007B/199